Early Film Noir

Early Film Noir

Greed, Lust and Murder Hollywood Style

WILLIAM HARE

Foreword by Ken Annakin

McFarland & Company, Inc., Publishers
Jefferson, North Carolina, and London

LIBRARY OF CONGRESS CATALOGUING-IN-PUBLICATION DATA

Hare, William 1942–
Early film noir : greed, lust and murder Hollywood style
/ William Hare ; foreword by Ken Annakin
p. cm.
Includes bibliographical references and index.

ISBN 0-7864-1629-7 (softcover : 50# alkaline paper) ∞

1. Film noir—United States—History and criticism. I. Title.
PN1995.9.F54H37 2003 791.43'655—dc21 2003010991
British Library cataloguing data are available

Cover photograph: Jane Greer and Robert Mitchum in the 1947 film *Out of the Past*

Manufactured in the United States of America

McFarland & Company, Inc., Publishers
Box 611, Jefferson, North Carolina 28640
www.mcfarlandpub.com

To my agent Robert Kendall and director Ken Annakin
for consistent generous assistance.

And to the memory of my parents, Leamon and Helen Hare,
for generous support and keeping the faith,
and Mervyn LeRoy and Rouben Mamoulian,
for helping to show me the way.

Table of Contents

Foreword by Ken Annakin ix

Introduction 1

ONE—Film Noir: Chandler and the American Institution with a French Name 7

TWO—A Blend of Three Great Talents: *Double Indemnity* (1944) 22

THREE—Women of Danger and RKO's Noir Factory 46

FOUR—Dmytryk and the RKO Team 63

FIVE—Jane Greer: Hollywood's Unforgettable Femme Fatale 80

SIX—*Laura* (1944) 106

SEVEN—An Obsession in White and a Final Reckoning: *The Postman Always Rings Twice* (1946) 130

EIGHT—British Noir: *The Third Man* (1949) and *Across the Bridge* (1957) 144

Synopses of Major Films 201

Bibliography 205

Index 207

Foreword

I have known Bill Hare for a number of years and admired his work as a critic, screenwriter and historian. *The Struggle for the Holy Land,* an objective account of the evolution of the Middle East from Biblical times to the present, shows his gift for research and that nothing or no one is going to stop him from making a success of any project in which he becomes involved.

Many years ago, as Bill was working on a "Great Directors" magazine series, he cultivated the friendships of Mervyn LeRoy and Rouben Mamoulian, both film creators on the very highest level. These associations gave him a unique understanding of how great directors get the best out of stars and casts, right down to the humblest of bit players.

In one of my first meetings with Bill, he remarked, "A director on top of his or her game needs to serve as a psychologist and often as a 'minder' for creatively fascinating, but often exceedingly volatile, temperamental, and insecure human beings [actors]." I found this a most perceptive analysis.

Over the years Bill has tried his hand at screenplays such as *The Sunset Boulevard Murders, Freud Meets Hitler, The Final Dawn* and *The Trials of Sir Walter Ralegh,* all fascinating and deeply researched dramas with a moral or message. Yet, like all of us, he has had to write and rewrite, then battle with agents, producers and studio heads, to get his work financed, filmed or published.

In *Early Film Noir,* Bill has succeeded brilliantly, and for my part, I feel honored to be included in his analyses and assessments of early film noir.

Ken Annakin, OBE
Beverly Hills, California
2003

Introduction

Film noir came into being following World War II and received its baptism in Paris, where realism in art assumed a position of prime importance. It was France and Britain where the detective stories of Dashiell Hammett and Raymond Chandler became prime sellers and influenced an author as prominent as Existentialist Albert Camus, a future Nobel Prize winner.

The European surge resulted not only in increased sales for the novels and short stories of hard-boiled detective authors Hammett and Chandler; it prompted Hollywood to take a look at a fresh, creative vehicle of expression at a time when the industry's productivity was reaching an all-time high, bolstered by expanding prosperity after World War II ended and the veterans returned home.

Film noir as a story vehicle appeared made to order for the studios during a period of intense competition. Great dramatic films involve stories about people caught in the throes of conflict. The characters are seen through the camera's eye enduring traumas, often immersed in struggles for their very survival. Film noir was a particularly welcome innovation by smaller studios such as RKO. The Melrose Avenue film factory rose to the occasion, using film noir to garner financial and artistic acclaim, taking advantage of the maxim that, in the film noir genre, less could often encompass so much more. A large musical such as the kind produced at MGM and Twentieth Century–Fox required larger budgets and more people than film noir, with its starkly realistic settings—a lonely street corner at midnight, a room in a sleazy hotel with neon light flashing, a stool or booth of an all-night restaurant or seedy bar. Studios realized that film noir projects were great levelers. Large talents could overcome small budgets as the focus shifted from splashy settings and costumes to a world embodied in Edward Hopper paintings, vignettes of people in conflict in confined settings.

John Huston, of Hollywood's big talents, used film noir as a springboard to transpose his creative talent as a major Hollywood scenarist to the directing realm, where he achieved enduring greatness. While the term film noir did not become a part of the cinema lexicon until 1947, the first movie given that label was *The Maltese Falcon* in 1941. It was considered to possess the qualities associated with the term spawned in Paris's prestigious *Cahiers du Cinema.*

Huston, son of legendary acting great Walter Huston, had been appealing to his Warner Bros. boss Jack L. Warner for the opportunity to direct after achieving an impressive record as a scenarist. Warner ultimately allowed his successful writer to assume the director's reins on the condition that his low-budget requirement was met. Huston hired as his leading man Humphrey Bogart, one of the stars from his last screenwriting success, *High Sierra*, directed by Raoul Walsh. Bogart used the opportunity to catapult himself from respected lead performer to dynamic superstar and would enhance it further by starring in future Huston-directed vehicles.

The Maltese Falcon was based on a novel by Dashiell Hammett and had been filmed unsuccessfully on two previous occasions. Hammett's detective novels and stories had a ring of spontaneous truth based on his earlier career as a Pinkerton detective. Fog-shrouded San Francisco streets provided the dramatic background for the conflicts of uncompromisingly tough private detective Sam Spade and his pursuit of justice as he sought to tame the wilder, more unrestrained elements of the city's populace.

Hammett formed a part of the energetic writing trilogy whose efforts launched film noir. The words became graphic pictures, tough and uncompromising. While Hammett had an authentic detective's background, an out-of-work oil executive with a strong penchant for alcohol who read Hammett's pulp fiction magazine stories found a way to earn some money and ultimately an unrivaled reputation for excellence as a wordsmith of the hard-boiled school. Raymond Chandler used Hammett as a model in developing his style, then proceeded to tap human dimensions beyond the San Francisco writer's efforts. Chandler's stories were set some 400 miles to the south of Hammett's San Francisco venue in Los Angeles. Chandler, who spoke with a British accent and had been educated at a prominent prep school near London, found his adopted home town of Los Angeles well beneath his sophisticated tastes. His prose contained a biting sarcasm and his detective Philip Marlowe stood as a knight battling windmills in Don Quixote fashion amid the corruption and anarchy of a city comprised almost exclusively of people who had come from other places.

The third member of the noir writing triumvirate who shaped Hollywood history was James M. Cain. Baltimore-born Cain shifted gears abruptly, turning away from his career as a journalist and writing prose with a mule's kick about people who battled society and lost, but did so with captivating flourish. When Vienna emigre director Billy Wilder became enchanted with Cain's novella *Double Indemnity*, an invigorating new movement toward incisive realism was created. Desiring a partner he felt had the credentials and abilities to undertake the task of adapting Cain's novella to the screen, Wilder turned to Chandler. The two great artists disliked each other throughout the time they worked together, and yet one of the greatest scripts ever penned by Hollywood writers resulted. Even before the 1944 Paramount release debuted in theaters, the word spread at local movie industry watering holes such as the Brown Derby that a blockbuster film which would rock the cinema field would soon be premiering. *Double Indemnity* lived up to its advance billing with Barbara Stanwyck turning in the performance of her career as the femme fatale who succeeded in driving Fred MacMurray to help her murder her husband. Edward G. Robinson was equally memorable as the insurance claims investigator with bloodhound instincts who was determined to solve the case.

Paramount and RKO were located no more than two blocks from each other. While Raymond Chandler was ensconced with Billy Wilder in the director's office at Paramount, a blockbuster noir epic was taking shape nearby at RKO. Ironically, while Chandler helped craft a script around James M. Cain's novella, RKO was adapting the Philip Marlowe novel *Murder, My Sweet*, based on Chandler's *Farewell, My Lovely*. Former song and dance man Dick Powell forged a new dramatic career playing Marlowe in a manner of which the frequently critical Chandler approved. Dogging every movement of Powell's was RKO contract player Mike Mazurki as the hulking, homicidal Moose Malloy. Claire Trevor became one of filmdom's most enduring femmes fatales in the 1944 release, playing a woman who will stop at nothing to achieve her aims, including murder. Anne Shirley played the contrasting sweet girl, Powell's love interest.

Impressing RKO brass enormously through his efforts on *Murder, My Sweet* was young director Edward Dmytryk, who began his film career as an editor and displayed a penchant for turning out first-class product with speed and economy. During his productive RKO phase, Dmytryk directed *Crossfire*, another noir classic. This film took a tough look at anti–Semitism and was based on a novel by Richard Brooks, who would later surge to greatness as a director with such memorable films as *Elmer Gantry* and *In Cold Blood*. Brooks was able to use his persuasion to generate interest on RKO's part in a fellow Marine friend striving to become an actor. Robert Ryan got rave reviews playing the homicidal anti–Semite Montgomery, who is finally trapped by the combined wiles of Washington, D.C., police captain Robert Young and the killer's fellow soldier, played by Robert Mitchum.

The same year that RKO released *Crossfire*, 1947, the Melrose Avenue film factory distributed another film noir classic, *Out of the Past*. Jane Greer, a 22-year-old performer from Washington, D.C., mesmerized audiences with her portrayal of the predatory Kathie Moffett, who cast her spell on Robert Mitchum and Kirk Douglas. French director Jacques Tourneur used shadowy photography for spectacular results as the devastating brunette beauty used her tactical wiliness to victimize those within her reach. Her all-consuming greed ultimately swallows up Mitchum and Douglas, and herself. Greer knew that her *Out of the Past* role was a once-in-a-lifetime opportunity and, until her death on August 24, 2001, she was in constant demand at movie nostalgia gatherings. Her pleasant, gentle, real-life demeanor was in sharp contrast to the Kathie Moffett character from *Out of the Past*.

During the war years, a jinx project beset Darryl F. Zanuck at Twentieth Century–Fox. It began as a B-film project which ascended to the A level upon Zanuck's entry. Feuds and angry recriminations abounded, the producer replaced the director, assuming the position himself, and for a time Zanuck wondered just what kind of predicament he had become involved in. When all was said and done, however, *Laura* became one of movie history's premier noir successes. Producer-director Otto Preminger beseeched Zanuck to cast New York stage performer Clifton Webb as the sophisticated, sardonically egotistical Manhattan columnist and radio commentator Waldo Lydecker. Zanuck finally relented and Webb delivered an unforgettable performance. Zanuck's misgivings extended to Dana Andrews, who played Detective Mark McPherson, and again his apprehension proved unjustified. Gene Tierney was far from the first choice to play glamorous Park Avenue advertising career girl Laura Hunt, but her captivating performance convinced viewers and critics alike that she was born to play the role, which became the most memorable of her career.

While the 1944 release *Laura* demonstrated upper crust New York society at its most rapacious, the 1946 MGM noir classic *The Postman Always Rings Twice* was a story about two survivors of the Depression who kill so that they may remain together. The film was adapted from a novella by James M. Cain. In an example of successful typecasting, John Garfield, who grew up tough on New York's mean streets in the Depression, was selected to play drifter Frank Chambers, who is provided with a job by Cecil Kellaway, a diner owner on the outskirts of Los Angeles. Garfield falls hard for Kellaway's young wife, played by Lana Turner at her most alluring. Garfield's memorable first scene with Turner is one of the sexiest in film history, the camera tilting upward as she looms as a sultry symphony clad in white. Garfield is hooked from that moment on, overcoming pangs of conscience to conspire with Turner and kill a man who had treated him like a son.

In the brooding land of Shakespeare, Marlowe and Jonson film noir attracted audiences. British noir is represented by two outstanding films done by a master director and the young man who received his formative training by him. With *The Third Man,* Sir Carol Reed captured postwar Vienna and its black market at its grimmest as opportunistic Orson Welles makes a prosperous living stealing penicillin from hospitals, diluting it, then selling it for monstrous profits. Vigilant British Army officer Trevor Howard seeks to capture him, while Welles's oldest American friend, Joseph Cotten, ultimately agrees to help Howard. Cotton, meanwhile, cannot make the hauntingly beautiful Alida Valli forget the faithless Welles and embark on a new relationship with him.

It was eight years after *The Third Man* was released that Ken Annakin, given his start in film directing by Reed, etched a film war masterpiece of his own, the 1957 release *Across the Bridge*. Utilizing Graham Greene, the same writer who penned the script for *The Third Man*, Annakin's gem provided Rod Steiger with an opportunity to display his wide range of talents shortly after he had impressed audiences and critics opposite Marlon Brando in *On the Waterfront.* A probing psychological drama, *Across the Bridge* details the degradation of international financial magnate Steiger, who ultimately sleeps in dusty culverts of a small Mexican border town. His only friend is a dog named Dolores who consoles him during his painful isolation after his money and power have been ruthlessly wrested from him by a corrupt local police chief.

The aforementioned selections represent significant breakthroughs in film noir and are examples of the genre at its best, using its captivating powers of presenting people in conflict in different avenues of life. Rich and poor, predators and victims, all comprise a part of the panorama of a genre which mesmerizes film viewers to such a degree that one viewing is scarcely enough to satisfy. The stories and characters contain such profound depth that these films are viewed with frequency, *a la* students of literature revisiting Tolstoy or Joyce. With such enduring interest, which extends to succeeding generations of cinema enthusiasts, these films have become justifiable classics representing the genre in a variety of different ways.

William Hare
Fort Lauderdale, Florida
Summer 2003

ONE

Film Noir: Chandler and the American Institution with a French Name

The name is French, but the detective writer who inspired the concept was decidedly American, his prose marked by gripping realism from the seedy hotels, back alleys, dimly lit bars, main streets, country clubs, mansions, apartments, corporate boardrooms and flophouses of America. Raymond Chandler was an author who scared people with his unnerving manner of peeling off the outer layer of society's veneer and digging into the uncertainties of modern existence—what remained after the superficial niceties had vanished.

Chandler's scorching realism was crafted from his own experiences. His shadowy adventures were set in the city where he had lived so long and which he knew so well that he could demolish the most carefully crafted buildup of the most determined Chamber of Commerce enthusiast with a few well-chosen pecks on his Underwood typewriter. This process occurred in a small, dark room with a bottle of whisky sitting nearby as his trusty companion. The corrosive prose that resulted carried a bite that demanded that the reader approach with extreme caution, if at all. Chandler was so much of an original that he even typed while wearing gloves.

Raymond Chandler, as reflective of any writing giant capable of capturing the period of which he or she is a part, looms as quasi-storyteller and quasi-prophet. In order to be a prophet in one's own time, as Chandler surely became, two forms of cooperation are essential: a public ready for what is delivered and a corresponding break in events. A writer needs to find a sympathetic editor and publisher before receiving the opportunity to sell his or her wares to the public. Often the determining factor regarding whether the writer-prophet will attract attention are the extrinsic events that shape the author's intrinsic subject matter. The mood established by Chandler was a by-product of events occurring in society which evoked a response within him and struck a concurrent chord with his readers.

There were numerous factors at play that made Chandler's brand of literary noir marketable to audiences and critics alike as film noir. A primary element was the blunt realization that what innocence the age may have held had vanished. Musicals and the festive gaiety evoked by screen darling Shirley Temple injected viewers throughout America and the world with the kind of stimulating relief from the devastation of economic uncertainty followed by the devastation of world war; but the realization was gradually setting in that, as technology advanced, there was the corresponding potential to destroy civilization as we and our forebears knew it. Albert Einstein wrote his famous 1939 letter to President Franklin D. Roosevelt warning him of the dangers inherent in Nazi Germany developing an atomic bomb before the Allied nations. This letter generated the response which led to the secret Los Alamos experiments and the ultimate release of the atom bomb on Hiroshima and Nagasaki. Einstein later regretted his decision. Though continuing to recognize, particularly as a Jew, the importance of stopping Hitler, he was plagued by burning apprehensions of what lay in the future. By the time the great man of conscience died in 1955, the United States and the Soviet Union were engaged in the Cold War, creating a mounting stockpile of weapons capable of wreaking world destruction. Such knowledge on the part of the world citizenry created widespread apprehension.

Another major element creating the type of climate in which literary and film noir were more likely to flourish was the solemn realization that once the Axis powers were defeated in World War II, a fresh enemy in possession of greater firepower remained to be confronted. No sooner had the celebrations ended following the end of one war than we were in another, termed the Cold War, a bitter recognition that a swift conflict for supremacy was foolish predicated on the ultimate cost to civilization. The result was an extended balance of terror through the mutual accumulation of weapons on the one hand coupled with political gambits on the other. While the democratic nations sought to preserve one philosophy, the Soviet Union's exponents of Marxism-Leninism, in the manner of the most ardent secular fundamentalists, expressed the inevitability of their system's global triumph. When Soviet strongman Nikita Khrushchev told a concerned United States "We will bury you," he was stating his confidence in the capacity of the Soviet Communist economic system to outproduce his capitalist rival.

Deep frustrations and grave doubts about where America and the world stood at the end of World War II were reflected in films. Two movies focusing on readjustment to a civilian world following military conflict reflected these uncertainties. Samuel Goldwyn's Oscar-winning blockbuster *The Best Years of Our Lives* included a tense scene in which a customer at a drugstore dramatically holds up a newspaper and tells Harold Russell, who lost both arms in the conflict, that, with the advent of the Cold War and the challenge presented by the Soviet Union, the United States had accomplished nothing in the recently concluded war. While an angry Russell bemoans the fact that his arms are gone and he has no means of physically expressing his burning displeasure over the remark, drugstore worker Dana Andrews, a fellow Army veteran, demonstrates anger for both of them by punching the man, then summarily resigning his soda fountain job with the remark, "I know, the customer is always right."

The second Hollywood film dealing with post war adjustment tackled a different theme. In the RKO release *Till the End of Time*, a certain veterans' group is mentioned periodically, planting curiosity in the minds of viewers, a standard suspense ploy. In the film's climactic scene, set in a Los Angeles bar, members of the controversial organization make a direct membership pitch to Robert Mitchum and Guy Madison, informing them that the group excludes Negroes, Jews and Catholics. The unflappable Mitchum describes a friendship with a Jewish Marine friend who died serving his country at Guadalcanal. He adds that if his fellow Marine were there at that moment he would spit in the other man's face, but since he is not, Mitchum is prepared to do it for him—and does. In the fierce battle that ensues, he is hit over the head with a bottle. (He has a plate in his head, the result of a war injury, so he survives.) Bill Williams, an ex-professional boxer who has lost both legs in the war, lands some solid punches from his wheelchair. The battle serves the purpose of soul cleansing for the returning Marines. They feel relieved after the release of tension and happy over the thought that their energies had been expended in a good cause.

Since art mirrors life, expressing what is in the minds and hearts of artists who are part of a broader community, the scenes from *The Best Years of Our Lives* and *Till the End of Time* expressed social concerns then felt in the community at large. The sentiments expressed in each film represented liberal thinking, but made opposite points. The director of *The Best Years of Our Lives*, William Wyler, was active in Directors Guild debates of the period concerning the perceived influence of Communism in the film industry. The point made on the screen by actors Andrews and Russell represented the view repeatedly expressed by Wyler that the world was a better place as a result of the defeat of Nazism and Fascism and that conservative forces within the industry were overreacting concerning the threat of Communism, at least at the domestic level. At one Directors Guild meeting when Cecil B. DeMille had exclaimed that some of the Guild's members were not good Americans, an angry Wyler responded tartly that he would punch the first director in the nose who questioned his loyalty, and that he would not care how old his accuser happened to be, a direct reference to the film pioneer.

The point addressed in *Till the End of Time* related to the uncomfortable reality that, while Americans had risked and often given their lives to thwart a megalomaniacal dictator committed to the perpetuation of a so-called master race, the same invidious viewpoint was being expressed regularly on the homefront. Concern was registered that those who had risked their lives to thwart tyranny were not being accorded decent treatment at home.

Till the End of Time, which drew attention to the idea of addressing injustices at home in the wake of fighting tyranny abroad, was directed by Edward Dmytryk. Two years later, in 1947, he achieved greater success on the same theme. *Crossfire* dealt with the brutal murder of a kindly Jewish man in Washington, D.C., by a crazed soldier who turned virulent anti–Semitism into a crusade. This gem has been consistently praised as one of the all-time great film noir classics.

Shortly after *Crossfire* was released, one of the great conscience films on the subject of anti–Semitism was brought to the screen by Darryl Zanuck: *Gentleman's Agreement*, with Gregory Peck starring as a magazine writer posing as a Jew to observe firsthand what it is like to be victimized by discrimination. It was an adaptation of Laura Z. Hobson's novel.

As America moved into the Cold War, innocence gave way to the terrifying reality that scientific achievement had outpaced humankind's ability to cope with increasingly awesome potentials. Sober-minded individuals began openly confronting the possibility that civilization as we knew it could be facing extinction in the foreseeable future. This chilling view appeared to be reinforced not only by Cold War tensions, but by the Korean War, with the emphasis on thwarting Communist expansion. With the existence of nuclear weapons hovering with silent muscularity somewhere in the abyss came the chilling reality that warfare had permanently changed. With the potential of unleashing such weaponry, the combative confidence with which Americans confronted two world wars had vanished.

In the 1948 U.S. presidential election, an entire leftist-oriented peace wing of the Democratic Party deserted President Harry Truman's bid for reelection to embrace the accommodationist views of Henry Wallace and the assumption that America would be better served by broader negotiation and fewer armaments in resolving U.S.–U.S.S.R. tensions. This view become particularly popular within Hollywood creative circles, and had a significant bearing on the subject matter of certain films produced during the period. Vigorous discussions took place on how to confront the menacing challenge of Communism. Some called for accommodation, others for negotiation accompanied by preparedness, and certain individuals believed that military superiority and a steadfast determination to use those weapons of destruction constituted the only sound response to the challenge the nation faced. In this environment, children were subjected to regular school drills to prepare against atomic onslaught: A screaming air raid siren warning was their signal to position themselves beneath their desks in a crouched position.

While politicians tackled the crucial issues of war and peace and children prepared for a dire eventuality, the hard-bitten prose of Chandler found an ever-inviting mood in film subject matter. The dark side of the human experience was explored in a manner which, in the coordinated mastery of a superb script, solid direction and eerily convincing dramatic performances, created a chillingly real poetry much like that dashed off by Raymond Chandler. Not only were lead performers provided with opportunities to broaden their talents by playing absorbing characters. While genre icons Robert Mitchum, Humphrey Bogart, Burt Lancaster, John Garfield, Fred MacMurray, Dick Powell and Robert Montgomery led us into the world of the dark, forbidding and brooding, we were fascinated to also find there the likes of Mike Mazurki, Sydney Greenstreet, Elisha Cook, Jr., Dan Duryea, Otto Kruger and Joseph Calleia, complicating and frequently terrorizing the protagonists' lives. As for the women, they led the loners, the residents of darkness seeking to cope with a world indigenously anarchistic, into mousetraps from which they frequently never escaped. This fascinating cinema type found expression in Jane Greer, Claire Trevor, Mary Astor, Rita Hayworth, Lana Turner, Ava Gardner and Yvonne DeCarlo. Viewers observed the step by step destruction within the imprisoning wiles of erotic glances and well-turned ankles.

A Society Losing Control

Even during eras of economic uncertainties, the reliable mainspring around which society revolved was the American family. The Hollywood fine-tuned message was clear: In times of economic hardship, the worst of tragedies could be surmounted through teamwork, family interlinking with community. It was no surprise that the staple product during the turbulent economic uncertainties of the Great Depression on the Culver City lot of Metro-Goldwyn-Mayer (largest of the dream factories) was the financially successful Andy Hardy series. It was set in small town America, where helping your neighbor and maintaining a solid family were the paramount objectives. Lewis Stone epitomized American solidarity as Judge Hardy; and the dreams and aspirations of the nation were symbolized by his irrepressible son Andy, played with the appropriate energy level by the peripatetic Mickey Rooney. It was natural enough for this energetic young man, unafraid to tackle any challenge, to have a sweet young girl with whom he could interact, someone with whom he could aim for the skies and enjoy triumphs. This person was symbolized by a petite and supportive Judy Garland. Given the box office bonanza studio chief Louis B. Mayer realized through the hugely popular Andy Hardy series and the indomitable Rooney character, it was no surprise that Mayer's all-time favorite film was Rooney's starring vehicle, *The Human Comedy*.

While family and community were the twin pillars relied upon to steer Americans through the Great Depression, in retrospect it was not surprising that a mood swing occurred in the wake of a world conflict resulting in the loss of 50 million lives. Many survivors would come home facing disillusionment, having seen and sniffed the stench of death in Europe and the Pacific. They would awaken in the middle of the night drenched with sweat after experiencing nightmares of conflict. The Nuremberg Trials brought home to an entire world how savage hatred and a megalomaniacal belief in a Nazi superstate designed to rule for 1,000 years resulted in the attempted extermination of the Jewish people along with others believed to be unfit to live in the state Hitler was fashioning for the future (Slavs, Gypsies, homosexuals, the mentally and physically handicapped). Now, in the wake of World War II, Americans were being asked to steel themselves for the Cold War, in which two systems, Communism and freedom, would vie for global supremacy. Little better than a decade after Mickey Rooney and Judy Garland had frolicked with carefree optimism in the sunshine, schoolchildren knelt beneath their desks as air raid sirens sounded, preparing them for what it would be like in the event of a nuclear attack.

Some of the most eminently representative film noir language ever spoken was written and later uttered for the RKO classic *Out of the Past*. It addressed the times and the subject matter with the same poetic fidelity as Shakespeare penning Elizabethan dramas. The dialogue was the polar opposite of that in the upbeat Andy Hardy family dramas. Shrewd, laconic loner Robert Mitchum replaced effervescent optimist Mickey Rooney. Two of Mitchum's most memorable lines from *Out of the Past* were "I've been afraid of half the things I've ever done" and "If I'm gonna die, I'm gonna die last." Could anyone ever conceive of Rooney as Andy Hardy uttering such dialogue?

The fatalism articulated by Mitchum is representative of the French literary influence that spawned the name film noir. A creature of darkness, the film noir male protagonist sees life as a struggle, but is determined not to be snared in life's deadly tentacles without waging ferocious battle.

The French Connection

While classic film noir adventures occurred largely within the eerie darkness of major American cities, it is understandable why French terminology was employed to define the U.S. cinema phenomenon. It was France which gave us the Lost Generation following World War I. The young Ernest Hemingway was an involved resident of the French cultural scene when he penned his powerful first novel, *The Sun Also Rises*, which reflects so many of the disenchantments pervasive in film noir. Regrettably, the 1957 film version starring Tyrone Power, Ava Gardner and Errol Flynn failed to capture much of the raw power of the literary work, which represented uncertainty toward the future based on a disenchanted reading of the past. The emerging question was whether humankind was headed toward anything beyond a series of disenchantments.

The crucial issue of where humanity was headed and what use, if any, we were to make of life are core issues tackled by Nobel Prize laureate Albert Camus and Jean Paul Sartre, who in 1964 refused the Nobel Prize for Literature, which the younger author had accepted seven years earlier. France's premier Existentialist thinkers sought to define life within the framework of a world groping for meaning, with a sketchy grip on the past, a confusing present and a hazily uncertain future.

Two defining works allow the discerning reader into the philosophical and psychological underpinnings of Camus' world. Of all the short works in literary history, one of the most powerful and widely read, along with F. Scott Fitzgerald's *The*

Great Gatsby, is an even shorter work, *The Stranger*, a potent novella whose first person protagonist does not begin to come to grips with life until he sits in his dank jail cell staring out of his barred window at twinkling evening stars while awaiting execution. Meursault, the protagonist, had routinely gone to the cinema to watch French comedy great Fernandel, then taken a young woman to his room for sex, in the immediate aftermath of his mother's funeral and burial. In his novel *The Plague*, Camus' first person protagonist is a doctor ministering to dying patients. While a deadly plague claims a number of victims, the doctor finds life within the realm of an existence in which he sees the footprints of the Grim Reaper on all sides. By facing the imminent reality of death, the doctor is able to confront responsibility and prolong his own life.

As for Sartre, the Left Bank Parisian intellectual who had a highly publicized split from his protégé, his renowned Existentialist play *No Exit* lucidly represents his viewpoint. The atheist Sartre presents a fictional hereafter totally dissimilar to that described by religious thinkers. Rather than the traditional Heaven and Hell dichotomy, Sartre presents figures confined to one room with "no exit," having to endure one another in a suffocating setting.

Raymond Chandler's detective novels featuring the indefatigable survivor Philip Marlowe found an interested reading public in France as well as other points across the Atlantic. Chandler biographer Tom Hiney links the creation of the term "film noir" to the American author's popularity in France. A 1949 Chandler novel, *The Little Sister*, sold 17,000 hardcover copies in the United States and another 27,000 in the United Kingdom, but achieved its highest figure in France with a total of 42,000. Chandler was also well received by French literary critics. *The Little Sister* was published in a cheap *Seerie Noire* edition, a series which also included Dashiell Hammett and Georges Simenon. Chandler biographer Hiney states that "it was from this hugely popular crime publishing venture that the term 'film noir' was derived."

One prominent author familiar with the *Seerie Noire* editions was Albert Camus, who claimed to have been influenced more by American detective writers in creating the solitary main figure of *The Stranger* than by literary novelists. The death of Camus resembled something that the Existentialist author or hard-bitten detective writer Chandler might have penned. A slender and youthful appearing 47–year-old Camus, who had won the Nobel Prize three years earlier, appeared to have a bright future, boasting a legion of devoted readers throughout the world. In the midst of fame, fortune and prospects of a luminous future, the Existentialist author met death in a freak automobile accident in a Paris suburb.

The Cost Factor

While rapidly shifting sociological factors of the post–World War II period had a strong bearing on both the creative impulses and audience demand of film noir cinema, another important element was also at work. Since simplicity was the hallmark of such productions, mood pieces set against the darkness of evening on deserted city streets, with illumination frequently provided by the flashing neon light of a cheap hotel or bar, studios could hold down budget costs and frequently shoot films entirely on the lot using cheap sets. A long chorus line of leggy dancers required considerably greater expenditures than a lonely detective sitting in the austere setting of a small office or on a deserted street past bewitching hour.

Noir vehicles provided an exciting *mano a mano* competition in which smaller studios could more readily compete against the giants. This competition warmed the creative blood of writers, actors and directors. In a frugal setting, creative filmmakers explored a narrower field than glossy productions meant to awe viewers. Film noir involved raw creativity.

During this period, a studio on Melrose Avenue excelled in film noir productivity. RKO specialized in the type of "lean and mean" fare that combined cost effectiveness with unadorned creativity. RKO's terse mood pieces put their bigger rivals on notice that dividends could be achieved without incurring major expenses. Understandably, this was a message that cost-conscious executives from the major studios were eager to hear.

No-frills directors such as Edward Dmytryk and Jacques Tourneur turned out classics that are better remembered and more frequently watched today than numerous high-budget vehicles loudly and expensively touted by the publicity mills of major studios. The sleepy-eyed, brooding Robert Mitchum, looming as a cinema creation who could have been ideally sculpted by Raymond Chandler, turned laconic dialogue and a brooding manner combined with brisk action into enduring international stardom.

Interviewed not long before his death on the Chandler segment of the Arts and Entertainment Network's *Biography* series, Mitchum revealed that he had once worked as a bartender at a Hollywood spot visited periodically by the detective writer. According to Mitchum, Chandler did not fit in at the bar; his tweed suit and cultured British accent did not mesh with the clientele. Such are the ironies of the creative world. While in real life Chandler embodied a demeanor more befitting of an Oxford University don rather than that of his celebrated private eye Philip Marlowe, in bartender Mitchum he encountered in the flesh the embodiment of what his brand of storytelling represented. The drooping eyes and melancholy stare along with a natural penchant for tossing off lines with the kind of Existentialist devil-may-care manner of someone familiar with the frequent dead ends of a social milieu overwrought with anarchy made him a natural for the genre. Mitchum was so convincing in *Out of the Past*, released in 1947, the very year that the term film noir came into vogue, that the movement appeared to have been invented for his personal use.

While the term film noir was not actually used until 1947, the tradition developed earlier. Those forces that synergistically converged at the close of the war with a cluster of film noir epics exploring the dark and dangerous sides of the human spirit had antecedents, creative ancestors without whose dynamic presence the movement would have had a much more difficult time being born.

Raymond Chandler's creative efforts are correctly cited as a major catalyst of the film noir movement. His creative predecessor, a former detective able to draw upon true-life experiences, served as an influence to Chandler when he was beginning his early career as a pulp magazine writer. It was a novel penned by Chandler's writing influence, a story that had already been filmed twice, which launched a new career for a restless young man who had recently clicked as a scenarist.

The restless young man, whose past exploits rivaled those of the young pre-superstar Robert Mitchum, cast a rising actor who soared meteorically with him. They became two of Hollywood's legends, working together frequently.

A Noir Morality Play

Cinema historians agree that the first movie in the genre was the 1941 Warner Bros. classic *The Maltese Falcon*, which was adapted from the novel by Dashiell Hammett. Hammett's legendary detective Sam Spade possessed a resemblance to Hammett himself, who had worked as a Pinkerton Agency sleuth before turning to writing. Hammett cautioned against making too close a comparison between himself and his fictional creation, envisioning Spade as a composite of how detectives saw themselves. The author explained that "Sam (Spade) had no original.... He's a dream man in the sense that he is what most of the detectives I worked with would like to have been and what quite a few of them, in their cockier moments, thought they approached."

The Maltese Falcon struck the fancy of John Huston, one of Hollywood's hottest screenwriters. In the words of Otto Friedrich, "Huston had reached the age of thirty-five and wanted to strike toward the center of Hollywood power." After working as a failed journalist, and having traveled the world as a self-described roustabout, Huston ultimately found a niche in Hollywood, just as his famous father Walter, one of the industry's most talented character stars, had done before him. After living more lives than the proverbial cat, John Huston was newly married when he settled into a long and rewarding cinema career. One of his first writing credits was a blockbuster film for two major talents, the 1937 release *Jezebel*, starring Bette Davis and directed by William Wyler. After penning the 1938 film *The Amazing Dr. Clitterhouse*, Huston then wrote two of Warners' major biopics, *Juarez* in 1939 and *Dr. Ehrlich's Magic Bullet* the following year. The latter netted an Academy Award nomination for Huston, as did his next effort, Howard Hawks' 1941 *Sergeant York*, starring Gary Cooper in one of his most enduring roles.

The screenplay that provided the springboard into the directing ranks for Huston was the 1941 release, *High Sierra*, on which he collaborated with novelist W.C. Burnett in adapting the latter's novel to the screen. *High Sierra* proved to be the crowning achievement in the colorful directorial career of Raoul Walsh, one of

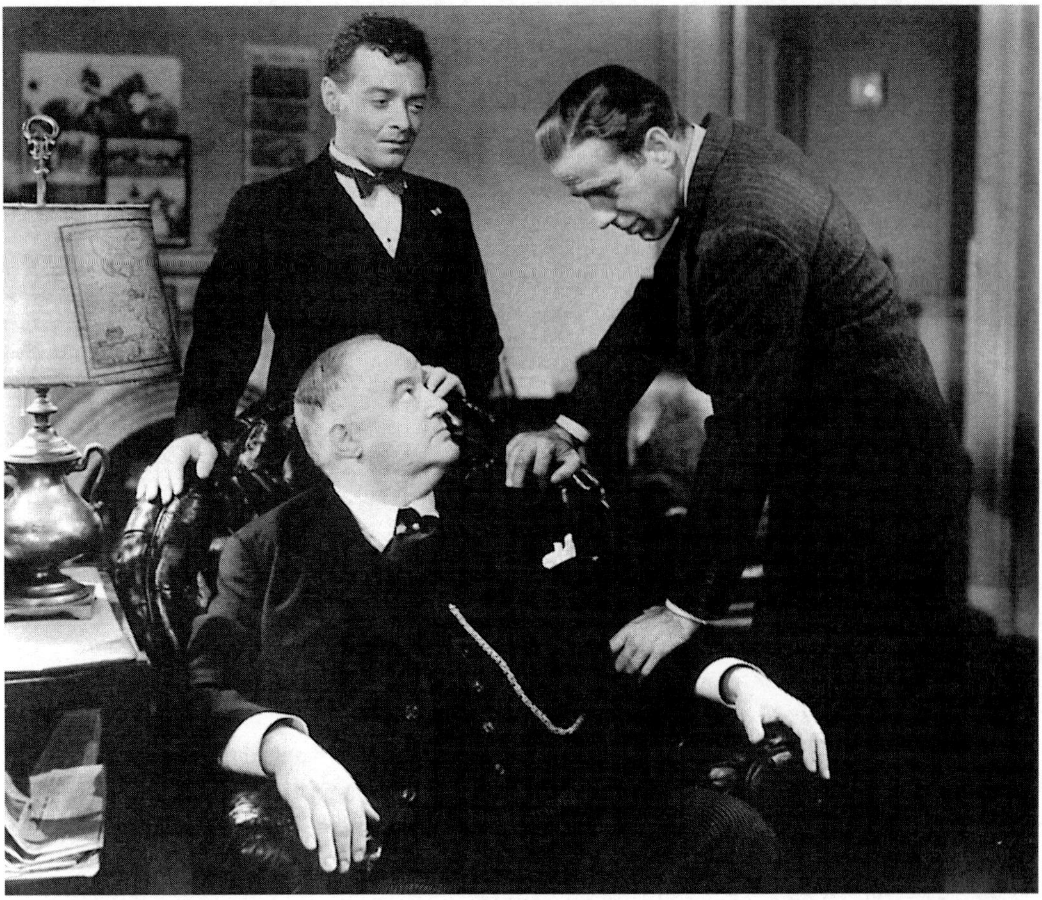

Tough, honest San Francisco detective Humphrey Bogart lets criminal mastermind Sydney Greenstreet know that he will tolerate no nonsense while Greenstreet's operative Peter Lorre stands by and listens in a scene from the 1941 Warner Bros. classic, *The Maltese Falcon*. John Huston, making his directorial debut, scored a casting coup in discovering Greenstreet, who had made a career out of playing butlers in New York theater, providing him with his film debut opportunity in the film.

Hollywood's larger-than-life figures. An individual who had moved around a great deal in various social circles, Walsh turned to directing after abandoning a film acting career after an accident left him minus an eye, after which he wore a patch. A two-fisted, boilermaker-swilling type, the adventurous Walsh teamed up with one of his own kind, Humphrey Bogart, who appeared in his first starring role as the fugitive hero who loses his life at the end of the film. It marked the beginning of what would be a long and mutually rewarding professional relationship between Huston and Bogart. Huston later directed Bogart in *The African Queen*, for which the actor won his only Best Actor Oscar; his co-star, Katharine Hepburn, received Best Actress honors. In another great Bogart-starring vehicle directed by Huston, *The Treasure of the Sierra Madre*, the director's father Walter earned an Academy statuette for Best Supporting Actor.

Bogart would be Huston's ultimate choice for the starring role in *The Maltese Falcon*, but not before it was turned down by Paul Muni, Edward G. Robinson, John Garfield and George Raft (who would later reject the lead in Billy Wilder's noir classic, *Double Indemnity*). Raft had earlier turned down the lead in *High Sierra*, providing Bogart with a golden opportunity. The name performers were leery about undertaking a starring role in what was designated a low-budget Warners film with Jack L. Warner mandating a brief shooting schedule. Also, Huston was making his debut as a director. And yet another point also concerned them: "[*The Maltese Falcon*] had been filmed twice before but never successfully," Huston revealed in his memoirs. "[Henry] Blanke and [Hal] Wallis [the producers] were surprised at my wanting to make a two-time failure, but the fact was that *Falcon* had never been really put on the screen."

Jack Warner was unenthused about a second remake of *The Maltese Falcon*. He agreed to Huston directing the film on the condition that he produce a satisfactory script. Huston's writing efforts had netted him earlier success.

Bogart was a kindred spirit poised to make a twin leap with Huston, after which he would emerge as a superstar and screenwriter Huston would emerge as one of the industry's premier directing talents. After receiving rejections from some of Hollywood's most notable screen tough guys, Huston was delighted by Bogart's laconic response when he approached him concerning his initial directing project: "Where the hell's the script and when do I start?"

Huston went to work immediately on the script of *Maltese Falcon*. The process resulted in the most bizarre Best Screenplay Oscar in Academy annals for Huston's adaptation of the Hammett detective novel.

Allen Rivkin, a veteran member of the leadership ranks of the Writers Guild of America, turned out such screenplays as Loretta Young's Oscar vehicle, *The Farmer's Daughter*. Huston asked Rivkin to collaborate with him on a *Maltese Falcon* script. "We were office mates, and we had a secretary between us," Rivkin said. Huston asked Rivkin to read Hammett's novel prior to embarking on the screenplay. After Rivkin finished the novel, Huston told him, "Let's give the book to the secretary to break it down into scenes and dialogue."

At that point, the fates intervened. Huston told Rivkin to ask the office secretary they shared to recopy the book, but from a scenarist's and director's standpoint, with establishing shots, scenes and dialogue. What was intended as a preliminary process resulted in a finished product. The Hammett novel converted into a script without changing either the novel's structure or dialogue. Rivkin explained that "in every studio, whatever a secretary types goes into the pool for copies. How it got to Jack Warner [prematurely], I don't know, but John came in one day all elated." Warner gave his approval for Huston to direct *The Maltese Falcon*; apprised of this, Rivkin responded that they had better get busy on the script. Huston replied, "No. The *secretary* did the script, and that's what he wants me to shoot!"

How the script reached Jack Warner's hands will almost certainly remain one of movie folklore's unsolved mysteries. Was big brother in the form of the Warners hierarchy carefully watching over Huston's activities? Was an ambitious secretary eager to let Warners officialdom see what Huston was doing? What can be said was that Jack Warner's new level of enthusiasm for *The Maltese Falcon* was high, as evidenced by his request that Huston begin shooting the film the following Monday. As Rivkin noted, Huston "took the credit on [the script], naturally, because he was the director.... And that made John."

A Detective and His Partner

The Maltese Falcon was released in 1941, just before America became involved in World War II after the Pearl Harbor bombing of December 7. It is thematically

Humphrey Bogart, right, stands next to the woman he loves, Mary Astor, but whom he believes he must turn in to the police for killing his partner in *The Maltese Falcon*. Astor is beguiling and resourceful while Peter Lorre (left), a lieutenant to Sydney Greenstreet throughout their criminal enterprise, constantly annoys Bogart.

interesting that *The Maltese Falcon* reveals a main character in detective Sam Spade who can appear corrupt on the outside but who, ultimately, relies on solid moral underpinnings. This puts him at odds with later film noir characters who succumb to evil, generally in the form of a tempting femme fatale such as Barbara Stanwyck, Jane Greer or Claire Trevor.

The thematic essence of the film boils down to a conflict which Bogart as Spade resolves in a moralistic manner. He has fallen in love with his client, aristocratically beautiful Brigid O'Shaughnessy (Mary Astor), and when he learns that she killed his partner Miles Archer (Jerome Cowan), he must choose between assisting the woman who makes his heart race, albeit a killer, or forgetting his personal feelings and taking the correct legal action. When the pivotal moment of the film occurs, Astor believes that Bogart, having fallen deeply in love with her, will cover up for the murder of his partner, someone he personally disliked. His shrewd mind had been in analytical operation from their first meeting, as evidenced by this brilliant piece of film dialogue: "We didn't believe your story, Mrs. O'Shaughnessy, we believed your $200. I mean you paid us more than if you had been telling us the truth, and enough to make it all right."

Hammett biographer William Nolan envisioned Sam Spade as a moral pragmatist caught up in the mire of a grimy netherworld where it was necessary to appear to play the criminal's game to secure ultimate victory for the cause of righteousness. Nolan concludes that in dealing with the sociopath Kasper Gutman (Sydney Greenstreet), "it is imperative that the fat man [Gutman] think him capable of anything; he must play villain to defeat a villain." This pragmatic maxim delineated by Nolan is evident when Spade later tells Brigid, "Don't be too sure I'm as crooked as I'm supposed to be. That kind of reputation makes it easier to deal with the enemy."

The beautiful femme fatale, one of the most unforgettable in cinema annals, learns ultimately that Spade's earlier comments about being "less crooked than I'm supposed to be" were sincere. "Don't be silly," Spade tells her bluntly. "You're taking the fall." He then provides his reasoning in the film's most important line in explaining the rigidity of the Sam Spade moral code. Even though he believes his deceased partner was a "louse" and makes no attempt to disguise his passionate feelings toward Brigid, he tells the coolly feminine beauty, "Listen. This won't do any good. You'll never understand me, but I'll try once and then give it up. When a man's partner's killed, he's supposed to do something about it. It doesn't make any difference what you thought of him. He was your partner and you're supposed to do something about it."

The character Sam Spade was drawn closely on the personal experiences of Dashiell Hammett as a Pinkerton detective, as were some of the other characters etched enduringly in *The Maltese Falcon* (crooks as well as police officers). It was understandable that a creative talent with the gifts of John Huston would select such a novel on which to make one of filmdom's most outstanding directorial debuts. A major reason for the film's popularity, along with the superb performance of Bogart as Sam Spade, was the fascinating ensemble of characters assembled by the fledgling director. Huston had watched 61-year-old, 285-pound Sydney Greenstreet playing butlers on Broadway. He signed him up for his first film role as the ruthless Kasper Gutman and the portly actor responded with a performance which resulted in a Best Supporting Actor Oscar nomination. Berlin refugee Peter Lorre was another excellent choice, having drawn earlier attention with his convincing portrayal of a compulsive child murderer in Fritz Lang's epic, *M.* Elisha Cook, Jr., became a standout in gangster films as an offbeat heavy, frequently corrupt and ruthless, yet ultimately vulnerable. The director's father Walter was summoned for a bit part *sans* dialogue as a dying ship captain who staggers into Spade's office with a package containing what was believed to be the valuable Maltese Falcon. Mary Astor proved a perfect femme fatale, seeking to convince with surface layer gentle femininity as she sought to fool a wily Bogart.

In addition to the dramatic interaction between Spade and the villains led by Greenstreet, the detective became involved in a cinema equivalent of a good cop/bad cop dualism represented by Detective Tom Polhaus, who was modeled on a former captain of detectives with whom Hammett in his detective days interacted, and Detective Lieutenant Dundy, Spade's bitter nemesis. Polhaus was played by veteran character actor Ward Bond, noted for his frequent association with director John Ford and his friendship with John Wayne. Barton MacLane played Dundy. On one occasion, an angry Dundy strikes Spade, with Polhaus quickly stepping between the angry pair before Spade can retaliate. The Dundy character is reminiscent of Raymond Chandler's invocation of the sharp continuing clash between his famous detective character Philip Marlowe and Lieutenant Degarmo of the Bay City Police.

While Raymond Chandler's detective, Philip Marlowe, is a tough, street-smart city detective with ethical standards, Chandler reveals a world of greater cynicism amid a sea of moral turpitude and overriding anarchy than that of Hammett. Hammett's Sam Spade learning about the enemy by attempting to play along, adopts a pattern of conventional morality. The famous dialogue (when a detective's partner is killed, he is expected to do something about it) summarized the code of Hammett. After being identified in 1951 House Un-American Activities Committee testimony as being a Communist, he was jailed for six months for refusing to divulge the source of funds he held as trustee of the Civil Rights Congress, cited as a Communist-dominated organization. He refused to disclose any information about his activities as trustee or reveal anything about his political affiliations or beliefs, basing his refusal on a bedrock principle that the information was nobody's business but his own. He would later be charged with tax delinquency by the Bureau of Internal Revenue.

The Huston blockbuster combined elements representative of film noir, but, as noted, in a milieu devoid of the anarchy, rapacity and often inevitable destruction which accompanied later film noir efforts. These elements included:

1) A street-wise, highly individualistic detective, tough and shrewd, who is determined to uncover the truth. His principles prompt him to reject the plea of

the woman he loves but knows to be guilty of killing his partner, someone he considered a louse. Bogart climbed the ladder to international stardom with his excellent portrayal of Sam Spade, playing the Hammett creation with just the right degree of physical toughness blended with steely intuition. He keeps Greenstreet and his gang off-balance with his machinations. One scene showing Spade as tactician occurred when, after going off on a tirade in Greenstreet's hotel suite, Bogart is seen in a revealing close-up in the hallway after his departure with a broad smile on his face, believing that his "angry" display had accomplished its desired purpose.

2) An alluring femme fatale with the beauty and feminine intuition to play havoc with the detective's emotions. Mary Astor was an accomplished veteran dating back to the silents. Had Astor been less appealing as Brigid, the decision that Bogart's Spade was compelled to make would not have been so agonizing.

3) A superb collection of villains. Just as Huston and Bogart used *The Maltese Falcon* to reach new heights, Sydney Greenstreet went on to become one of the most unforgettable villains of the screen. Peter Lorre used his role to enhance the momentum he generated through the highly acclaimed *M*, while the youthful Cook would become one of the most sought-after character performers in Hollywood. Each Cook role underlined a boyish vulnerability. Even as an older man, he performed brilliantly as the cuckolded husband of Marie Windsor in Stanley Kubrick's 1956 noir gem, *The Killing*.

4) Tension with the police. Bogart and MacLane harbor a strong mutual dislike which threatens to flare into physical violence each time they meet. Ward Bond supplies a master touch as peacemaker between the hot-blooded adversaries. One senses a genuine liking for Bogart on Bond's part, and that he understands him in a way that MacLane never will.

5) Tension of a large city at night. Just as Raymond Chandler made Los Angeles his noir venue, Dashiell Hammett immortalized the San Francisco whose pavement he had earlier pounded as a Pinkerton operative. Even though the low-budget film was shot entirely on the Warner Bros. lot, the flavor of San Francisco resonated in *The Maltese Falcon*. Huston used the City by the Bay's noted element of fog when Miles Archer steps into it early in the film for an appointment he will never keep. The camera follows stealthily and we see Archer fall to the ground after a gun is fired. The action is revealed through the victim's viewpoint. Given the density of the fog, viewers are unable to see the killer.

TWO

A Blend of Three Great Talents: *Double Indemnity* (1944)

Question: What is the ultimate result of a combination of the following forces? 1) An embittered beginning screenwriter who terms the novel; 2) a screenwriter walking out on his partner due to revulsion at the story; 3) a replacement screenwriter and partner-director who cannot abide each other; 4) a story considered so conspicuously amoral as to rattle censors and create apprehension from performers considered for starring roles; 5) a leading man strongly tempted to turn down the part; 6) an original work in which the dialogue appears made to order for the screen but cannot be successfully lifted off the printed page, and 7) a cynical screenwriter with an excessive taste for alcohol who looms as a perpetual, temperamental loose cannon.

Answer: In Hollywood fashion, the rocky aforementioned collaboration results in one of the greatest films ever made!

The 1944 Paramount classic *Double Indemnity* enjoys increasing attention as one of Hollywood's greatest efforts, bolstered by keen current interest in film noir. It would be intriguing to view a movie about the interactions of the participants who brought the controversial story to the screen.

By the mid-twenties, writer James M. Cain had left his native Baltimore and become a member of the editorial page staff of the prestigious *New York World.* He worked there alongside Walter Lippmann, who would ultimately reach the plateau of America's leading political editorial writer, and Allan Nevins, destined to become one of the nation's most eminent historians. Cain, considered a Lippmann protégé, learned to make magazine and book sales through the distinguished political journalist.

Having excelled in journalism and the freelance magazine market, it was understandable that Cain would eventually make the trek to California to work in the film industry. After a brief and uneventful period at Paramount, Cain had a comparable stint at Columbia. When he was terminated at Columbia, Cain decided it was time to sit down and write his first full-length book manuscript. Just when he needed an encouraging hand, one of the film industry's most talented and beloved scenarists was there to assist him.

Charming and engaging Vincent Lawrence was referred to by Cain biographer Roy Hoopes as "probably the prototype of the Hollywood writer of the 1930s, the kind of guy who called everybody 'pal' and 'laddie' and 'lassie.'" Lawrence had a special gift for words and was someone who could write the kind of masculine dialogue that would sound believable in love scenes when delivered by a macho leading man like Clark Gable. In Eastern detective magazine fiction, Cain (described by Maurice Zolotow in his biography *Billy Wilder* as "a stocky gentleman with hornrimmed glasses, who talked out of the side out his mouth like a stevedore and knew more about grand opera than any Viennese") developed a tough prose which befit ruggedness in the region of the country where the Baltimorean had been raised, encompassing as well the New York where he had spent a good deal of his professional career. Now that he had migrated West, the idea struck Cain to use the language of the western roughneck.

Cain and Lawrence developed a home-and-home operating basis for their joint efforts. Cain would spend evenings with Lawrence at his apartment at the Chateau Elysee on Franklin Avenue while, on other occasions, Lawrence would climb into his big Packard convertible with its separate windshield for the back seat and drive out to the San Fernando Valley to Cain's Burbank residence for creative sessions. Former journalistic colleague and friend Lippmann helped the fledgling novelist find a home for his short 35,000 word novel through his own publisher, Alfred K. Knopf, in 1934. After much creative straining the initial title of *Bar-B-Que*, disliked by Knopf, was scuttled in favor of another.

When Cain was musing on the amount of work involved in the publication of a first novel, recalled a period of anxiety he had encountered while living in Boston after sending his first play to New York. Lawrence recounted his daily ritual of walking over to the window to watch for the postman. When the process became unendurable, he would proceed to the backyard, always listening intently for the ring. "And no fooling about that ring," Lawrence said. "The son of a bitch always rang twice, so you'd know it was the postman."

The wheels in Cain's creative brain started turning. "Vincent, I think I've got my title," Cain said.

"What title?" Lawrence asked.

"*The Postman Always Rings Twice.*"

"Hey, that is a title, he sure did ring twice for Chambers, didn't he?"

Lawrence immediately caught the author's drift: Cain's street-wise anti-hero, Frank Chambers, had succeeded in escaping punishment after committing a murder, only to be sent to California's gas chamber after an automobile accident resulting, with supreme irony, in the death of Cora, his earlier accomplice in homicide.

Postman established Cain as a new star in the hard-hitting fiction realm. It became a 1946 film success, provided Lana Turner with her most memorable role and is also remembered as one of the celebrated efforts of co-star John Garfield.

While *Postman* was Cain's first fictional work, his initial book adapted to the screen was *Double Indemnity*, released in 1944.

While Hammett's *The Maltese Falcon* marked the debut of film noir, *Double Indemnity* marked a major transition into the genre. Hammett's Sam Spade remained a throwback to the old hero-villain sharply delineated lexicon in which virtue ultimately prevailed and evil was punished. *Double Indemnity* and the works that followed (down to more recent efforts such as *Chinatown* and *Body Heat*) did much more than blur the old Sam Spade distinctions represented in the detective's underlying code of honor; they eliminated them altogether, forging a new world predicated on an anarchy of the spirit in which protagonists are gripped by obsession, generally represented by a chillier-than-ice femme fatale. The netherworld of the streets, generally at pitch darkness, further accents this somber mood. Actions here are governed by the will to survive. On an ultimate philosophical level, this brand of film noir more closely represents the "pawns of fate" early twentieth century fiction of Theodore Dreiser in his defining works, *Sister Carrie* and *An American Tragedy*, both of which were successfully adapted to the screen.

A career turning point arose for Cain not long after he finished writing a screenplay for Universal's Maria Montez-Jon Hall vehicle, *Gypsy Wildcat*. An anthology of Cain stories entitled *Three of a Kind* contained a yarn in a community frightened by the power and rigidity of the Breen Office and its top watchdog, Joseph Breen, a founder of the Legion of Decency of the Roman Catholic Church. *Three of a Kind* had been a tough studio sell in the first attempt. A determined Cain had his new agent launch a fresh effort, and also furnished written suggestions on ways to placate the Breen Office. The new Hollywood agent H.N. Swanson, began shopping *Three of a Kind* around the studios in stitched-up galley form. One man who became interested was a Viennese.

According to James M. Cain, Wilder's initial interest in the selection from the trilogy that he would ultimately shepherd to a great directorial triumph, *Double Indemnity*, resulted from not being able to locate his secretary. After asking repeatedly for her, one of the other girls in the office replied, "I think she is still in the ladies' room reading that story."

"What story?" a curious Wilder asked.

"Some story Mr. Swanson left here," was the reply.

At that moment, Wilder's secretary emerged with the stitched galleys pressed against her bosom. By then the boss's curiosity had peaked. Wilder took the story home to read and immediately informed Paramount producer Joseph Sistrom that he wanted to adapt *Double Indemnity* to film.

Animosities Overcome

Wilder's first hurdle to overcome was the loss of his writing collaborator on most of his hits, Charles Brackett. The team embodied one of the interesting "odd couples" of cinema. Brackett was a highly educated, straight-laced Easterner from a distinguished family. His father had been a member of the New York Legislature. Brackett followed in his dad's scholastic footsteps by attending Harvard, ultimately graduating from its law school. He looked askance at Wilder's irreverence, particularly his flowery language. All the same, the unlikely duo had already carved out an impressive niche as a writing team. Brackett found the Cain story disgusting, and refused to have anything to do with developing it for the screen. Wilder saw things in a totally different way. Before deciding to embark on *Double Indemnity*, he had been contemplating directing a musical to avoid being typecast as a bitter, headline-oriented dramatist. During that same period, *Cover Girl* with Rita Hayworth premiered. Wilder explained to an interviewer, "I realized that no matter how good my musical might be, most people would say it was no *Cover Girl*. This *Double Indemnity* looked like a better chance to set Hollywood on its heels. Even my own studio said I was crazy to attempt it."

Paramount executive William Dozier surfaced at a strategic point, getting the *Double Indemnity* project launched through an initiative involving two famous writers, the book's author, Cain, and Wilder's eventual screenplay collaborator, Raymond Chandler. Dozier, then in charge of Paramount's writers, was a dapper executive resembling Hollywood leading man Joseph Cotten. Called upon by Paramount to negotiate the rights for *Double Indemnity*, Dozier offered Cain and Swanson $15,000, half upon signing and the remainder if Breen approved the final script. The agent urged his client to accept, telling Cain, "If we keep this thing in suspense, Wilder might just turn away." Cain bitterly complained for years afterward that the Breen Office cost him $10,000 since the going price for a screen property had been $25,000 in 1935. Dozier came into the picture again after Wilder was frustrated in his first attempt to secure a writing partner to replace Brackett. The director opted for Cain, but the creator of *Double Indemnity* was then under contract to Twentieth Century–Fox.

The frustrated Viennese filmmaker then received a timely suggestion from Dozier, who offered the name of Raymond Chandler. Dozier's creative instinct proved sensible since Chandler was (like Cain) a popular and respected generators of two-fisted realistic novels revealing the anarchistic and seamy underbelly of Southern California's netherworld. Wilder had never heard of Chandler, but after reading the detective master's first novel, *The Big Sleep*, which was given to him by producer Joseph Sistrom, he gave his approval for Dozier to initiate contact.

Dozier wrote to Alfred Knopf, publisher for Cain as well as Chandler, seeking Chandler's address. Dozier was surprised to learn that Chandler, who had never been previously employed by a film studio, was living in Hollywood. Chandler was residing with his wife Cissy (18 years his senior) only a short distance from Paramount.

When Chandler naively offered to furnish Wilder with a script for a few hundred dollars, Dozier concluded that he was in need of representation, calling in Cain's agent, a man who people in the industry referred to as "Swanny," to negotiate for him. He eventually signed for $750 a week for 13 weeks.

A Surprising Reaction

In theory it appeared to be the perfect blending: hard-boiled Chandler adapting the same "poke in the gut" realism of master stylist Cain to the screen. If case-hardened cynic Chandler could empathize with any writer, that person would seemingly be Cain. Such a theory would be dead wrong. Instead of empathizing, Chandler initially excoriated the author of *Double Indemnity*.

Perhaps Chandler's initial revulsion toward Cain stemmed from the inherent duality within the fascinating yet bizarre detective author. Considering his potent, two-fisted prose, people meeting him for the first time were often astonished by the individual they met. A Paramount writer H. Allen Smith expected a hulking, broad-shouldered football player type in the image of Chandler's fabled Philip Marlowe, and was astonished to meet a "mild-mannered guy of medium size with wavy black hair, horn-rimmed glasses, and a sensitive face." In Smith's opinion, Chandler looked "like a poet is supposed to look." Dressed in his traditional tweed jacket, bespectacled, with his equally traditional pipe resting between his teeth, Raymond Chandler, if he were to be typecast, it would be as a soft-spoken Professor of Literature on a leafy college campus in rural England or small town New England.

While born in Chicago, Chandler was raised by his mother in England. He would retain his English accent throughout the remainder of his life in America. The creator of Philip Marlowe was educated in the distinctly non–Marlowe setting of Dulwich College, five miles south of Central London. Marlowe would have let out a groan if he had ever cast his eyes on young Chandler clad in black coat and Eton collar! Years later, when Chandler wrote the screenplay for *The Blue Dahlia*, he would empathize with the film's producer, John Houseman, based on their common British prep school links. Dulwich, though lacking the prestige of upper class pacesetters Eton and Harrow, produced numerous achievers in the creative arts. P.G. Wodehouse had left Dulwich the year of Chandler's arrival. C.S. Forester, author of the Horatio Hornblower novels, and A.E.W. Mason, who penned *The Four Feathers*, both attended Dulwich, as did Michael Powell, who co-wrote and directed the British film classics *The Life and Death of Colonel Blimp* and *The Red Shoes*.

Chandler's early reaction to Cain was reminiscent of what a British country squire might say about someone seen as coarse and low-class. Rather than observing similarities in their writing, Chandler instead referred to Cain in a letter to their joint publisher, Alfred Knopf, as "Faugh." The Dulwich man further exclaimed, "Everything he touches smells like a billygoat. He is every kind of writer I detest, a faux naif, a Proust in greasy overalls, a dirty little boy with a piece of chalk and board fence and nobody looking. Such people are the offal of literature, not because they write about dirty things, but because they do it in a dirty way.... A brothel with a smell of cheap scent in the front parlour and a bucket of slops at the back door." Chandler ended his diatribe against Cain with an interesting question: "Do I, for God's sake, sound like that?"

On that note, Chandler and Wilder embarked on the process of adapting *Double Indemnity* to the screen. Wilder received an early jolt when he realized that the dialogue he had loved in the book was not successfully translatable by spoken word. Initially Wilder and Chandler stuck close to the original material until concluding that what read fine was not necessarily acceptable to the ear. To test their early suspicions that the dialogue did not sound right, a group of studio actors were hired by producer Sistrom to read the lines, which, in Chandler's estimation, sounded like "a bad high school play."

Eventually Chandler's opinion of Cain improved somewhat, perhaps altered at least in part by meeting and speaking with the author in a conference with Wilder and Sistrom also present. Cain biographer Roy Hoopes credits Chandler for coming "as close as anyone ever has to diagnosing why James M. Cain never developed as a scriptwriter or a playwright." According to dialogue master Chandler (in a letter to Cain), "Nothing could be more natural and easy and to the point on paper and yet it doesn't quite play.... It had a remote effect that I was at a loss to understand. It came to me then that the effect of your written dialogue is partly sound and sense. The rest of the effect is the appearance on the page. These unevenly shaped hulks of quick-moving speech hit the eye with a sort of explosive effect. You read the stuff in batches, not in individual speech and counter speech. On the screen, this is all lost, and the essential mildness of the phrasing shows up as lacking in sharpness. They tell me that is the difference between photographable dialogue and written dialogue. For the screen, everything has to be sharpened and pointed and wherever possible eluded."

By the time Cain received the detective writer's letter, he was operating on a $1,250-a-week contract at MGM and receiving many plaudits for *Double Indemnity*. In his reply to Chandler, he explained that the dialogue in his novels and short stories was "calculated." He explained that he employed a different system in movies than in books, and that in films, "I dictate for the ear and pay almost no attention to how it appears to the eye. I have been secretly amused at picture producers who tell me: 'And don't forget to give me plenty of that fast Cain dialogue.' The truth is the fact that Cain dialogue wouldn't play at all, but I think it advisable not to tell them." Cain then alluded to *Double Indemnity* and the dialogue experiment involving the Paramount actors. "Your description of the vague, cloudy way the dialogue sounded when you had it tried with actors is wholly interesting, for in *Double Indemnity* I was trying to capture some of those bellowing unrealities you get in a fever dream, and if the dialogue sounded as you say it did, quite possibly I succeeded."

It is possible that Cain was shrewdly attempting to bluff away his dialogue deficiencies by drawing differences that were contrived rather than real between his

Claims investigator Edward G. Robinson, right, reveals his suspicions to Fred MacMurray that criminal activity is afoot. It so happens that insurance agent MacMurray is deeply involved in the criminal conduct Robinson suspects, and is barely able to prevent the wily claims investigator from discovering him with his accomplice, femme fatale Barbara Stanwyck. This is one of the craftiest scenes from the brilliant, hard-hitting *Double Indemnity*. Billy Wilder directed, penning a taut script with crisp, acid-laden dialogue in tandem with famous detective author Raymond Chandler.

book-writing strategy and the one that he employed for the screen. Cain never cracked the top ranks of screenwriting whereas the Wilder-Chandler team received an Oscar nomination for its only effort, *Double Indemnity*.

The spoken effect of screen dialogue aside, Cain and Chandler were masters of the laconic, tough, no-nonsense masculine prose that served each author well. Given their perspectives, Southern California became the perfect base for their characters and their disingenuous lives of frustration.

The brilliant interpreter of film noir, Robert Mitchum, stated that "Los Angeles was a town for losers." Mitchum, the perfect Philip Marlowe, was describing Los

Angeles in particular but Southern California in general as a polyglot encompassing people who had encountered difficulties elsewhere. The land of sunshine was a perfect place to throw away the memories of painful experiences and begin anew. Los Angeles became the perfect spot to acquire new identities, an ideal location in which to lose oneself, a distinction separating honest arrivals who had encountered misfortune elsewhere from shadowy figures seeking to prey upon others. So often the first group, people seeking to lift themselves by their bootstraps and generate a fresh start in the town they called "The City of the Angels," would be directly confronted by the second contingent, eager to squeeze money from honest citizens through nefarious deeds. This minefield of activity set against the backdrop of a desert sun provided an ideal creative atmosphere for two master craftsmen to weave their tales of struggle, set against the backdrop of a sea of amorphous faces.

It was Cain's objective to create a central roughneck Southern California drifter for his first novel, which he did in the person of Frank Chambers, portrayed with unforgettable conviction by John Garfield in *The Postman Always Rings Twice*. The first paragraph of his great novelette sets the tone of the book by establishing Chambers' rootlessness:

> They threw me off the hay truck about noon. I had swung on the night before, down at the border, and as soon as I got up there under the canvas, I went to sleep. I needed plenty of that, after three weeks in Tia Juana, and I was still getting it when they pulled off to one side to let the engine cool. Then they saw a foot sticking out and threw me off. I tried some comical stuff, but all I got was a dead pan, so that gag was out. They gave me a cigarette, though, and I hiked down the road to find something to eat.

Cain's first chapter of *Postman* serves as a definitive model for creative writing instructors for several basic reasons. First, as mentioned, Chambers identifies himself in tough laconic prose as a California drifter seeking to find his way amid hard times. He is hungry and without prospects. A second crucial element immediately identified is that of fate in the development of the story. By discovering Chambers at the point where they did, the truck drivers enabled the story's anti-hero and first person narrator to make swift contact with Cora, and involve himself in an ultimate web of murder. The short and power-packed paragraph provides a significant example of why Existentialist author Albert Camus modeled *The Stranger* in part on the writing of Cain. Existentialism is built around the concept of fate in human existence. Its more rigid adherents believe in the doctrine of mechanistic predetermination, embodying a "pawns of fate" Dreiserian existence to the ultimate, in which we are at the total mercy of mechanized fatalism.

The second paragraph quickly establishes a Southern California sociological base, in which drifter and local rootlessness converge. This same combination is also extensively delineated by Chandler, along with New York transplant and Los Angeles area sociological chronicler Nathaniel West in his classic work, *The Day of the Locust*. Cain writes, "That was when I hit this Twin Oaks Tavern. It was nothing but a roadside joint, like a million others in California. There was a lunchroom part, and over that the house part, where they lived, and off to one side a filling station, and out back a half dozen shacks that they called an auto court. I blew in there in a hurry and began looking down the road. When the Greek showed, I asked if a guy had been by in a Cadillac. He was to pick me up here, I said, and we were to have lunch. Not today, said the Greek." The Greek proprietor set a place for the drifter, who proceeded to order a huge meal consisting of orange juice, corn flakes, fried eggs and bacon, enchilada, flapjacks and coffee.

Cain's second paragraph also identifies the uncertainty of the Depression period. The book was published in 1934 but *Postman* did not ultimately reach the theaters until 1946. Once more Cain demonstrates a unique genius of establishing character, mood and setting within the space of just a few well-chosen words. He makes the process look deceptively easy, resembling something one could easily dash off in letter form. The genius is reflected by the deceptive appearance of ease. Cain mentions that the roadside sandwich joint was "like a million others in California," telling his readers about the numerous individuals eating on the run, moving freely from place to place in the open spaces of the sunny Golden State. After mentioning the filling station, he then refers to the "half dozen shacks that they called an auto court." Once more we are reminded of people on the move, transients, individuals on the run.

The brilliantly succinct first chapter, encompassing two pages, sets the stage for the tragic noir dilemma that will follow. The kind-hearted Greek stakes Chambers to the meal after Chambers guiltily informs him that there really is no man in a Cadillac. He then meets Papadakis' wife Cora and is asked by the proprietor of Twin Oaks if he would like a job. At the behest of femme fatale Cora, the drifter will ultimately agree to kill Nick, a man who has been kind to him. Cain strikes hard and fast, setting a dramatic stage quickly, proceeding to hypnotically drive his readership forward until the final page, symbolizing his trenchant verbal craftsmanship.

Chandler as Pungent Social Critic

Raymond Chandler, in speaking through his fictional alter ego, the redoubtable detective, Philip Marlowe, became a pungent social critic of Los Angeles in particular and the vagaries of humankind in general. At his acerbic peak, Marlowe seems to be echoing that most bleak assessment of humanity penned by Robinson Jeffers, the poet of Big Sur, not long before his death. Jeffers defined humanity as "a botched experiment run wild that ought to be stopped."

The critical Chandler wit is at its trenchant best in his description of a Marlowe drive from Los Angeles north to the San Fernando Valley in the 1949 novel *The Little Sister*, which would be made into a James Garner film (*Marlowe*) two decades later. Also to be noted is the Chandleresque metaphorical skill cleverly at work: "I drove East on Sunset but I didn't go home. At La Brea I turned north and swung over to Highland, out over Cahuenga Pass and down on to Ventura Boulevard, past Studio City and Sherman Oaks and Encino. There was nothing lonely about the trip. There never is on that road. Fast boys in stripped-down Fords shot in and out of the traffic streams, missing fenders by a sixteenth of an inch, but somehow always missing them. Tired men in dusty coupes and sedans winced and tightened their grip on the wheel and ploughed on north and west towards home and dinner, an evening with the sports page, the blatting of the radio, the whining of their spoiled children and the gabble of their silly wives. I drove on past the gaudy neon joints that look like palaces under the colors, the circular drive-ins as gay as circuses with the chipper hard-eyed car-hops, the brilliant counters, and the sweaty greasy kitchens that would have poisoned a toad. Great double trucks rumbled down over Sepulveda from Wilmington and San Pedro and crossed towards the Ridge Route, starting up in low-low from the traffic lights with a growl of lions in the zoo."

Chandler the social critic and acerbic sociologist was dissecting the post–World War II Southern California scene, with its floodtide of changes. People from all parts of the country were descending there to find their personalized places in the sun. The situation was compounded by the arrival of many young men, some with new families, who had first seen and lived in the area when they were being trained to go abroad to fight in the great global conflict. The biting prose demonstrates the disgust felt by Chandler as evidenced through his reliable alter ego Philip Marlowe.

From the highway scene, narrator Marlowe describes a dinner stop near Thousand Oaks. Ironically, this was the same town north of the San Fernando Valley where Cain's narrator and protagonist Frank Chambers was thrown off the truck in which he had been riding. Chandler through alter ego Marlowe describes the mentality behind the restaurant, which is expected to serve as a microcosm for many more businesses in the burgeoning Southern California of the late forties:

> I ate dinner at a place near Thousand Oaks. Bad but quick. Feed 'em and throw 'em out. Lots of business. We can't bother with you sitting over your second cup of coffee, mister. You're using money space. See those people over there behind the rope? They want to eat. Anyway they think they have to. God knows why they want to eat here. They could do better home out of a can. They're just restless. Like you. They have to get the car out and go somewhere. Sucker-bait for the racketeers that have taken over the restaurants. Here we go again. You're not human tonight, Marlowe.

In addition to spotlighting a callous business attitude, Marlowe is also focusing on what Harvard sociologist David Riesman wrote about in his illuminating work, *The Lonely Crowd*. People seek to go out to avoid the loneliness of staring at four silent walls, only to get lost in a crowd of others of a like mind, doomed to concurrent frustration. This theme of aimless, wandering frustration is continued one paragraph later after Marlowe has left the restaurant where he has eaten dinner and maneuvered himself back onto the highway. He writes, "I drove on to the Oxnard cut-off and turned back along the ocean. The big eight-wheelers and sixteen-wheelers were streaming north, all hung over with orange lights. On the right the great fat solid Pacific trudging into shore like a scrubwoman going home. No moon, no fuss, hardly a sound of the surf. No smell. None of the harsh wild smell of the sea. A California ocean. California, the department store state. The most of everything and the best of nothing. Here we go again. You're not human tonight, Marlowe."

The Philip Marlowe who excoriated California as "the department-store state" was almost optimistic compared to the detective's conclusion of his first novel, the 1939 masterpiece *The Big Sleep*. His concluding sentiments extend beyond his views of Southern California to the naked purposelessness over how we exit life's highway:

> What did it matter where you lay once you were dead? In a dirty sump or in a marble tower on top of a high hill? You were dead, you were sleeping the big sleep, you were not bothered by things like that.... You just slept the big sleep, not caring about the nastiness of how you died or where you fell.... On the way downtown I stopped at a bar and had a couple of double Scotches. They didn't do me any good.

The writings of Chandler and Cain entered a fresh dimension beyond that in which Dashiell Hammett traveled. While Hammett is customarily acknowledged to be a high level genre craftsman, creating interesting characters like the Continental Op and Sam Spade, then employing the same narrative skills to hook readers, carrying them along to a story's conclusion, Chandler and Cain have won places in college classrooms denied to Hammett.

Chandler and Cain emerge as a part of American literature alongside giants such as Melville, Twain, Faulkner, Wolfe and Fitzgerald while Hammett has earned a niche outside that notable pantheon as a skilled genre technician. The distinction arises from literary and sociological impact due to depth of characterization and sociological substance. Great writers have a way of dominating the periods in which they live by capturing through commanding verbal skills the sights, sounds and events of the contemporary scene. As Shakespeare commanded the Elizabethan stage through graphic portrayal, leaving a massive imprint, Herman Melville was able to do the same for the mid-nineteenth century in which he wrote. One astute student of Melville wrote that his classic work *Moby Dick* should be read three times by all serious students of literature: 1) in youth, 2) in middle age, and 3) later in life. The differing periods of life enabled the reader to analyze a complex and fascinating literary work from various perspectives.

The genius of Chandler and Cain was in their unique talents in analyzing a region of the country in a state of flux during the Depression period and its aftermath, culminating in the post–World War II period with its myriad changes. The Southern California of the roughly 15-year-period starting in the middle '30s and extending to the end of the '40s saw the aftermath of a great migration of settlement,

Tom Powers is literally signing his life away when he affixes his signature to a double indemnity accident policy he has been coaxed into signing by insurance agent Fred MacMurray. Paramount's 1944 blockbuster *Double Indemnity* is a film that shattered conventional barriers in helping etch noir drama as a notable film genre. Powers' unfaithful spouse, Barbara Stanwyck, watches with cunning approval.

embodying all the problems that such rapid growing pangs entail. Dynamic clashes of forces are observable in the graphic characterizations found in the pages of Chandler and Cain fictional works. The laconic prose they strategically employ impacts upon the reader in the manner of a no-nonsense voice of experience relating events in the bluntest manner.

In 1965, Lawrence Clark Powell, a librarian at the University of California, addressed the question of Chandler's greatness: "What makes [Chandler's novels] so good? Why are they among the few mystery stories of our time, and among the few novels about Los Angeles, that have achieved the distinction of literature? The answer is contained in a single word: *style*. Chandler's prose style has what he said Dashiell Hammett's lacks—overtones, echoes, images."

Chandler revealed his own perspective on what lifted a book to the level of literature in a letter to fellow Southern Californian Erle Stanley Gardner, the creator of the popular Perry Mason mystery series. According to Chandler, "When a book, any sort of book, reaches a certain intensity of artistic performance it becomes literature. That intensity may be a matter of style, situation, character, emotional tone, or idea, or half a dozen other things. It may also be a perfection of control over the movement of a story similar to the control a great pitcher has over the ball."

A Clash of Giant Egos

Great creative artists are known for their individuality. As highly developed individuals listening to the tune of their own distinct voices, they are often far less amenable to joint work endeavors than people in less individualized pursuits. Raymond Chandler and Billy Wilder were men of enormous talent, prodigious creativity and sturdy convictions. Their collaborative effort in the shaping and ultimate completion of the brilliant *Double Indemnity* script resulted in an often-violent clash of egos.

Chandler biographer Frank MacShane acknowledged that "Chandler himself did not take easily to working in the studio. He was shy and insecure in its strange atmosphere and bridled at anyone who put on airs. Above all, he could not bear to be patronized. His relationship with Billy Wilder was cool and polite, with occasional rows that would require the intervention of [producer] Joseph Sistrom." Wilder later called Chandler "one of the greatest creative minds" he had encountered and that the detective author had adapted himself very quickly to the film medium. The director later speculated that Chandler may have disliked him because he was German. It is more likely that the communicative difficulties were of a different origin. As Frank MacShane wrote, "More probably, the tension of the two working together made Chandler oversensitive and suspicious."

Chandler was a loner. By traveling to a studio daily and working with a co-writer, Chandler was withdrawing from ingrained working conditions in an isolated habitat. The nadir of the Chandler-Wilder relationship came when a sharply penetrating ray of Southern California sunlight poured through the Venetian blind onto the script, and Wilder requested, "Go and fix that, will you, Ray?" Chandler responded by rising, announcing that he would no longer work with Wilder, and stalking out of the office.

John Houseman, then an assistant producer at Paramount who would later team up with Chandler on the Alan Ladd-Veronica Lake film, *The Blue Dahlia*, as producer and screenwriter respectively, recalled observing a long document typed on yellow paper in which Chandler catalogued the purported indignities he had suffered from Wilder, urging that they cease immediately. Among the listed demands were: "Mr. Wilder was at no time to swish under Mr. Chandler's nose or to point in his direction the thin, leather-handled malacca cane, which Mr. Wilder was in the habit of waving around while they worked. Mr. Wilder was not to give Mr. Chandler orders of an arbitrary nature such as 'Ray, will you open that window?' or 'Ray, will you shut that door, please?'"

A Terrifying End Result and a New Film Reality

Despite their differences of opinion and dislike for each other, Wilder and Chandler remained consummate professionals and devout believers in the Shakespeare maxim that "the play's the thing." Once that they completed a taut shooting script, an "all bite and no bark" adaptation of James Cain's novel, fears abounded within Paramount and outside its gates that the creative duo had gone too far in presenting an uncompromising realism that would cause problems with the Breen Office as well as a shocked public if and when a finished product made its way into the nation's theaters.

The precedent-shattering film would ultimately weather all storms. The finished product was a new reality, a step well beyond the traditionally ethical private detective Sam Spade of *The Maltese Falcon*, a leap into an orbit of the rapacious and anarchistic, where blood lust and greed could be microscopically examined through a sharply honed script, defining camera angles and uncompromisingly honest performances. *Double Indemnity* can be broken down into the following story components:

1) A male lead (Walter Neff) who, unlike Sam Spade, was not just pretending to be corrupt to defeat a ruthless villain, but succumbed fully to a woman. He finally concedes that she is thoroughly rotten and without redeeming social value. Neff is a well-dressed, smooth-talking, thoroughly superficial insurance salesman who gets by on his gift of gab and is devoid of any real ambition. He has an eye for women and enjoys flirtation.

2) Neff becomes putty in the hands of femme fatale Phyllis Dietrichson. She is in psychological control over Neff from their first meeting, but must convey the impression that she is disgusted with and does not understand Neff's overt obviousness in pursuing her through un-subtle flirtation. In this area, Neff is anything but fooled by Phyllis's expressions of surprise, but this awareness avails him nothing as he becomes her victim, feeling a burning lust that propels him to a daring level he had never previously scaled.

3) The emergence of a would-be father figure, a voice of knowledge and uncompromising honesty. Barton Keyes is a walking actuarial encyclopedia of the insurance business, which represents his entire life. When Neff plots, it is with the knowledge that, if there is just one slip, the brilliant Keyes will crack the case. The Keyes relationship receives an interesting dramatic spin with the older man's feeling for Neff. The intense Keyes recognizes the younger man's aimlessness. Keyes

offers him a job as an assistant in the claims department over which he singly presides. It entails a drop in pay, but Keyes hopes to give some purpose to Neff's life, and instill in him some of the burning idealism that fuels the older man. Neff declines. After he and Phyllis Dietrichson kill her husband, Neff is forced to sweat through the subsequent investigation, always wondering if the wily Keyes will solve the case.

4) The emergence of a "good girl," a contrast to Phyllis Dietrichson. This plot concept is woven adroitly into the story with the appearance of the sweetly sensitive, sincere stepdaughter of Phyllis, Lola Diedrickson. After making Lola's acquaintance, Neff learns disturbing facts about Phyllis, beginning with Lola's conviction that the predatory femme fatale killed her mother. Lola feels a need to get some details off her chest and Neff proves to be the ideal confidante. The more she confides the greater the realization that he has been taken in by a ruthless woman who will stop at nothing to get what she wants.

5) The emergence of the next victim of Phyllis Dietrichson. One of the reasons why Lola is so melancholy and eager to confide in Walter Neff is that the amorally wily Phyllis has found a victim to step into the shoes previously occupied by him. Nino Zachette, a hot-tempered former medical student, is Lola's boyfriend until Phyllis steps into the picture. She proceeds to poison the vulnerable young man against Lola, working him into the same web occupied by Neff, who quickly understands the implications. The insurance salesman concludes that it is only a matter of time before Phyllis convinces Zachette to do away with Neff. After that, Neff reasons, she will find a way to do away with Zachette. Neff sees the vicious cycle of greed, murder and lust continuing as long as Phyllis Dietrichson lives. While Lola provides some clues regarding Phyllis and her developing relationship with Zachette, he draws his own conclusion concerning his own vulnerability as a prospective victim of the amoral femme fatale after receiving a vital piece of information.

6) Merging objectives. Neff sneaks into Keyes' office one afternoon after the claims manager has left for the day. Eager to learn what is on Keyes' mind regarding the Dietrichson claim, he turns on Keyes' Dictaphone and learns that he has been cleared of suspicion. Neff then hears that the prime murder suspect is Nino Zachette, who has been seen making frequent evening visits to Phyllis. Neff concludes that the web is closing in on him fast and that soon Zachette, under the same hypnotic influence of Phyllis, will be uniting with her to take his life. He brings matters to a head by visiting Phyllis. His objective is the same as hers: Each individual wants the other out of the way. As a result, each individual has a gun and each fires with devastating results.

Double Indemnity rocked the film world with its chilling predatory realism as lust, greed and passion overrode conscience and decency. Almost 40 years after the initial release of *Double Indemnity*, a young screenwriter preparing for his directorial debut saw within the framework of the basic story the idea for a chilling drama of his own. While *Double Indemnity* had broken new ground in storytelling realism in the 40s, Lawrence Kasdan's *Body Heat* (1981) took the thread of the earlier story and embellished it in ways that Wilder and Chandler could never have done with the Breen Office such a dominating factor.

One basic area wherein Kasdan was able to extend his story beyond *Double Indemnity* was that of sexual expression. Prevailing censorship prevented showing Phyllis turning Walter into a helpless victim by physically revealing her animal seductiveness. Kasdan faced no such obstacle in the updating of the original story as femme fatale Kathleen Turner in her film debut reduces William Hurt to putty. Hurt becomes so keenly aroused that he smashes a window to get inside her house and ravish her for the first time, after which they ultimately plot and kill her wealthy husband (Richard Crenna). Whereas *Double Indemnity* showcased a bustling, rapidly growing Los Angeles during the war, *Body Heat* was set in the small town of Lake Worth, Florida, located only a few miles south of Palm Beach. Kasdan emphasizes heat on heat at Hurt's lust for Turner, represented in the film's title of *Body Heat*, as the torrid romance is symbolically played out during a sticky Florida summer heat wave.

The new freedom available to filmmakers like Kasdan was also revealed in another area where Wilder and Chandler could never dare to traverse. Deputy District Attorney Ted Danson and police detective J.A. Preston both strongly suspect that their friend, unsuccessful criminal lawyer Hurt, was involved with Turner in Crenna's death. They beg Hurt to cut off his association with Turner. Crenna was a syndicate operator, and Danson and Preston believe society in general and Florida in particular are better off without him. They explain that at a certain point, if he continues to visit widow Turner in the evenings and evidence is amassed, there is no way they can continue to help him. Wilder and Chandler could never consider making Barton Keyes complicitous. The industry morality code established by the Breen Office would never allow it.

A final area where *Body Heat* parted company with films of the 40s was that femme fatale Kathleen Turner's brilliantly hatched plot totally succeeds. Her high school yearbook reveals a yearning to travel to exotic lands. As the film concludes, the shapely Turner is seen lying in a bathing suit at poolside in the sun at an undisclosed tropical paradise as a handsome young male admirer hands her a drink. Meanwhile Hurt sits in Florida State Penitentiary after being convicted of the crime she induced him to commit. Whereas Phyllis Dietrichson selects Walter Neff as an accomplice due to his familiarity with the insurance business, improving the chances for a major financial score upon her husband's death, Turner picks Hurt due to his conspicuous deficiencies as an attorney. She draws up a phony will in the name of her husband which she plants in Hurt's office. It is purported to have been written by Hurt and violates the Rule Against Perpetuities governing wills, invalidating the document. As a result, Turner as widow receives all of her dead husband's assets. Turner's research before meeting Hurt uncovers information that he was disciplined by the Florida Bar for malpractice pertaining to an earlier will he wrote, making his second apparent mistake plausible. The freedom to allow the crime perpetrator in a movie to ride off into the sunset unpunished, as Turner does in *Body Heat*, did not exist in the 40s when *Double Indemnity* was filmed.

MacMurray's Good Luck Charm

After the team of Wilder and Chandler completed what was destined to be acknowledged as one of the most potent shooting scripts in cinema history, the director moved on to the crucial casting phase. Wilder's initial choice to play Walter Neff was, predictably enough, the top male star on the Paramount lot, Alan Ladd. But Ladd was averse of taking a chance in a highly controversial role in Wilder's daring project.

Once more, as occurred so often in casting suspense dramas in the early forties, the name of George Raft surfaced. The former dancer from New York's Hell's Kitchen turned the part down. The role was unappealing to Raft for the same reason that the lead in *High Sierra* was; he did not want to die at the end of a film in which he starred. Raft said he would play the part of Walter Neff if he turned out to be an FBI agent at the end. Wilder found this hilarious. As a result, history repeated itself and Raft lost out on a superb film role.

After having been nixed by Raft, Wilder turned his attention toward Fred MacMurray. The tall, dark-haired actor refused the part for a time. He had made his mark in the film capital as a light comedy lead, and wondered if he could handle a part that was such a radical departure from past roles. Wilder's instincts with MacMurray in *Double Indemnity* are reminiscent of Rouben Mamoulian's conviction that a light comedian by the name of Fredric March was capable of mastering a challenging dual role in *Dr. Jekyll and Mr. Hyde.* Mamoulian's judgment would be validated by March's ultimate Oscar win for that 1931 film.

At one point, an uncertain MacMurray told Wilder, "I'm a saxophone player. I do little comedies with Carole Lombard." Wilder, sounding like a coach giving an apprehensive athlete a pep talk, told the reluctant actor, "You've got to take this big step."

The wily Wilder strategized in a manner suggesting he would make an excellent poker player. Wilder had set his sights on Barbara Stanwyck as the coolly calculating, ruthless Phyllis Dietrichson. Stanwyck biographer Al DiOrio revealed that since Phyllis Dietrichson, a sociopathic murderer, was different than any part the great actress had ever played, "For the first time Barbara was unsure of herself. She wasn't sure she could carry it off or what the public's reaction would be to her portrayal of an out-and-out bitch."

At that point, Wilder the strategist went to work. Stanwyck and MacMurray had respect for each other, which gave the cagey director maneuvering room. Wilder told Stanwyck that if she would agree to do the film, he could obtain the services of MacMurray. Stanwyck then agreed to consider taking the role. The next step in Wilder's ploy was to contact MacMurray, informing him that Stanwyck would agree to perform in the film on his acceptance. MacMurray stated, "There being nobody, then or now, whom I respect more, not only as an actress but as a person, I said okay." MacMurray's triumph in *Double Indemnity* forged a new career beyond the light comedy roles in which he had been previously typecast.

MacMurray and Stanwyck can thank Wilder for his shrewd gambit since *Double Indemnity* is generally thought to constitute the peak performance of each star. Stanwyck received an Academy Award nomination (Ingrid Bergman would ultimately win for her performance in *Gaslight*) while MacMurray, though overlooked in the Oscar sweepstakes, received a Best Actor nomination from the New York Film Critics Circle. They constituted on-screen dynamite. In the words of Al DiOrio, "The eroticism between these two can almost be touched."

Wilder achieved another casting coup by tapping Edward G. Robinson for the role of Keyes, the indefatigable claims manager. The shrewd factotum receives analytical assistance from "the little man" living within him, who informs the investigator whenever a claim carries a fishy scent.

Verbal Stylization

The laconic "battering ram" dialogue that was the joint product of Wilder and Chandler, particularly evidenced in the first double entendre-laced conversation between Stanwyck and MacMurray, carries the impression of a biting realism more apparent than real. The dialogue of *Double Indemnity* that is also evident in other film noir masterpieces such as RKO's *Out of the Past* with Robert Mitchum could be classified as verbal stylization. The lean dialogue with the pit bull bite is to the ear what the cinematic stylization embodied by shrewdly positioned camera shots is to the eye.

The essence of what dialogue crafters accomplish was explained by a law professor to an interested class years ago. The wily professor, who as a lawyer had many times argued before the United States Supreme Court, explained the true essence of the compliment that a barrister "thinks fast on his or her feet." The professor said that "thinking on your feet involves being prepared." The brilliant response on the part of an attorney during a tense moment of a trial is the product of lengthy hours of preparation. What seems to be a spontaneous comment stems from painstakingly covering the subject matter involved from every standpoint.

In spontaneous conversation, even among intelligent and articulate people, one's best thoughts almost invariably occur afterwards. In only rare instances are even clever individuals able to spontaneously register the type of verbal bull's-eyes generated by MacMurray and Stanwyck in the course of a conversation such as the meeting between Neff and Phyllis. To be able to provide such sharply focused repartee necessitates advanced knowledge of the subject or subjects to be discussed.

The spontaneous ring generated by the *Double Indemnity* dialogue represents joint reflection over a lengthy period by two of the most gifted dialogue masters in American history. While long reflection is necessary to produce results such as that heard in the film, the magic that is produced through verbal stylization, the appearance of spontaneity, is part of the special make-believe magic of films.

Verbal and visual stylization entertain through engaging ear and eye in an entertaiment process revealing sharpened speech and images presented as spontaneous behavior.

Cain's novella was based on the 1927 Snyder-Gray case set in New York, but the adaptation was perfectly situated to Southern California. The pervasive air of an area then consisting almost entirely of migrants gives it, as drawn out in the skillful creative hands of Cain and Chandler, the same aura as the inimitable British master cynic Somerset Maugham gave to Monte Carlo. Maugham referred to the great French resort as "a sunny place inhabited by shady people." The irony evidenced by films like *Double Indemnity* is how the dark presence of film noir is felt even in the bright desert sun of Los Angeles. It is the byproduct of the people, so often the aimless confronting the ruthless, as in the classic confrontation between Neff and Phyllis. Neff is a bachelor of 35 making a good living as an insurance salesman through conditioned indifference. A spark is ignited within him when he meets the quintessential femme fatale Dietrichson.

Wilder helped make Barbara Stanwyck all she was meant to be in her stirring role as a literal and figurative man killer. Wilder outfitted the brunette actress in a blonde wig, prompting Paramount mogul Buddy DeSylva to quip with dismay, "We hire Barbara Stanwyck and here we get George Washington." Wilder explained, "I wanted her to look as sleazy as possible."

The blonde wig was the starting point for the Stanwyck transformation. Premier Hollywood dress designer Edith Head was brought in by Wilder to enhance the effect. She responded by presenting Stanwyck initially in a silky robe, then in appropriately confining tight skirts and sweaters. The clincher was a gold ankle bracelet which Neff spots early in their first meeting.

Controlling the Temperature

The first meeting between the femme fatale and her victim involves the combination of 1) using animal magnetism and the appropriate level of suggestiveness to seize the intended victim's attention, and 2) controlling the temperature in such a manner as to enhance the animal urges within that individual while maintaining a studious enough aura of standoffishness to spur the potential victim onward, conveying the impression that ultimate conquest involves a challenge. A shrewd femme fatale can never convey the impression of a sexual pushover if the game is to be played in the most adroit manner. That is why married women make good fatales in that the husbands they seek to dispose of or cheat on can be used as psychological tools to wave in the faces of their lusty pursuers.

When Neff, responding to the golden anklet, silk robe and come-hither manner of Phyllis, makes suggestive remarks, she reminds him, "There's a 45-mile-per-hour speed limit in this state." When he asks her, "How fast was I going, officer?" she replies, "I'd say about 90." He becomes cryptically skeptical after he makes an appointment to return to the Dietrichson home the following night. The dialogue moves with blistering Chandler speed:

NEFF: You'll be here too?
PHYLLIS: I guess so, I usually am.
NEFF: Same chair, same perfume, same anklet?
PHYLLIS: I wonder if I know what you mean.
NEFF: I wonder if you wonder.

Neff knew that his pursuer understood his comment, but controlling the temperature is an inherent element of the game orchestrated by a Phyllis Dietrichson. As Pauline Kael wrote regarding the Stanwyck character, "With her bold stare, her sneering, over-lipsticked, thick-looking mouth, and her strategically displayed legs, she's a living entrapment device." The snaring of the femme fatale's victim is generally a foregone conclusion; the elements of cinema fascination are embodied in how the game is played up to the victim's capture and the pattern of activity proceeding from that critical juncture to the film's conclusion.

In many ways, the hapless Neff emerges as a yo-yo manipulated from conflicting sources, the evil personification of Phyllis on the one hand and the incorruptible father figure displayed by Edward G. Robinson as Keyes. While Neff is being seductively coaxed toward murder by Phyllis, loyal Pacific All-Risk company man Keyes, who needs a sharp and reliable assistant, offers the younger man the position at a pay cut from his salesman's post. He cites the creative challenge of the job, which Keyes explains requires more thought than the organized persistence of his salesman's job. When Neff declines, a disappointed Keyes quips that he had previously held the opinion that the salesman was smarter than the other fellows around the office, but in reality was "just taller."

Thinking Through Keyes

Billy Wilder used a flashback structure to enhance two of his greatest dramatic hits, *Double Indemnity* and the 1950 classic *Sunset Blvd.* The opening scene of *Sun set Blvd.* (scripted by Wilder and Charles Brackett) has been the subject of frequent discussion among film zealots, cinema historians and writers in general for its unique creativity. The murdered body of hard luck screenwriter Joe Gillis (William Holden) is seen floating in the swimming pool of former silent screen legend gone mad Norma Desmond, portrayed commandingly by bona fide silent star Gloria Swanson. Film audiences look and listen with rapt attention as the deceased scenarist now begins narrating (!), telling in flashback a story that begins with his first meeting with Norma Desmond and ends with his murder at Norma's hands. The technique serves a twofold purpose, (1) a visual and narrative hook to grab the viewer's interest, in a cinematic equivalent of the way that literary detective and suspense masters like Chandler, Cain and Hammett used it to capture immediate interest in their books, and (2) the establishment of narrative pull by leading audiences into important scenes, giving them the kind of enhanced perspective that book authors can provide through the aid of the written page, and that are generally denied to filmmakers given the differences between the two realms of creative expression. By allowing a narrator to provide interesting story input, the narrative pull that accompanies the narrative hook of a Chandler, Cain or Hammett can be employed through film.

For *Double Indemnity*, the team of Chandler and Wilder cleverly instituted a vehicle for implementing the mystery author's narrative hook-narrative pull duality. Action commences on a dark and deserted Olive Street in the heart of downtown Los Angeles, where a lone car pulls to an erratic stop at the curb in front of a large office building. The tall figure of Fred MacMurray as Walter Neff steps out of the car and walks with obvious difficulty into the building, where the offices of Pacific All-Risk Insurance Company are located. When Neff enters the elevator, the night watchman registers surprise at seeing the insurance salesman at that hour. The watchman makes some small talk that fails to bring Neff out of his introspection, which is registered in his troubled expression. Neff enters Keyes' office, picks up his Dictaphone and begins to tell his story, beginning with a seemingly routine visit to the upper middle class Los Feliz neighborhood to renew a lapsing automobile insurance policy. It is there that Neff encounters Phyllis Dietrichson.

The sharp narrative from Neff describing his ordeal features the clashing forces reflected in Phyllis and Keyes. Neff reveals to Keyes that his planning at each stage involved thinking like his father-figure office compatriot. The manner in which he describes the morbid details is enhanced by the agony he suffers from the bullet wound sustained during his final climactic meeting with Phyllis.

Neff calls on every bit of experience, bolstered by his association with Keyes, to fashion a plan to kill Phyllis' husband, a stolid, humorless oil executive (Tom Powers). Even after Dietrichson suffers a broken leg in an oil field accident, Neff presses Phyllis to convince him to make his annual trek north to Palo Alto for a class reunion. Neff even sees an added attraction: a double indemnity clause in the life insurance policy that Dietrichson was tricked into signing covers deaths in falls from moving trains, an insurance company come-on applied to rarely occurring events.

Neff kills Dietrichson, then takes his place on the train, jumps off, then places the dead man's body on the railroad tracks. An ironic story twist is that, after killing Phyllis' husband so he can be united with her, the murder leaves them compelled to separate as Keyes, the claims adjuster with the bulldog instincts, investigates the claim with broadened fascination. Irony is piled atop irony as, after shrewdly concluding that Dietrichson's death resulted neither from suicide nor accident, the adjuster decides that the killer is Nino Zachette, a hot-blooded former USC medical student and former boyfriend of Phyllis' stepdaughter, Lola.

Another point of irony is that Neff, who would otherwise be expected to be elated at having a designated fall guy to be punished for his crime in Zachette, someone he disliked from their one brief and brusque meeting, is alarmed to learn through eavesdropping on Keyes' Dictaphone that the conclusion has been reached through tracing the movements of the young man in concert with those of Phyllis, with whom he has been spending a great deal of time.

A Dramatic Clash of Opposites and a Stirring Climax

A frequent element of noir suspense films is the direct clash of evil between a good and often at least somewhat naive woman and that of a more experienced, hardened female. This clash is often plausibly aided by having the good woman younger than that of the wily, experienced femme fatale. A facsimile of this contrast has been successfully used in romance novels.

In *Double Indemnity*, Neff ultimately turns against Phyllis through the disclosure by Keyes along with revelations by a thoroughly shaken Lola, sensitively portrayed by Jean Heather, a last-minute replacement for Mona Freeman. Lola explains how her ruthless stepmother has lured Zachette away from her with her feline adroitness and poisoned his mind at the same time. She drops a bombshell on the victimized insurance salesman by revealing just how her father met Phyllis. She tells him that Phyllis had worked as a nurse when Lola's mother was ill, after which the earlier Mrs. Dietrichson died, with the new woman quickly stepping into her shoes after a whirlwind courtship with Mr. Dietrichson. Lola also observed her stepmother trying on her funereal black mourning outfit before her father's demise.

Many suspense films are capable of maintaining a brisk pace up to the conclusion, when all too often writers using clever ploys to enhance audience interest have painted themselves into corners with disappointing results. Wilder did a great deal of experimenting before filming a memorable conclusion.

The breakneck pace relentlessly continues as Neff, feeling pathetically used and with blood reaching a boiling level, decides to finish off Phyllis, leaving Zachette to pay the price for his joint murder endeavor with the seductive blonde. His effort is enhanced by his knowledge that Zachette is due to visit her 15 minutes later. Their memorable meeting occurs in the darkness as befitting a film noir classic. An instrumental version of a popular hit song of the period, "Tangerine," wafts in through an open window. The laconic dialogue contains its same bite, as evidenced by Neff's sadly resigned comment, "It's just like the first time I came here, isn't it? We were talking about automobile insurance, only you were thinking about murder. And I was thinking about that anklet." A dramatic exchange has Phyllis sneering, "We're both rotten." Neff responds, "Yeah, only you're a little more rotten."

Always the cold realist, Phyllis recognizes the impasse she has reached with Neff. When he steps across the room, she removes the gun she has hidden beneath her chair and fires. In her warped and tormented way, she held a love for Neff, so she is unable to fire again as he moves toward her, grabs the gun, and kills her. He waits outside for Zachette. Displaying a decent instinct, he hands him a nickel and coaxes him into going to the nearest pay phone to call the brooding Lola, who cares for him.

The Final Ending

Wilder spent much time and reflection on how to end the tense and taut masterpiece. Neff would ultimately pay the price for his misdeeds, a result mandated by the Breen Office, but the question remained as to just how to bring the story to a fitting conclusion.

The rapidly paced Cain novella ended with the murderers of the oil company executive simultaneously meeting death through a suicide pact. The novella focused much more strongly on the insurance salesman's involvement with stepdaughter Lola than depicted in the film. Wily claims investigator Keyes agrees in the book to provide his surrogate son-ultimate killer with a head start toward the Mexican border, but not until he has signed a confession to his involvement in the murder. The partners in crime, called Walter Huff and Phyllis Nirdlinger in the book, are spotted by the captain early on the cruise ship they have boarded for Mexico (not long after Keyes has given bride Lola away as she marries Zachette). First person narrator Walter wrote: "The captain knows us. I could tell by his face when he came out of the radio room a little while ago. It will have to be tonight. He's sure to put a guard on us before he puts into Mazatlan."

Walter and Phyllis decide to kill themselves when the moon comes up that evening. At the very time that Walter has started bleeding internally again, he thinks about the shark a sailor had pointed out to him in the water earlier. He writes, "The bleeding has started again. The internal bleeding, I mean, from the lung where the bullet grazed it. It's not much but I spit blood. I keep thinking about that shark." When Phyllis joins him that afternoon in the stateroom, he pens, "She looks like what came aboard the ship to shoot dice for souls in the *Rime of the Ancient Mariner*." The final words Walter writes before the joint rendezvous with death are "The moon."

Deliberating Over an Execution

Intent upon providing the proper ending to his groundbreaking noir epic, Wilder initially decided that Neff's ultimate fate should be death in the gas chamber after a last meeting with Keyes. After the long walk to the execution chamber, Keyes witnesses the death of the man he loved like a son. Following Neff's demise, a stunned, traumatic Keyes stands transfixed, long after the final execution viewer has left the witness room. He has to be summoned by a guard to leave before he can bring himself to turn and slowly walk away.

Paramount spent $150,000 to reconstruct the gas chamber, execution room and witness gallery of San Quentin Prison. It took five days of intensely concentrated shooting. Wilder would later remark that the execution scene was one of the best segments he had ever filmed. Despite its inherent dramatic greatness, this ending would be seen only at a single preview. Wilder made the ultimate decision that the execution sequence would be cut, despite its raw power (not to mention the money Paramount spent on it). He decided it was too strong and had Chandler write another ending. The ultimate conclusion of Neff sprawled out in the corridor, badly bleeding, unable to make it to the elevator and at least temporary freedom, used the staple dialogue exchange summing up the relationship between the two men:

> NEFF: Know why you couldn't figure this one, Keyes? I'll tell ya. The guy you were looking for was too close. Right across the desk from ya.
> KEYES: Closer than that, Walter.
> NEFF: I love you, too.

The helpless figure of Neff sits sprawled on the floor as Keyes watches at the fadeout. The audience knows that the best Neff can hope for, as expressed in earlier dialogue, is to be pieced together in the hospital and ultimately die in the so-called "Little Green Room" where lethal executions by gas were held in Northern California's San Quentin. Knowing how and where to impose cuts is as intrinsic an element of a great director as the knowledge of the scenes to retain. The final scene of *Double Indemnity* would win its rightful place as one of the most dramatically memorable in cinema history.

It is likely that by the time the film was concluded Wilder, as well as Chandler, Stanwyck, MacMurray and the production's other contributing forces, had an idea that some Hollywood history had been made. Cain biographer Roy Hoopes wrote years later: "The movie was shot in a little over forty days in the fall of 1943, and all winter long the talk at the Brown Derby and other bars and restaurants was about a movie, then being edited, that would rock Hollywood and the country."

Double Indemnity proved such an epic *tour de force* that even Paramount did some cautious hedging. Perhaps smarting from the official censor's verdict that the film was "a blueprint for murder," the studio pushed a different film for Oscar recognition: *Going My Way*, a feel good story about the lives of two parish priests (Bing Crosby and Barry Fitzgerald) and a glamorous nun (Ingrid Bergman). On Oscar night, *Going My Way* secured a Best Picture statuette over nominee *Double Indemnity* with its director, Leo McCarey, winning over Billy Wilder. In terms of staying power, *Double Indemnity* has aged like great vintage wine while the Paramount film with the cheerful message is rarely shown.

As for the historical significance of Wilder's daring film, during the same period that *Double Indemnity* was being conceived and ultimately filmed, exciting things were happening at the neighboring studio two blocks southwest on Melrose Avenue. RKO was doing a groundbreaker of its own that would generate considerable thunder for its hard-boiled realism in 1944.

THREE

Women of Danger and RKO's Noir Factory

The major success of *Double Indemnity* resulted in triumph and vindication for two major suspense authors finding increased audiences and critical praise along with harsh criticism from censors. James M. Cain's controversial novella had been converted into a film triumph through the visual mastery of director Wilder and a script laced with TNT dialogue. The irony for Raymond Chandler was that at the very time he was successfully adapting the work of another writer to the screen, just a few blocks from Paramount on the RKO lot on Melrose Avenue a major project was being developed, one which bore an intimacy beyond adapting Cain's work to the screen.

Charles Koerner, RKO's dynamic studio boss, was as daring as Billy Wilder. His objective was a significant $400,000 budget devoted to adapting Chandler's *Farewell, My Lovely* to the screen under the revised title of *Murder, My Sweet*. Even though Chandler was working only a short walking distance away, rights would be secured and the creator of Philip Marlowe would not even be invited to the party since he was then under contract to Paramount.

The blueprint for *Murder, My Sweet*, which was also released in 1944, was akin to *Double Indemnity* in that the plot revolved around the ruthless activities of a beautiful femme fatale with the same amorality as Barbara Stanwyck's Phyllis Dietrichson. There would also be a sincere good girl to furnish dramatic contrast, as Lola Dietrichson portrayed in the Paramount film. Film noir was rapidly providing new opportunities for glamorous actresses with one cautionary caveat: Challenging parts were involved. The leading lady was obligated to simultaneously make herself interesting while audiences expressed a natural revulsion toward the loathsome, anti-social behavior displayed.

The successful paths trodden by the creative forces molding *The Maltese Falcon, Double Indemnity* and *Murder, My Sweet* resulted in actresses moving from conventional images of supportive housewives and law-abiding working girls into daring temptresses intent on staying ahead of their victims and the police. In 1946, two of the screen's greatest beauties, Lana Turner and Rita Hayworth, rendered their most memorable screen performances in *The Postman Always Rings Twice* and *Gilda*, respectively. If blonde Turner and redhead Hayworth garnered bouquets as the femmes fatales for 1946, honors went to gorgeous brunette Jane Greer in 1947, as ruthless and cold-blooded in *Out of the Past* as any hoodlum portrayals generated by the likes of Cagney or Robinson.

It would be helpful to now analyze content similarities of film noir. It is ultimately impossible to present a reliable, much less definitive, checklist of elements incorporated into the films since there were too many variables. All the same, supplying a list of elements enhances understanding of this exciting cinema realm.

Basic elements of film noir often include the following:

1) A leading male figure, often a private detective, who becomes victimized by an opposing force, generally a femme fatale, sometimes a powerful syndicate led by a corrupt and ruthless boss, and on many occasions a combination of those forces. Sometimes the male is a vacillating type more easily manipulatable. Primary examples of this type are Fred MacMurray in *Double Indemnity* and William Hurt in *Body Heat*. MacMurray and Hurt were a salesman and lawyer respectively. The Robert Mitchum detective figure manipulated by Jane Greer in *Out of the Past* was a stronger, less controllable individual than either MacMurray or Hurt, but became ensnared in the wily clutches of Jane Greer even as he repeatedly discerned her pattern of amorality, which he found morally contemptible while he sexually succumbed. He repeatedly stands up to his rival for her affections, syndicate boss Kirk Douglas, as Greer's feminine wiles overwhelm his better instincts.

2) The ruthlessly calculating femme fatale. This type has a judicious mixture of beauty, raw sensuality and an intelligence and amorality that allows her to strike like a panther with no guilt compunctions.

3) A male force or forces actively pursuing the victim. This is often a syndicate, sometimes in concert with a ruthless boss who orchestrates activities. The cynical Whit portrayed by Kirk Douglas in one of his earliest film roles, *Out of the Past*, is a classic example of a sociopathic syndicate boss who believes that you buy and control people in the same way one does furniture or automobiles. Douglas is inflamed by Mitchum and Greer uniting because it marked a departure by two people he had presumably bought and paid for as a private detective and mistress respectively. In *The Maltese Falcon*, John Huston breathed life into the film through his casting coup of the fascinating three-man criminal ensemble of Peter Lorre, Sydney Greenstreet and Elisha Cook, Jr., who convey personas exceedingly offbeat as well as ruthless. The pursuing force need not be corrupt or negative. It can be the police or even an authority figure such as claims manager Edward G. Robinson as he seeks to unravel the story behind the allegedly accidental death of Mr. Dietrichson in *Double Indemnity*. On some occasions, the victim is pursued in a crossfire involving

policemen convinced he has done wrong and a killer or syndicate seeking to silence him.

4) The good girl as a dramatic contrast to the generally older, wiser, more experienced femme fatale. This innovation is effective because it generates dramatic tension within the leading man while demonstrating the differences between good and evil to audiences within the framework of the evolving story. The innocent are often less complicated and considerably less prepared than the coldly calculating individuals who make a science of laying intelligently constructed traps in a methodical manner. Since the femme fatale exudes such a glamorous facade and calculates many steps ahead in the manner of a skillful chess champion, the male victim is often more likely to react positively to the possessive overtures of the woman of experience in contrast to the importunings of the honest but less calculating good girl, who operates on genuine instinct rather than methodical preparation. A cornerstone of many dramas is the manner in which the intended male victim is gradually won over by the woman of virtue. This plot development worked to brilliant effectiveness in *Murder, My Sweet*, as will be examined forthwith.

"Find My Velma!" *Murder, My Sweet* (1944)

A policy of watchful waiting, the correct blend of patience mingled with fervent determination, finally won the day for a character actor hungrily sniffing the scent of a role he knew could make a major difference in his career, one of those parts from which other opportunities would spring.

Mikhail Mazurwski was brought to America by his immigrant parents early in the twentieth century not long after his birth in Tarnopol, Austria. The young Ukrainian grew up in upstate New York and, like so many ambitious people, decided to seek fame and fortune in the big city. He went to school at Manhattan College and, through an interesting series of twists and turns, would ultimately achieve fame as a film actor after changing his name to Mike Mazurki. An actor with Horatio Alger roots, Mazurki's steadfastness of purpose enabled him to overcome many obstacles during the Great Depression and gain ultimate success.

An incident from early in his Manhattan College days was of unique significance. Here was a young man who had never seen a football game in his life, but who decided to attend a game to watch a college friend play. At a sturdy 6' 4", Mazurki was certain to be noticed by a football coach. At halftime, when Mazurki visited the Manhattan College dressing room, the coach took one look at him and exclaimed, "Son, I'd like to put you in."

"The first football game I ever saw as a spectator was one I ended up playing in at Manhattan College," Mazurki recalled. "It was the only time I ever heard about somebody ending up playing in the first college football game he ever saw."

Mazurki thrilled his immigrant parents by securing a college degree, but the timing was inauspicious when he sought to enter the job market. His ambitions ran headlong into the Great Depression. He did some amateur boxing and played professional football in the early fledgling days of that sport, when the pay level was considerably removed from what the current heroes of the National Football League television era receive. Mazurki got a job working on Wall Street. While this could have represented an opportunity for riches during a more opportune period, this was the Depression, when stock market employees were known to while away otherwise empty time playing catch with baseballs and gloves on the stock exchange floor.

While Mazurki was and would remain an educated, intelligent, erudite man who could converse on virtually any topic, it was that huge, muscular physique that his Manhattan College football coach spotted that provided him with a ticket out of the Depression doldrums. A professional wrestling promoter spotted him and made Mazurki an offer.

"The promoter told me that he would train me, supervise workouts, and give me a chance to see if I could develop into a professional wrestler," Mazurki explained. "He said that after I had worked under him for about a month he would tell me whether he thought I had what it took to be a wrestler. After working under him, he gave me the go ahead and got me my first match."

An ecstatic Mazurki had his first match on an outdoor promotion at the Polo Grounds in the Coogan's Bluff section of uptown Manhattan.

"It all really thrilled me, happening the way it did, having my first professional wrestling match before all those people in that large outdoor stadium," Mazurki reminisced. "I won my first match with a flying tackle, a popular maneuver in that period, and made $250. As a young guy trying to survive during the Depression, it seemed like a fortune to me. After that, I got a guy to book my matches and jumped into my new profession with glee."

Mazurki's wrestling prowess enabled him to benefit from the ironic phenomenon linked to the Depression period. While unemployed men sold apples on street corners of big cities and knocked on front doors of residences in small town America offering to perform work chores in exchange for food, there were long lines outside movie theaters and arenas. The desire to escape at least for a time the bleakness of an economically tragic period prompted those who could to scrape together money to attend movies and wrestling events. The thriving film industry garnered spectacular dividends with products expressing America's polarity. On the one hand, the delightful Shirley Temple, the princess of the "feel good" realm of optimism, played to huge throngs. The highly publicized activities of real life mobsters Al Capone, John Dillinger, Baby Face Nelson and Dutch Schultz spawned a wave of successful gangster films which garnered lasting stardom for James Cagney, Edward G. Robinson, Humphrey Bogart and George Raft.

Mazurki quickly moved to the top of the professional wrestling world and was pitted in competition with world champions such as Ed "Strangler" Lewis, Jim Londos and fellow Ukrainian Bronco Nagurski. His successful efforts generated demand for him to appear in all regions of the country. Wrestling and boxing both enjoyed wide popularity in Southern California so it was only a matter of time before

Mazurki headed west. The Friday night fights at the Hollywood Legion Stadium on El Centro Avenue a couple blocks northwest of Hollywood Boulevard and Gower Street not only drew top celebrities such as Al Jolson and George Raft; the heated action prompted the rich and famous to often engage in brawls of their own, frequently surpassing the intensity of the ring competition. A highly excitable Lupe Velez, living up to her screen image as "The Mexican Spitfire," frequently took off her shoes and pounded them on the ring apron when she believed that action needed acceleration. During the Depression, wrestling was also big at the Hollywood arena located beneath the pepper trees, on which a Bally fitness center now sits. It was popular too at the Olympic Auditorium situated at 18th and Grand just south of the heart of downtown Los Angeles and at Ocean Park Arena near the waters of the Pacific Ocean in Santa Monica.

Not long after Mazurki arrived in Southern California, he received an opportunity to work in the film industry. Saucy screen comedienne Mae West had received a death threat. When she was slated to work in *Belle of the Nineties* at Paramount in 1933, the blonde actress sought protection in the event that the anonymous individual who sent the message sought to personally or through an emissary or emissaries carry out the threat. Mazurki was employed by the actress as a bodyguard during the shooting of the film.

"My instructions were simple and clear," Mazurki revealed. "I was to be near Mae West during the entire film. I was told to keep a constant watch for anyone or anything out of the ordinary. Since I had to be near Mae West, it meant that I was in every scene. I was an extra working in every scene of the film without any dialogue. Mae West was very kind to give me a screen credit even without dialogue at the end of the film. As for the threat, thank goodness nothing happened. Whoever made the threat never tried to make good on it."

Mazurki had received a taste of the Hollywood cinema scene. Within a decade he would receive an opportunity to join the acting ranks. His big moment occurred one evening after he had finished his match at the Olympic Auditorium and had returned to the dressing room.

"I had just finished showering and was getting ready to leave when somebody told me there was a guy who wanted to talk to me," Mazurki recalled. "The dressing room visitor turned out to be Josef von Sternberg. He explained that he thought I was right for a part in an upcoming film he would be directing and asked if I would be interested. I told him I was definitely interested."

Mazurki made his film debut as a performing actor in the 1941 Sternberg film *The Shanghai Gesture*, amid a celebrated cast including Gene Tierney, Walter Huston, Victor Mature, Ona Munson and Maria Ouspenskaya. The famous European director who had selected a little-known German revue artist to star in *The Blue Angel*, propelling Marlene Dietrich to ultimate superstar status, had launched Mazurki who, from that point until shortly before his 1990 death would remain a stellar and highly active character performer. Until his retirement from the wrestling mat in the '60s, he would function as both actor and wrestler.

On the heels of his debut for von Sternberg, Mazurki was cast in an action biography at Warners, a 1942 release based on the life of former world heavyweight boxing champion James J. Corbett: *Gentleman Jim*. The studio's most popular leading man, Errol Flynn, portrayed the San Francisco fighter who brought finesse to boxing. Mazurki was cast as one of Corbett's ring opponents.

The cinematically active '40s marched on with Mazurki cast in films such as *Mission to Moscow*, *Lost Angel* and *The Missing Juror*, but the part he found the most intriguing was one that was seemingly out of reach. "Here I was under contract at RKO at the time and the part I felt I was ideally cast to play was one that seemed to elude me. There was this great story Charles Koerner had just bought and there was a terrific part in it for a big guy, a menacing heavy. I thought I was perfect for it and talked to the director, Edward Dmytryk, about it. The problem was at that time he considered me a professional wrestler and not an actor so he would say things like, 'Mike, you're a good wrestler. Stick to your wrestling.'"

Convinced that he was ideal for the part of the menacing Moose Malloy in *Murder, My Sweet*, Mazurki decided to exercise a posture of watchful waiting, hoping that his quiet determination would result in receiving a role he knew would enhance his career.

"I kept checking and hearing that they still hadn't cast the part of Moose Malloy," Mazurki explained. "I mean, here they were looking all over and here I was just waiting for the chance. I sat around the commissary at RKO hoping that somebody would notice me and put two and two together where the Moose Malloy part was concerned."

Mazurki was hard to miss as he maintained his posture of watchful waiting at RKO. Finally the strategy paid off. "It was Charles Koerner, the head of the studio, who finally told Dmytryk, 'You know, you've been looking around all this time trying to cast the part of Moose Malloy when we've got the perfect guy for the role right here at this studio, Mike Mazurki.' When Mr. Koerner mentioned me, Dmytryk finally saw the light and cast me for the part."

Kindred Spirit Powell

During the making of the film, Mazurki encountered an equally determined leading man intent on turning his career around during a critical phase. Whereas Mazurki was seeking prominence in the film arena, Dick Powell had been in the cinema limelight from his twenties. His career crossroads stemmed from the fact that he had made his mark as a perpetually youthful song and dance man but was now entering his forties.

Powell, seeking to shift his career into drama, lobbied unsuccessfully for the part of Walter Neff in *Double Indemnity*. He possessed the actor's instinct to know when a pivotal opportunity had surfaced. Just as Mazurki was eager to grab the villain's role of Moose Malloy, Powell saw rainbows and silver lining in the challenging

Philip Marlowe lead in *Murder, My Sweet.* According to Mike Mazurki, "When I first met Dick Powell he told me, 'Mike, we're in the same boat. You're trying to move up the ranks as a character actor and this will be your most important part. Yes, I've been a leading man, but that was in musicals. I'm moving into a new field to play this part so let's work closely on this and we can help each other.'"

Powell had many major film credits in the musical field. He appeared in three of the hugely popular *Gold Diggers* musical variety films in 1933, 1935 and 1937. He starred in two 1933 winners, *42nd Street* and *Footlight Parade*, both opposite dancing star Ruby Keeler, and in 1937 he wowed blonde glamour girls Alice Faye and Madeleine Carroll in *On the Avenue*. Powell appeared opposite Rosemary and Lola Lane, Frances Langford and Benny Goodman and His Orchestra in the Busby Berkeley–directed musical *Hollywood Hotel*. The RKO hierarchy knew Powell had a big name, which provided marquee luster as he retooled his image.

Despite the advantage of economic budgeting in film noir, in the case of *Murder, My Sweet*, the Charles Koerner commitment of a $400,000 budget for the project represented a muscle flexing on the part of RKO indicating its desire to compete with the major studios. This news surely reached the ears of Raymond Chandler, who was working just a couple blocks away at Paramount and was known to visit nearby watering holes like Lucy's, where Hollywood production activities were daily conversational grist.

Chandler remembered that he had received $2,000 from RKO in 1941 for an earlier production of *Farewell, My Lovely*, which was ultimately released under the title of *The Falcon Takes Over* starring George Sanders. The film represented an obvious attempt to reap benefits from the immensely popular John Huston adaptation of Dashiell Hammett's *The Maltese Falcon*. In May 1942 the Chandler novel *The High Window* was sold to Twentieth Century–Fox for $3,500. The result was a second feature programmer, *Time to Kill*, starring Lloyd Nolan.

Since *Murder, My Sweet* was another version of *Farewell, My Lovely*, to which RKO had purchased rights in 1941, Chandler received no additional compensation. As earlier mentioned, his contract with Paramount prevented him from working on *Murder, My Sweet*, but the knowledge that RKO had ticketed it for major production release, along with his co-writing status with Billy Wilder on *Double Indemnity*, doubtlessly provided happy moments during those informal luncheon discussions with writers in which he unofficially presided as senior member at the Paramount commissary. Chandler and his subject matter had permanently vaulted out of their earlier B film status. Both productions still endure as suspense classics studied eagerly by film historians, critics and aficionados.

The Giant from the Shadows

One of the primary elements which invests *Murder, My Sweet* with its classic film noir look is the manner in which director Edward Dmytryk utilized dark shadows to advantage. By making him a creature of darkness, Dmytryk furnished Mike Mazurki's Moose Malloy with an aura that made him one of the screen's terrifying psychopathic killers. From the time that Mazurki initially appears in Dick Powell's small Hollywood office, illuminated only by the brightly flashing lights of Hollywood Boulevard several stories below, he remains a lurking presence. Despite his hulking demeanor, the determined Malloy surfaces with the stealthiness of a circumspect hunting dog. Marlowe realizes that he is likely to pop up at any time and any place. The detective is aware of another paramount reality: The psychopathic ex-convict who has been released after serving eight years in prison is maniacally zealous in his pursuit of his old girlfriend, his hungry urges substantially enhanced by the time he has spent away from her and by the fact that she has failed to keep in touch with him.

The incessantly repeated exhortation, "Find my Velma!" is drummed into Philip Marlowe without letup. Malloy is there to remind him at virtually every unscheduled opportunity of the importance of locating the woman the cretinous giant calls "as cute as lace pants." Not only are dark shadows utilized to make Mazurki appear menacing, his swarthy appearance and matching suits and hat enhance the effect. Despite the ease with which he becomes ruffled and homicidally violent, Malloy never sees fit to raise his voice, the violence appearing all the more terrifying. This is no evil giant who loses his temper; he is an easily programmed homicidal tool. Malloy responds like Pavlov's dog when the shrewd and polished villain of the film, Jules Amthor, portrayed by veteran character actor Otto Kruger, tells him during a meeting in Kruger's Sunset Towers penthouse apartment that he believes Marlowe has information about Velma's whereabouts. Such disclosures result in Malloy grabbing his victim by the throat. Fortunately a gasping Marlowe is spared death when Kruger informs him that the detective was really not withholding information on the elusive Velma, whereupon he turns his victim loose. To use Malloy in such a manner, however, is like waving a red cape before an angry bull. Ultimately Amthor is a victim of Malloy's maniacal pursuit of his elusive girlfriend and is strangled when the hulking giant becomes convinced that he has been withholding news about Velma.

Montage Sequence

The tense confrontation in Kruger's apartment sets the stage for one of the most effective scenes in noir annals. It is preceded by an angry Powell punching Kruger. The cynically grinning criminal, never abandoning his suave demeanor, responds by pulling out a gun and hammering Powell on the head, knocking him unconscious.

The collision involving Powell's head and the butt of Kruger's gun is followed by an eerie montage sequence serving as an explicit example of what film noir is all about. The woozy pool of black uncertainty into which the detective is hurled is represented in the unforgettable sequence. The viewer can readily empathize with

Powell's tortured state of helplessness through the use of camera techniques revealing his dazed condition, along with the confining walls in which he is imprisoned. Amid the spinning vortex, Powell stares at a piercing white light above the bed where he lies. Thick stationary smoke surrounds him as taut narration commences in Marlowe's voice: "The window was open but the smoke didn't move; it was a gray web woven by a thousand spiders. I wondered how they got them to work together." Marlowe was plunged by the shrewd criminal into the cruel hypodermic needle world of a sleazy clinic run by a heartless quack, Dr. Sonderborg, effectively rendered by Ralf Harolde. As needles pierced his skin, the cold-blooded Amthor hopes to use the drugs as a truth serum to force information out of Marlowe about a missing jade necklace (he wrongly assumes the detective knows its whereabouts). During the torturous inquisition, the omnipresent Moose Malloy also stands by. Marlowe is not able to escape until after he has knocked a male nurse unconscious with a steel bar he has removed from the bed and has wrested a gun away from Dr. Sonderborg. After he has staggered out of the house in the residential neighborhood where the clinic is located, Marlowe is greeted on the sidewalk by none other than Moose Malloy, who immediately presses him for more information concerning Velma.

Good Girl-Bad Girl Syndrome

Murder, My Sweet employs the effective ploy of numerous mystery stories, the good girl-bad girl syndrome. The two female leads pitted in psychological warfare against each other are ruthless blonde femme fatale Claire Trevor and the dark-haired, innocent Anne Shirley. They are natural competitors in that Shirley is the daughter of an enormously wealthy businessman and Trevor is a gold digging stepmother. The second Mrs. Grayle is ostensibly seeking to locate a stolen jade necklace, which Jules Amthor also seeks. The mutual antipathy evident on the surface is shrewdly emphasized in their competition for the affections and professional assistance of Powell. Shirley was at the time of *Murder, My Sweet* as the wife of the film's producer, Adrian Scott. Her girlish good looks and sweet demeanor blend as a shrewd casting contrast to the blonde temptress Trevor, and are representative of an actress who had been a successful ingenue previously. Shirley was nominated for a Best Supporting Actress Oscar by playing an ingenue in a 1937 release, *Stella Dallas*, after securing her big break three years previously when given the lead in *Anne of Green Gables*. She retired from films after appearing in *Murder, My Sweet* and two other 1944 films while still in her twenties. Her marriage to Scott ended in divorce and endured tragedy when he was called to appear before the House Un-American Activities Committee and was ultimately sent to prison as one of the Hollywood Ten.

Trevor had a much lengthier career. A product of New York City, Trevor made a transition from the New York stage to films. She moved from a series of early roles as a hardened but sympathetic victim or gun moll in a host of B productions into the ranks of stardom with her memorable performance as a likable saloon girl in the 1939 John Ford Western classic *Stagecoach*, which also provided a career rocket thrust for male lead John Wayne. Trevor secured an Oscar for Best Supporting Actress in the 1948 John Huston film adaptation of the Maxwell Anderson Broadway play *Key Largo*.

In *Murder, My Sweet*, Trevor possesses the same cold, calculating manner as the ruthless blonde image conveyed by Stanwyck in *Double Indemnity*. The difference is that, when she enlists the aid of Powell to commit murder on her behalf, he spurns her. The incorruptible detective was not about to engage in murder in the first place while, additionally, by then he had decided that he prefers the piquant youthfulness of Anne Shirley. A strong plot element of the film is the internal jousting of the two women for the affections of the wealthy Mr. Grayle, (Miles Mander), who freely admits to Powell in front of Shirley that, while he loves his daughter, his wife is the most important person in his life. He tells Powell that he plays a mind game of make believe with himself that blonde temptress Trevor would have married him even if he were not rich, and that he has somehow managed to convince himself of its reality.

The Mixed Ensemble

In terms of providing a varied mixture of fascinating characters, the ensemble assembled for *Murder, My Sweet* is among the most interesting in noir annals. The creative birth and development to fruition of fascinating and frequently offbeat characters is reflective of the Chandler touch, enhanced by his absorption of the amorphous Southern California landscape of the early '40s, of which he was a part. The migration wave was in full swing to the land of palm trees and beaches as the new wave of pioneers, transported by cars, trains and buses rather than covered wagons, converged on a land of sunshine popularized by its best-known industry, that of film. The ensemble of supporting players is reminiscent of *The Maltese Falcon* in terms of sheer fascination as well as their contrasting virtuosity of activities. The omnipresent Mazurki as Moose Malloy is the very quintessence of film noir with his tendency to surface soundlessly from the shadows of darkness. Otto Kruger as a sophisticated jewel thief and blackmailer seeks to use cunning in dominating the Moose Malloys of the world, but is foiled in his own devious machinations when the cretinous giant suspects him of withholding information on Velma, a crime punishable in the ex-convict's offbeat morality code by instant death. Marlowe is battered for the first time in the story by a blackjack in a foggy beach area after being asked to ride along with a homosexual dandy criminal type, Marriott (Douglas Walton). Marriott is killed with the same death instrument that rendered Marlowe unconscious. He turns out to be a subordinate of Jules Amthor, a professional escort of women who lures them into fancy clubs while thieves steal their expensive jewelry.

Dick Powell as wisecracking Los Angeles detective Philip Marlowe spurns beautiful blonde temptress Claire Trevor in a scene from *Murder, My Sweet*, the film which marked RKO's emergence into the film noir sweepstakes. Powell instead has romantic designs on Trevor's stepdaughter, Anne Shirley. Ironically, the film was shot virtually next door to neighboring studio Paramount and released the same year (1944) as that studio's noir giant, *Double Indemnity*. The RKO release was adapted to the screen from Raymond Chandler's novel, *Farewell, My Lovely*. With Chandler under contract to Paramount, where he penned the *Double Indemnity* script with Billy Wilder, he was able to be no more than an interested observer of the *Murder, My Sweet* project, but registered his pleasure with Powell as an ideal Philip Marlowe.

Dewey Robinson is appropriately sleazy as the boss of a rundown Los Angeles club where the sought-after Velma had worked, and is ultimately tossed around the room like a toy doll by Malloy. Esther Howard as Mrs. Florian, the widow of the club's former owner, is induced to talk by Marlowe through alcohol, but turns out to be cold sober and provides the detective with a false lead as he grabs a picture he presumes to be that of Velma, but is not. There is the aforementioned quack doctor running the drug establishment, Ralf Harolde as Dr. Sonderborg. Powell is vigilantly pursued throughout by Don Douglas as Lieutenant Randle and Paul Phillips as Detective Nulty.

A Faithful Chandler Portrayal

Screenwriter John Paxton, RKO's noir specialist, was astute in following the old Southern saying, "If it ain't broke, it don't need fixing" in his script adaptation. The Chandler recipe for suspense is embodied in the combination of fascinating characters, generally turning on each other with the speed of light, along with zesty one-liners, often delivered by the author's alter ego, Philip Marlowe. The superb formula was followed by Paxton as he utilized some of Chandler's best dialogue while weaving a fascinating screenplay that took advantage of every labyrinthian plot twist that master Chandler had executed.

Powell scored his triumphant breakthrough into the dramatic field in large measure due to his shrewd performing instinct, building on a style that had worked in the lighter story realm of musicals. While Powell was entering an age when he could no longer play some of his boyish roles of the past, there was no reason to abandon a puckish youthfulness that audiences had grown fond of, as evidenced by the popularity of his films. Rather than invest Marlowe with a tough "in your face" physicality, Powell played the detective as an essentially vulnerable but honestly plodding individual who seeks to win out despite being overwhelmed by numerically superior forces. He uses humor to throw his ruthless and sordid contacts and enemies off balance, along with hiding the inner vulnerabilities of which the common sense detective is aware. On one occasion when Malloy is shaking him with his gigantic claws, a disgusted Marlowe requests that he "stop dancing with me." Mrs. Florian is narratively described as a "charming middle-aged lady with a face like a bucket of mud." He passes judgment on her alcoholic inclinations: "She'd knock you down to get the bottle." When Marlowe insults his heavily perfumed office visitor Marriott and is threatened with a punch in the nose, he coolly responds, "I tremble at the thought of such violence." The breezy style was reflective of the old musical Powell successfully transferred to a new area of exposure. Pauline Kael wrote, "There was a time when Raymond Chandler regarded this movie ... as the most successful film adaptation of his novels, and thought that Dick Powell came the closest to his conception of Marlowe."

It is no surprise that Chandler would admire the finished product due to the

Dick Powell takes an unexpected nap while the criminal duo of Mike Mazurki, center, and Johnny Indrisano look on, guns drawn, in a scene from the hard-boiled noir gem *Murder, My Sweet*. Mazurki and Indrisano enjoyed prominence as a professional wrestler and boxer, respectively. Their swarthy, rugged visages made them ideal film heavies.

fidelity of adaptation as well as the manner in which the honest, wisecracking detective is portrayed by Powell, who conveys the same human vulnerability incorporated by Chandler into his books. After all, Marlowe was never intended to be a superman, just an honest detective working his way through the dangerous labyrinth of Southern California's underbelly. *Cinebooks' Motion Picture Guide Review*, in awarding *Murder, My Sweet* a perfect 5-star rating, states, "no one else could ever match Powell's personification of the down-and-out but highly principled gumshoe. He takes only $25 a day and expenses for wading through the worst kind of human mire." *Cinebooks* further declares: "This tough, sardonic, and unusually witty film brought onetime movie crooner Dick Powell back from the brink of career catastrophe and made him a superstar; it also established him as an actor of immense ability."

Final Confrontation

A great suspense story demands a great final confrontation. Symbolic of Southern California, the final confrontation of *Murder, My Sweet* occurs at the Grayle beach house retreat, adjacent to the rumbling shores of the Pacific Ocean. Marlowe has wisely allowed the perpetually lit fuse, Moose Malloy, to cool his heels on the sandy beach as he speaks with the former small time nightclub performer Velma, who has executed a leap onto the society pages as a presumably respectable Mrs. Grayle. After the calculating blonde seeks Marlowe's cooperation in her murder plans, Mr. Grayle and daughter Ann emerge. Mrs. Grayle has sought Marlowe's assistance to kill Amthor. The detective strategically withholds his knowledge that Amthor has already been strangled to death by Malloy. In all the excitement, enhanced by Mr. Grayle's sudden anger on learning what the woman he loves is really like, Marlowe proves himself human by letting it slip about Amthor's demise. This leaves him staring ominously at the butt of the icy blonde's gun as she concludes that the detective knows too much and must be disposed of by her in the manner of Marriott earlier.

A moral resolution is quickly obtained as Mr. Grayle kills his wife rather than let her extend her evil machinations by killing Marlowe. Ann beseeches Marlowe not to call the police to report the death of the ruthless blonde, exclaiming, "He saved your life." The flow of action continues as Moose Malloy, curious to learn what has been happening inside, arrives to find his beloved Velma dead. "You shouldn't have done that," he informs Grayle, moving menacingly toward him. Grayle makes a quick move toward his gun, shots are fired, and Marlowe sprawls floorward, blinded by the exploding gunfire. The confrontation ends with both Grayle and Malloy dead.

A skillful transition next displays the interior of Lieutenant Randle's office as Marlowe explains the resolution of events. He wears an eye patch as a result of the damage sustained through contact with the flashing light from the exploding bullets. Marlowe is unaware of the quiet emergence of Ann Grayle into the room. When he finishes his account of the events, he is accompanied out the door by

Detective McNulty, with Ann moving along in the background. It is not until he is inside the cab that he realizes that Ann has arrived to accompany him home. The time has arrived for the perfect fadeout as RKO enters the noir blockbuster sweepstakes.

As RKO moved forward as a producer of extraordinary black and white suspense thrillers, Powell and Mazurki proceeded to enduring careers with the former propelling himself into solid dramatic leads and the latter becoming an enduring character performer. In the case of the former cherubic crooner Powell, fresh from the *Murder, My Sweet* triumph, producer Adrian Scott sought to put his winning team on the field again as soon as possible, with *Cornered* the next project. The 1945 war thriller starred Powell in what Leonard Maltin called "high-tension drama" as he played a grieving widower seeking to track down the man who killed his wife during World War II in Buenos Aires. In addition to producer Scott, the director and screenwriter of *Murder, My Sweet*, Edward Dmytryk and John Paxton, were also reunited in *Cornered.* A tortured Powell, seeking to avenge the death of his wife, is finally able to track down her killer. Providing the Nazi killer with a brutal self-righteousness and doctrinal rigidity is Broadway stage great Luther Adler, who is ultimately beaten to death by an enraged Powell.

Noir in a London Fog

Mazurki's career moved into high gear after *Murder, My Sweet* with two impressive Twentieth Century–Fox dramas standing out. Each film starred a dynamic young leading man seeking to outsmart his contemporaries, and ultimately being done in by his con artist ways.

The 1947 release *Nightmare Alley* showcased the brightest star in Darryl F. Zanuck's constellation, Tyrone Power, who portrayed a circus wiseguy devoid of scruples. He uses Joan Blondell as a stepping stone, then moves on to a younger, more vulnerable Coleen Gray. Mazurki is cast in the role of a circus strongman who befriends Gray and seeks to impose integrity on Power in their relationship. The film provided Power with the opportunity to expand his dramatic horizons as a daring young man who oversteps his bounds and, at the film's end, is reduced to the station feared by circus employees, that of geek. The movie concludes with Power being provided with all the free liquor he can drink to serve the sad and dark purpose involved.

Mazurki lavished praise on both Power and the film's British director, Edmund Goulding, whose last effort prior to *Nightmare Alley* had been the notable adaptation of the Somerset Maugham novel, *The Razor's Edge*, in which Power starred opposite Gene Tierney. "Tyrone Power was so incredible in *Nightmare Alley* that I thought he deserved an Oscar," Mazurki reflected. "So did everybody else working in the film. Unfortunately he never even received a nomination. I liked working with Edmund Goulding. He was like so many of those great directors of the 40s.

Goulding always was patient enough to break things down for you so you always understood the characters in the film and their motivations."

Mazurki traveled to England in 1949 to appear in the most typically cast role he would ever play, that of a professional wrestler, in the noir crime adventure *Night and the City*. This was the year that the House Un-American Activities Committee's activities reached their zenith and the term Hollywood Ten was paramount in the minds of those involved with and following the cinema.

"The director of *Night and the City*, Jules Dassin, had left the U.S. because of the Committee hearings and was making films in England," Mazurki revealed. "Edward Dmytryk, the director of *Murder, My Sweet*, was one of the Hollywood Ten and he'd also left America to make pictures in England. I'd heard that Dmytryk's wife, the actress Jean Porter, had just given birth to a child so I went over to take a gift and express my congratulations."

While Mazurki was cast in the familiar role of a wrestler, his part in the 1950 release provided him with one of his foremost acting opportunities. Richard Widmark, in the early days of his career, plays an unscrupulous American promoter who has targeted London to apply his nefarious talents. Widmark strings along two women, Gene Tierney and Googie Withers, and eventually becomes involved in London's professional wrestling scene. He coaxes crime boss Herbert Lom into letting his wrestler father work for him as a trainer. The role of the older wrestler was played by Stanislaus Zbysko, a Polish-born former world heavyweight champion who became one of the legends of the mat world. Mazurki was cast as a rival wrestler abhorred by purist Zbysko as representing the new wave of entertainment and showmanship.

The ruthless Widmark is destined to sustain ultimate disaster through his unsavory activities. He works Zbysko and Mazurki into such a competitive frenzy that the two engage in a grudge match, after which Zbysko dies of a heart attack. Such a result produces an obvious response from a crime boss such as Lom: a death contract on Widmark.

Central London's old city with its small, winding streets extending back to the days of Queen Elizabeth, Sir Walter Ralegh and Shakespeare, along with its notable fog, provides the perfect dramatic backdrop for classic film noir. *Night and the City* builds to a stirring dramatic conclusion with Mazurki invested with the same kind of eerie presence he provided in *Murder, My Sweet*. Realizing that he has been used by Widmark, who seeks to flee London before he is murdered by Lom, an enraged Mazurki sets out to resolve the con man's fate, as hell-bent on destruction as he had been to avenge the death of Velma in *Murder, My Sweet*.

The movie's conclusion is definitive noir in which the London locations are adroitly utilized. Out of the shadows of darkness Mazurki follows Widmark along the Thames. When he catches up with him, the glib words of the desperate con man are in vain. Mazurki uses his gigantic hands to menacing advantage. Widmark suffers the same demise as Otto Kruger, the con artist of *Murder, My Sweet*, death by strangulation, with one difference. One of the world's most famous rivers beckons as a burial place for the dead con artist. After Mazurki strangles Widmark, he hurls him into the Thames. Not long thereafter the police descend and Mazurki is led away to jail.

Mazurki would act with Widmark again in *Cheyenne Autumn*, which culminated a longstanding ambition to work with director John Ford. A specialist in outdoor action films, many of which starred his close friend John Wayne, Ford's story choices fell directly into the path of the rugged Mazurki. For years, one obstacle prevented Mazurki from joining the group known as the "Ford repertory company."

"Ford was known for using the same people in his films and what prevented me from working in his films for years was that I resembled Victor McLaglen," Mazurki revealed. "I found out how closely I resembled him one night when I was traveling in the East and had stopped at a hotel for the night. I decided to go to the bar and have a drink before going up to my room. All of a sudden this good-looking woman comes up to me and plants a kiss on my lips. I was startled and my expression showed it. The woman said with great disappointment, 'Victor, don't tell me you don't remember me.' You know, I had the hardest time getting her to believe that I wasn't Victor McLaglen."

Murder, My Sweet continues to enjoy international success. In December 1996, it was attracting audiences in a special showing in London's West End.

FOUR

Dmytryk and the RKO Team

With two successful noir thrillers behind him, *Murder, My Sweet* and *Cornered*, RKO's Edward Dmytryk was establishing himself as an exciting young directing talent. The shadowy land of black and white in which the forces of good are involved in a life and death struggle with those of evil found Dmytryk in a comfortable habitat. His films embodied the breakneck pacing of a technical craftsman who knew what he wanted and managed to keep his films on schedule and within budgetary limits.

Dmytryk was born in Grand Forks, British Columbia. Like Mike Mazurki, his parents were Ukrainian immigrants. The second of four sons, he was taken as a very young boy by his parents to the Ukraine, where his parents still owned a farm. His father owned a small truck farm in Grand Forks and also worked winters at the local copper smeltry. After Edward's devout Catholic mother died when he was only five or six, his father moved to San Francisco and remarried, working as a streetcar motorman, then finally relocating to Los Angeles. Young Edward was forced to pull his economic weight in the family at an early age, explaining, "I had peddled papers on street corners, delivered them morning and evening, [and] caddied at the Los Angeles Country Club, where I learned that the richer the player, the smaller the tip."

When the future director was 12, a psychologist identified him as well as his brother Arthur as gifted children possessing IQs of 140 or better. Two years later he was on his own, leaving home with the sweater on his back and 35 cents in his pocket. When he was picked up by authorities, his assertions of having left home due to repeated beatings were apparently corroborated to the point where it was agreed that Dmytryk would be better off living in a rented room and working his way through Hollywood High School. By the time he was 15, he was already working at Famous Players-Lasky Studios as a messenger boy. When he graduated from high school with straight A's, he was rewarded with acceptance into the prestigious California Institute of Technology, bolstered by a gift of $1,000 from a studio executive who had taken an interest in his exceptional academic record.

While his freshman year at Cal Tech enabled him to indulge his passion for athletics (he earned letters in five different sports), Dmytryk had too much of an independent creative bent to conform to the discipline of a rigid academic life. Rather than wishing to concentrate on physics and mathematics prior to achieving an engineering degree, he left Cal Tech before the end of his freshman year. It was 1927 when he returned to his old employer, which by now had undergone a name change from the previous Famous Players–Lasky to Paramount Studios. During his earlier studio phase, when he was earning $6 a week, he had progressed in one year from messenger boy to a film splicer and part time projectionist. While working in the viewing room, he was able to study the rushes of a variety of films and eavesdrop on the comments of directors such as Erich von Stroheim, Cecil B. DeMille, James Cruze, Raoul Walsh and William Wellman.

Dmytryk immediately took up where he left off on the studio scene, progressing fast with the aid of additional maturity. He became a Paramount editor and worked in that capacity at the studio throughout the '30s. Dmytryk directed a very low-budget 1935 Western, *The Hawk*, shot in five days for $5,000, but did not regard this as his official directorial debut, explaining that he "just took a few days off from editing" to help a friend. In his autobiography, *It's a Hell of a Life but Not a Bad Living*, Dmytryk explained that "it was in the cutting rooms that I learned the rudiments of filmmaking." He has consistently stated that editing is "the only film craft that is entirely indigenous to the cinema" and integrally relates to every other facet of the art.

In 1939 Dmytryk made the move toward directing at Paramount, beginning with B level productions. He then directed low-budget features at Columbia, including Lone Wolf and Boston Blackie series entries as well as a Boris Karloff horror film. When he moved to RKO in 1942, his career progressed as he followed up his first film there, *Seven Miles from Alcatraz*, with the highly regarded 1943 release, *Hitler's Children*, a powerful anti–Nazi film. That same year he did a companion anti–Japanese piece starring Tom Neal, *Behind the Rising Sun*. As earlier mentioned, his career then soared with the back-to-back Dick Powell vehicles *Murder, My Sweet* and *Cornered*.

As the war concluded, Hollywood prepared for the return of the American fighting men with story vehicles focusing on the adjustment period back to civilian life. The potent William Wyler film *The Best Years of Our Lives* (1946), with an all-star cast headed by veteran performers Fredric March and Myrna Loy, would secure Oscar recognition, but an alert RKO was able to get out its own veteran readjustment film a few weeks earlier than the Wyler blockbuster and Dmytryk would be handed the directorial reins. *Till the End of Time* follows some Marines from mustering out at Camp Pendleton back to civilian life in rapidly burgeoning Los Angeles. Robert Mitchum won critical praise for his vivid portrayal of William Tabeshaw, who must endure life with a steel plate in his head resulting from war injuries.

The film held great personal meaning for Dmytryk in that one of its feature performers, Jean Porter, who played the next door neighbor and unsuccessful romantic pursuer of Guy Madison, would become his wife not long thereafter. While

Dmytryk's first marriage in young adulthood was unsuccessful, the union with Porter was destined to become one of filmdom's most enduring, lasting until his 1999 death.

With Dmytryk and his RKO repertory compatriots having scored so many hits, it was only natural to team them up some more, which occurred with two successful 1947 releases. The first, despite its success, would provide a sad harbinger of the near future. The second became the most acclaimed production of RKO's series of suspense adventures.

The team of producer Adrian Scott, scenarist John Paxton and director Dmytryk shifted the terrain from the RKO back lot to a small town in rural England in adapting the James Hilton novel *So Well Remembered* to the screen. Hilton's works had been successfully translated to the screen earlier in *Goodbye, Mr. Chips* and *Random Harvest*. Now that the war and accompanying travel restrictions had ended, RKO decided to shoot *So Well Remembered* in an authentic British location.

The film is a moving account of the efforts of an idealistic newspaper editor (John Mills) in strike-torn Northern England between the wars. It was released in Britain in 1947 with successful results, but was not shown in the United States until years later. The storm clouds were swiftly surfacing in what would culminate in the Hollywood Ten and prison sentences being served. The Cold War was in full swing and political sensitivities were acute. Howard Hughes, who had acquired control of RKO, detected what he perceived to be Communistic attitudes displayed in the film and insisted on major cuts. The controversy surrounding *So Well Remembered* was a premonition of the tragedy that would soon directly confront RKO as a studio hit hard in the area where it can be least afforded, in its creative department. All that lay just over the horizon, but before the tragedy occurred the studio would enjoy its greatest artistic triumph of a fruitful period. It would be accomplished by tackling sensitive subject matter theretofore untouched by Hollywood, at which point RKO and Darryl Zanuck each struck at the forces of bigotry with memorable film products.

Striking Directly at the Beast: *Crossfire* (1947)

RKO produced *Till the End of Time*, released just ahead of the Sam Goldwyn production covering the same subject matter, *The Best Years of Our Lives*. Now in 1947 RKO would release what became its most artistically lauded film noir effort, *Crossfire*, shortly before Twentieth Century–Fox premiered one of the most highly received films in the history of that studio, *Gentleman's Agreement*. Each film tackled the then verboten theme of anti–Semitism with refreshing candor. Equally refreshing was the fact that both films offered freshly insightful versions that were in no measure imitative of one another.

The *Crossfire* story involved the triumph of two Marines fresh from military duty. An ambitious young writer, Richard Brooks, had authored a sociologically probing novel, *The Brick Foxhole*, in which Hollywood had expressed interest. Brooks revealed to a tall, athletically trim fellow Marine interested in an acting career a desire for him to appear in the potentially starmaking role of Montgomery, the short-fused homicidal killer with a powerful propensity for anti–Semitism. Marine Robert Ryan launched a productive screen career with one of his two top dramatic efforts.

The Brick Foxhole was constructed around the ironic premise that, while fighting a war against a tyrannical Nazi system predicated on a "master race" theory with the objective of doing away with those deemed "unfit" for human existence, notably Jews, America simultaneously both supported and tolerated elements of that same morbid philosophy. The novel is set in the nation's capital at the end of the war, where Brooks with his sensitive narrative eye demonstrates the fundamental irony of segregation and other forms of racial injustice rife in what should be a model showplace for justice. He reflects as well on the segregation policy then in place in America's military, where African American men were deemed fit enough to risk their lives in combat abroad, yet were not allowed to be trained, housed or to fight alongside white allies in the same cause. It was through conscientious efforts such as Brooks demonstrated in *The Brick Foxhole*, which was published the year the war ended, 1945, that two years later, the same year that both *Crossfire* and *Gentleman's Agreement* premiered, President Harry Truman ended America's lengthy military segregation policy by integrating the armed forces.

Brooks finished his novel in January 1945, while America and its Allies were in the closing stages of winning the great war abroad. The author reflected on the fine line separating heroism from cowardice, epitomized in military conflict:

> The peculiar chemistry that often goes into the making of a hero is pretty generally understood, for the bravest men are usually the first to admit that when they were seemingly most brave they were also afraid. But many of us do not realize that a similar chemistry, compounded of other tensions, may also lead to actions just as strange and unpredictable in the more sheltered arenas of military life. For the disillusioned soldier who finds himself trapped in a brick foxhole is a victim of another kind of fear. From day to day he wonders whether he will be able to hold up under the corroding strain of slow disintegration. He is too far away from the battlefront and at the same time too far removed psychologically from the home front to become conditioned to either. He lives in a limbo of his own where he is bedeviled by frustration, loss of dignity, and all the most fantastic shapes that rumor can breed." He concludes with the comment, "So I can say, long after Sherman, that if war is hell, then a brick foxhole is damnation.

In that a novel is a narrative experience while a film is a visual entity, condensation and intelligent reshaping are necessary to translate a fictional work to the screen. Richard Brooks' novel tackled bigotry against Jews and blacks along with the realm of sexual preference. In the book a raging Monty unleashes his venomous fists against a homosexual in his drunken fury rather than killing a Jew, as occurred in the film. The novel earlier demonstrated Monty's delight when a Jewish soldier named Max Brock was beaten in an exhibition bout at the Army base by a ruggedly constructed semi-professional. Brock is presented as someone who decides to box to prove a point to his fellow soldiers in the anti–Semitic camp where he is stationed. When his more experienced opponent begins to overpower him and administer punishment the bigoted Monty reacts with supreme delight, venting his hatred. Later that same night, a drunken, raging Monty murders a homosexual in his apartment with his bare fists. In the film his victim is a kindly, soft-spoken Jewish man named Samuels, portrayed by Sam Levene. Another change between the novel and film involves the ultimate death of Monty. In the book, the Sergeant Keeley character played by Robert Mitchum in the film kills the crazed bigot in a battle to the death in the appropriately symbolic setting of Washington's War Museum. Had this been a large-budgeted production in the hands of someone like Alfred Hitchcock, the setting with all its attendant irony would probably have been scenically played out as two modern-day soldiers fight to the death amid the relics of yesterday's warriors, but the film's conclusion is anything but a disappointment as the Scott-Dmytryk-Paxton triumvirate scored an impressive triumph.

It was fitting that two of the film industry's most articulate voices of political activism, Richard Brooks and Robert Ryan, launched successful film careers on the heels of the notable success of *Crossfire*. Brooks' two most notable film contributions in his traditionally threefold function as producer-director-writer were *Elmer Gantry* and *In Cold Blood*. He won an Oscar for Best Adapted Screenplay for *Elmer Gantry*. The searing adaptation of the Sinclair Lewis novel netted Burt Lancaster a Best Actor Oscar. It explored the blatant commercialization of religion and the hypocrisy of those who preach virtue to hypnotized audiences with pearly words of wisdom, then conduct their personal lives in a disparate manner. *In Cold Blood* involved equally passionate subject matter, a lucid examination of crime and punishment in America with a focus on the death penalty. It was a brilliant adaptation of the probing novel by Truman Capote based on the Kansas murders of the Clutter family which provided comprehensive sociological analysis of the killers leading up to their executions.

Ryan was an active supporter of the Committee for a Sane Nuclear Policy and the American Civil Liberties Union. In the political arena he spoke on behalf of the presidential candidacies of Adlai Stevenson in the 50s and John F. Kennedy in 1960. A sensitive intellectual with an Ivy League education, Ryan abhorred bigotry of any kind. The highly motivated actor reached inside himself to invest the character of Monty Montgomery with a chilling air of impassioned reality in which the killer's tormented psyche is put on full display.

A Rousing Opening and a Masterpiece of Swift Pacing

John Paxton, a seasoned master of cinema suspense writing, brilliantly adapted *The Brick Foxhole* by establishing the kind of breakneck pacing necessary to obtain winning results in a noir film done with sharp budgetary restraints. Once that the symphony was handed to the conductor, Edward Dmytryk wielded his baton flawlessly. The film begins in the shadowy confines of an apartment, where a uniformed soldier is observed administering a deadly beating to a man in a suit. Dmytryk effectively uses shadows to hide the features of attacker and victim. The sound effects are chilling, initially those of fist crashing against face; ultimately, the thud of the deceased victim hitting the floor carries a ringing finality. His deadly deed accomplished, the soldier quickly departs.

A skillful transition finds a soft-spoken, methodical police officer, Detective Finlay (Robert Young), examining the murder scene. A masterful touch is then applied as the brutal killer is first observed as an officer assisting Young happens to open the apartment door and observes Robert Ryan standing there, explaining that he has returned to investigate the whereabouts of his "friend," Corporal Mitchell. This combined with the police having located Mitchell's wallet, which he had left behind before leaving the apartment, prompts Finlay to suspect the young corporal of killing Joseph Samuels.

The interrogative process heats up in Finlay's office as he summons Mitchell's superior, Sergeant Peter Keeley, played with brilliant low-keyed nonchalance by Robert Mitchum. Keeley is adamant in his belief that the sensitive commercial artist Mitchell, who has been depressed and drinking heavily due to the enforced military separation from his wife, is incapable of killing anyone. He explains that, while he had actually killed men "where you get medals for doing it," that Mitchell was restricted to stateside duty due to doubt concerning his battlefield mindset. Shortly thereafter, Montgomery enters the room, telling Keeley how shameful it is that the police are trying to pin a murder on their friend Mitchell. He proceeds to loudly rant and insult Finlay, exclaiming that the Washington police are "hick cops" as he proclaims himself to be a shrewd and experienced policeman from St. Louis, where he learned life the hard way by working on the tough East Side of the city. Keeley later observes that the only way Montgomery could try any harder to help Mitchell would be to string him up.

The role of Sergeant Keeley was one of the more interesting of Mitchum's long career. He plays a savvy newspaper reporter who leads his younger enlisted men (George Cooper, William Phipps, Lex Barker and Richard Benedict) through quiet example rather than bluster. He is a patient listener who, when he speaks, does so with laconic intelligence. Good examples of solid reactive acting are Mitchum's facial reactions to the blustery tirades of the pathetically paranoid Montgomery, played with such stirring believability by Ryan.

A Fascinating Ensemble

It was earlier observed that a familiar trait demonstrated in the works of suspense masters such as Chandler, Hammett and Cain is the mixture of fascinating characters interacting with the major players in the drama. Some appear only briefly but make indelible impact. Such opportunities abounded during the prolific 40s era of filmmaking, where actors like Sydney Greenstreet, Ward Bond, Leonid Kinskey, Otto Kruger or Elisha Cook, Jr., appeared in numerous films, becoming familiar sights on the screen. Some character performers such as Peter Lorre and Walter Huston ultimately rose to the ranks of character stardom. The mixture of a fascinating ensemble, often of sharply contrasting demeanors and temperaments, particularly in the equation of good as opposed to evil, enlivened stories.

When a distraught Corporal Mitchell leaves Joseph Samuels's apartment not long before Montgomery kills him, he wanders into a bar and meets Gloria Grahame, cast in the role of hapless Ginny Tremaine, who makes her living as a B-girl, a profession growing out of servicemen's loneliness of the war period. With lonely ex–GI's like Mitchell roaming city streets, opportunistic bar owners would station women like Ginny to sit and dance with them, just as long as they continued to buy watered-down drinks at high prices. Initially Grahame calls Mitchell "corny" for telling her that she reminds him of his wife, but eventually she considers it a compliment, softening to the point of dancing with him for free. She ultimately gives him the key to her apartment, telling him to make himself comfortable until she is able to return home. Their meeting is a psychological interlocking of two distraught people attempting to provide comfort to one another in their shared despondency.

Grahame's sensitive performance as a woman skittering on the edge of depression once more underscores her unique value to filmmakers of the post war period. The Hollywood High graduate who performed in school plays with America's future Secretary of State, Warren Christopher, provided the kind of dominant film presence that enabled her to stand out in the minds of film patrons after even a brief period on screen. In *The Bad and the Beautiful* she garnered a Best Supporting Actress Oscar with the briefest screen appearance of any recipient of that award to that point. She rendered an unforgettable portrayal as the untamed and restless wife of screenwriter Dick Powell.

Grahame exuded the sexuality of a restless kitten fearlessly slinking along uncharted streets in evening darkness. There was an underlying enigma about her that made her ultimately impenetrable, but such a fascinating challenge that men took the bait. Her female persona was as effective for film noir as was Robert Mitchum's as a male. Grahame was at her best appearing opposite Humphrey Bogart in Nicholas Ray's noir classic *In a Lonely Place.*

Grahame effectively portrayed rattled, vulnerable women on the verge of exploding. This is her persona in *Crossfire*, the irony being that she looks to an equally troubled Paul Kelly for companionship. Kelly serves as a centerpiece of two of the film's most interesting scenes, the first when a besieged Corporal Mitchell, seeking to clear himself of murder suspicions, visits Ginny's apartment, hoping she will supply him with a needed and legitimate alibi. Kelly's performance is fascinatingly enigmatic, leaving both a befuddled Corporal Mitchell as well as audiences seeking to tap his bewildering interior. He initially jolts Mitchell by telling him that he is Ginny's husband. Kelly quickly changes his story, informing the distraught soldier that he saw Mitchell with Ginny at "the joint." The longer he talks, the greater the recognition that he is constantly spying on Ginny. He tells Mitchell that he was drummed out of the Army due to a "bad ticker." Moments later he ponders the idea of joining the Army, where he believes he can make rank in the new post war military. Kelly, while looming on the surface as a harmless psycho type compared to the homicidal Montgomery, nevertheless injects nervous uncertainty due to his unpredictability. Confused enough prior to Kelly's appearance, Mitchell leaves Ginny's apartment more distraught than ever.

The Perfect Noir Setting

Film historians have lavished praise on the *Crossfire* scenes set in an all-night theater, as ideal a film noir setting as anyone could construct. Screenwriter Paxton adapted the concept from the Brooks novel. The ploy was the work of the shrewd Keeley, who engineers confusion when Washington and Army MPs converge at the Washington hotel where the sergeant and his men are staying. When an enervated Mitchell appears, having come from Ginny's apartment and his confusing conversation with Kelly, Keeley shoves him to the ground and ignites pandemonium, then helps him to escape out the back door. Needing a safe place for Mitchell to hide out from authorities until he is assured that he can convince them that his corporal friend is innocent, Keeley decides that the best possible hiding place for him is an all-night theater.

Keeley, always the soft-spoken, "take charge" man, telephones Mary Mitchell, played by Jacqueline White, to come quickly to Washington, explaining that her husband needs help. Keeley can see that, without his loving Mary, Mitchell will go to pieces. He explains to Finlay during their first conversation that he had not seen his wife for two years and did not know if they would pick up married life when they ultimately met or not, but that he could adjust to that type of situation whereas Mitchell could not.

A Female Confrontation and the Sting to Trap Monty

An important element in understanding *Crossfire* and its dramatic significance is that we are dealing with a brief time frame beginning in roughly the middle of the evening and ending early the next morning. (For breakneck story pacing over a brief span of time, *Crossfire* is reminiscent of the 1950 low-budget sleeper *D.O.A.*, in which an ultimately fatally poisoned Edmond O'Brien has one day to solve his own murder.) The compact, rapid fire sequences resulted in a breakneck thriller

Robert Ryan, right, smiles warmly between takes on the set of RKO's release of *Crossfire*, but once shooting resumed he assumed the grim-faced look of the ruthless anti-Semitic character he played. Robert Mitchum, center, would also stop smiling as he concentrated on helping Robert Young snare Ryan. Young looks like he is already into his character Capt. Finley as he exudes a somber demeanor. The 1947 release, directed by Edward Dmytryk, was released the same year as Twentieth Century–Fox's film about anti–Semitism, *Gentleman's Agreement*, and propelled the Melrose Avenue studio into the front ranks for successfully exploring social consciousness themes.

directed by Dmytryk with shrewd economy, never wasting a moment of film. Dmytryk shot roughly seven setups per six-and-a-half hour workdays. The entire 20 days of shooting consisted of 140 setups on a budget of $550,000. The quick pace never hurts the film. Instead it enhances its raw dramatic believability as characters are put in tense spotlights with little time to react, building dramatic tension to the point of ultimate explosion.

A confrontation occurs after Jacqueline White has convinced Robert Young to accompany him to the apartment of Gloria Grahame after common sense realist Mitchum realizes that the meeting with the B-girl must be brought into the open to supply Cooper with his needed alibi. Mitchum reveals the meeting in front of the young wife. A telling close-up reveals her noticeable wince at the disclosure, but the sturdy-willed wife knows she must carry on to help her husband, telling Young that she would like a few minutes alone with Grahame for "woman to woman" conversation.

A cheap melodrama would have displayed the women shouting at each other, if not culminating in a hair-pulling physical confrontation, but the meeting between White and Grahame pits a shrewdly tactful wife hoping to assist her husband by extracting an alibi from the nightclub girl. Grahame complicates matters by informing White that she knows nothing and wishes to be left alone, which she states with even louder adamancy when Young enters the room.

Just as Young has convinced White that she will receive no help from Grahame, the enigmatic Kelly reenters the scene, having eavesdropped from an adjoining room. He confirms Mitchell's statement to Keeley that the soldier was in the B-girl's apartment at the time that the killing occurred. As Young and White depart, Kelly calls out that he had been in the Army but had been drummed out on a dishonorable discharge. For tensely compacted dramatic interest, the scene is letter perfect, pitting a wife determined to help her husband, a dark woman of the evening fearful of being involved in a police matter, and an enigmatic psycho willing to help a man he has met once briefly and knows is telling the truth.

Back at headquarters, Young discusses developments with Keeley, deciding on an ultimate course of action. Both men conclude that Ryan is the killer on the basis of simple motive. While Ryan, a former policeman, is familiar enough with the investigative process to focus the spotlight on the hapless Mitchell under the pretext of helping him, in the manner of psychopathic types, he has talked too much and aroused suspicion. In his earlier freewheeling conversation with Young and an attentively listening Mitchum, he brings his virulent anti–Semitism to the surface by bitterly asserting that individuals such as the man he killed were clever enough to avoid military service. When an interested Young asks him to elaborate, Ryan declares that the "guys with funny names" were clever enough to avoid combat, people with "names like Samuels" and some "even funnier."

While Mitchell had left the apartment of Samuels before the murder, one Army associate of Montgomery's who was there to witness the cold-blooded crime was Floyd Bowers, played by Steve Brodie. Montgomery pays a visit to Bowers' apartment, threateningly reminding him of the need for them to stick together on their stories. He sees that witnessing the brutal murder of Samuels has shaken Bowers and filled him with guilt. Bowers tells him he will say nothing, go away to Mexico and forget about the incident. His conscience pangs prompt him, however, to tell Monty that there was no reason to murder Samuels. Montgomery realizes that Bowers poses a potential danger, knocks him out, then strangles him with a necktie.

The death of Bowers provides Young with an opportunity to trick the psychotic Ryan into revealing himself. Ryan was the only person with a motive to kill his kindly Jewish host, but proving it is another matter. Detective Finlay's deductive reasoning is simple: People kill for hate or money. Samuels had no money and did not even know the men with whom he was drinking, but he was Jewish and Montgomery angrily declared his anti–Semitism, providing him with the motive for the killing.

Finlay summons Keeley to bring one of the men in his outfit, a naive and self-conscious country boy from Tennessee named Leroy, to see him. When William Phipps, portraying Leroy, arrives at the police station, Finlay enlists his support. He is asked to trap Montgomery into revealing himself. As typical of such situations, the young soldier, who has been the frequent butt of Monty's sarcastic ridicule, does not wish to become involved in a gratuitous act that could cost him his life. His commanding officer, played by Kenneth MacDonald, assures him that he will not be doing a disservice to a fellow soldier, and that Montgomery is someone of whom the Army is not the least bit proud. Leroy remains adamant to the point where he is about to depart from Finlay's office when the officer strikes home by telling him that his own immigrant Irish grandfather was killed by forces of bigotry one century earlier as a result of coming to the aid of a priest being attacked by virulent anti–Catholic forces. He explains a fundamental moral to Leroy: As long as people look the other way and do not aggressively fight back, tools of social frustration such as Montgomery will always exist. As Finlay perceives it, Montgomery makes fun of Leroy as a Tennessean while he has never been in Tennessee. Whatever Montgomery and his ilk do not know and, henceforth, appears strange to them, they attack and belittle.

Leroy agrees to tackle the delicate assignment. While Montgomery is shaving, he drops word that he had just seen Bowers, who expressed his desire for his presumptive killer to see him at his apartment. Finlay staked his belief in the success of the plan on the assumption that the primitive Monty will believe that Leroy, someone he perceives to be entirely ignorant, would lack the imagination and cunning to conceive an outlandish lie. The psychopathic killer is further jolted when Leroy, carefully following the plan, tells him that Bowers wished him to convey the message that "the tie didn't hold." He hands a now rattled Ryan a piece of paper containing an address, which the psychopath peers at, then discards. Ryan sternly warns the younger man not to mention a word of what he has just been told.

When an agitated Montgomery appears on the scene minutes later, Finlay and associates are there to greet him. Finlay coolly asks him what brought him to the apartment. Montgomery mentions the conversation with Leroy, revealing that the address of Floyd Bowers' apartment was written on a piece of paper that the young Southerner had given to him. Finlay calmly produces the piece of paper, which Montgomery concedes was the one Leroy had given to him. An always cool Finlay exclaims, "The address I wrote down is the house across the street."

Like a cornered animal, Montgomery shoves Finlay, then makes a quick break. He runs down the stairs and into the street. Ignoring police warnings to halt, the two-time murderer is promptly gunned down. As sirens sound and a crowd quickly gathers, a still nonchalant Keeley, who has arrived with Leroy, pats the young soldier on the back and invites him for a cup of coffee at the fadeout.

Triumph Followed by Sorrow

Crossfire achieved more Academy recognition than any other film RKO did during the period, the cornerstone achievement of the repertory triumvirate of Adrian Scott, Edward Dmytryk and John Paxton, garnering five nominations. It failed to win any Oscars, hardly a surprise in view of the Academy practice of bloc voting among the major studios. Adrian Scott lost out in the Best Picture category to Twentieth's Darryl Zanuck for *Gentleman's Agreement*, the other 1947 blockbuster dealing with anti–Semitism. Often when two notable films tackle the same theme they are at least somewhat imitative of each other. In the cases of *Crossfire* and *Gentleman's Agreement*, the movies complemented each other. *Crossfire* demonstrated the result of subtly condoning bigotry, the emergence of an angry psychopath as that brilliantly depicted by Ryan willing to kill to sustain his warped beliefs. Moss Hart's highly literate *Gentleman's Agreement* screenplay tackled anti–Semitism from the opposite pole, focusing on the hypocrisy of the better educated set who, on the one hand, verbally denounce bigotry, then tacitly condone its perpetuation by refusing to speak out or confront a social evil.

Robert Ryan received an Academy nomination for Best Supporting Actor along with a Best Actor nomination by the New York Film Critics. Ryan's *Crossfire* performance was one of two epic efforts of his successful career. The other came two years later with his brilliant portrayal of a professional boxer in Robert Wise's superb low-budget drama, *The Set-up*. Gloria Grahame was nominated in the Best Supporting Actress category. Five years later she would win in that category in *The Bad and the Beautiful*.

Dmytryk and John Paxton rounded out the *Crossfire* Academy Award nominees in the Director and Screenplay categories. Dmytryk lost out to Elia Kazan, director of *Gentleman's Agreement*. He was also nominated by the New York Film Critics. John Paxton was nominated along with Moss Hart, the scenarist of *Gentleman's Agreement*, but in that category the winner was George Seaton for a film of a completely different nature, the Christmas holiday heartwarmer, *Miracle on 34th Street*, which produced the Best Supporting Actor Oscar winner with Edmund Gwenn.

The RKO repertory group appeared to be riding high with the celebrated reception accorded *Crossfire*, which won in the Best Social Film category at the Cannes Film Festival and was named one of 1947's ten Best Films by *The New York Times*, *Film Daily* and the National Board of Review of Motion Pictures. It appeared that the trio of Scott, Dmytryk and Paxton would be reuniting for many more triumphs. Instead *Crossfire*, the group's most creatively acclaimed product, represented the last time that the talented trio would work together.

The industry entered a stormy period in the late 40s, and as the specter of Communism hung as an ominous cloud pitting creative giants against each other at Directors and Screen Actors Guild meetings, culminating with Congressional investigations, two members of the RKO triumvirate, producer Adrian Scott and director Edward Dmytryk, became immersed in the center of controversy.

In October 1947, director Sam Wood testified before the House Un-American Activities Committee that several members of the Directors Guild, including Dmytryk, had attempted to assume control of that body on behalf of the American Communist Party. When called upon to testify, Dmytryk refused to say whether he had ever been a member of the American Communist Party. Scott also refused to furnish the Committee with such information about himself. In the words of film historian Otto Friedrich, "Edward Dmytryk and Adrian Scott, who had attracted considerable attention by directing and producing *Crossfire*, one of Hollywood's first movies on anti-Semitism, did their best to lecture the committee on civil liberties."

Dmytryk and Scott became members of the Hollywood Ten. Each would ultimately spend time in federal prison for contempt of Congress, but before that occurred, while on the heels of their greatest artistic triumph, *Crossfire*, they were fired by RKO. Dore Schary sought to avoid the responsibility, which ultimately devolved upon RKO President Peter Rathvon.

"Rathvon called Scott and me into his office and asked us once more to recant and to purge ourselves," Dmytryk recalled. "With hardly any sense of martyrdom at all, we refused. In that case, he informed us, we were no longer employees of RKO. So much for ironclad contracts. We went back to clean out our respective offices. The next day was Thanksgiving. Even a B writer wouldn't have dared that bit of bathos...."

Firings were the order of the day at the studios during the troubled period. A backlash of discontent evidenced in America's heartland, where scattered boycotts and demonstrations had already been directed against films involving the Hollywood Ten in California, Kansas and North Carolina, while the American Legion threatened a nationwide boycott. Fearful of widespread repercussions at ticket windows across America, the studios moved quickly to dampen the flames of any citizen brushfires. MGM suspended a $1,250-per-week contract that Eddie Mannix had given Lester Cole scarcely a month earlier, while fellow scenarist Dalton Trumbo's $3,000-per-week contract was not only suspended—the studio refused to pay him $60,000 for work already completed! Eventually Trumbo and Cole would sue MGM under the terms of those contracts and obtain a $125,000 settlement.

Jane Greer, left, and Robert Young, seen snuggling up to Susan Hayward, had two gigantic RKO successes in 1947. They are shown on the set of *They Won't Believe Me*, directed by Irving Pichel. Young received praise for his portrayal of the kind and efficient Captain Finley, who was able to trap killer Robert Ryan into revealing himself in *Crossfire* that same year. Greer impressed Young and Hayward so much that, at the end of the filming of *They Won't Believe Me*, they requested that she be given star billing alongside them. Greer then went from her initial starring role to the film for which she would be best known, *Out of the Past*. The irony in Young's case is that, while he gave perhaps his finest screen performance as a philandering husband in *They Won't Believe Me*, the film was initially a flop since audiences rebelled against accepting him as anything other than the nice guy he generally played.

When Twentieth Century–Fox head Darryl F. Zanuck could not bring himself to fire immensely popular writer Ring Lardner, Jr., his board of directors promptly met in New York and did so.

Scarcely a week after the purge of the Hollywood Ten, a Philadelphia organization, the Golden Slipper Square Dance Club, staged a dinner to present its annual humanitarian award to the makers of *Crossfire*. Scott and Dmytryk had been recently fired and, as such, were unlikely candidates to appear, despite their enormous contributions to the film as producer and director respectively. Dore Schary was invited to receive it but was reluctant to do so, having opposed the RKO firings. In another example of Hollywood irony, Eric Johnston, president of the Motion Picture Association, who had presided over the Waldorf-Astoria Hotel meeting of film executives that sought and obtained joint studio action in firing the Hollywood Ten posthaste, appeared to accept the award. Irony compounded upon irony as Johnston used the opportunity to salute Hollywood's "openness": "Hollywood has held the door of opportunity open to every man and woman who could meet its technical and artistic standards.... What [our industry] is interested in is his skill or talent, ability to produce pictures for the joy and progress of mankind."

Blacklisted in the American film industry, Dmytryk did the same as fellow director Jules Dassin and departed for England in 1948 to make films. When he returned to America two years later after being ordered back to renew his passport, Dmytryk, expecting a brief visit before returning to England and his film work, was tried in June 1950 and sentenced to six months at Mill Point Prison Camp for contempt of Congress. Upon his release from prison in November 1950, confronted with indefinite blacklisting in America, he reached a decision to cooperate with the Committee.

"I was being forced to sacrifice my family and my career in defense of the Communist Party," Dmytryk exclaimed, "from which I had long been separated and which I had grown to dislike and distrust." When he ultimately testified before HUAC in April 1951, Dmytryk provided many names of people he knew to be Party members, most of them already known to the Committee. One of that number was none other than Adrian Scott, his RKO repertory partner with whom he had worked on *Crossfire, Murder, My Sweet, Cornered, Deadline at Dawn* and *So Well Remembered.* Scott, a former magazine editor who joined RKO as a screenwriter, with the Cary Grant 1943 winner *Mr. Lucky* among his credits, was unable to shake the blacklist and never worked again. He died in Arlington, New Jersey, in 1973.

It can only be speculated how many screen triumphs might have awaited the RKO triumvirate of Dmytryk, Scott and screenwriter John Paxton had the association not ended abruptly at the very point in time when its most critically saluted vehicle, *Crossfire*, was achieving commercial and artistic success. Dmytryk would go on to direct films such as *The Caine Mutiny, The Young Lions* and *Raintree County* while Paxton, the only one of the three unaffected by the political tempest, worked into the early 70s, with his premier later credit being Stanley Kramer's 1959 release *On the Beach* with Gregory Peck and Ava Gardner.

Social Message Noir

Dmytryk and RKO broke new ground in moving from the rock-ribbed suspense of Chandler vehicle *Murder, My Sweet* to a different kind of social message film noir with *Crossfire.* While maintaining the same kind of swift pacing which marked the 1944 film starring Dick Powell and Claire Trevor, the 1947 release

Crossfire presented a taut drama redolent with social meaning about where America stood in the pivotal post war period.

It is instructive to examine the story elements of *Crossfire* in contrast to those of the more conventional noir hit of three years earlier, *Murder, My Sweet*:

1) A vigilant detective. Dick Powell as Philip Marlowe and Robert Young as Lieutenant Finlay of the Washington D.C., police were equally determined to put killers behind bars. In the case of Powell, the quest went from the darkened quicksand of Los Angeles by night as Claire Trevor sought to use her beauty to seduce and entrap the resourceful and honest detective. With Powell, the hunt was more physical while in Young's case more cerebral as he seeks to snare a killer he fears may elude him due to lack of evidence. Young as well as the crafty Mitchum are both strongly convinced that Ryan is the killer of Levene. His anti–Semitism is blatant and vocal. What Young needs in an evidentiary sense is what would be termed a "smoking gun," a way to tie him to the murders of Levene and fellow soldier Steve Brodie. A compelling motivator for Young in snaring the hateful anti–Semitic killer is the knowledge that his own grandfather, as an Irish immigrant, met his death through an act of anti–Catholic bigotry at the hands of a Washington mob.

2) A deranged killer. Montgomery had some of the psychopathic traits as the hulking Moose Malloy of *Murder, My Sweet*, but the bigoted soldier was a more complex and shrewder character than the omnipresent figure of darkness of the earlier film. Malloy had one overwhelming desire, to be reunited with Velma, the woman for whom he longingly pines. His hunger is magnified by the years he has spent in prison constantly fixated on her presence. Ryan is also removed from the greed that often dominates film noir killers, especially the femme fatales such as Stanwyck in *Double Indemnity* and Trevor in *Murder, My Sweet*. Montgomery is a seething cauldron of combustible hate, a time bomb ready to explode at recurring intervals. As Young explains at a pivotal moment of the film, when he is enlisting help from a frightened young soldier to trap the killer, the volatile Montgomery hates anything he fails to understand. Where Montgomery differs from a less complex killer such as Moose Malloy is that his knowledge of police interrogation invests him with a certain cleverness in seeking to turn an investigation in another direction. In this case, he is seeking to turn suspicion away from himself and toward the sensitive, tragical figure of Corporal Mitchell. This strategic facet is overwhelmed, however, by his clashing side, that of his towering psychopathic rage. As a result, he inadvertently lets Young and Mitchum know he is the killer when he launches into a bitter anti–Semitic diatribe.

3) An experienced force operating for good. Robert Mitchum as Sergeant Keeley remains a voice of reason throughout the film. A newspaperman by trade, his comments make it clear that he is a shrewd analyst of character. Having correctly analyzed George A. Cooper, who portrays Corporal Mitchell, as someone who could not commit murder, Keeley sets out in his quiet, probing, methodical way to help Finlay solve the crime. Realizing that he needs time as his ally, Keeley knows it is

imperative to keep Mitchell out of harm's path. He uses cunning to prevent his arrest through creating a commotion in a hotel lobby, allowing Mitchell and himself a quick escape, and through the clever noir technique of hiding the melancholy soldier, whose life hangs at a critical crossroad, in an all-night theater, where he and his compatriots check up on him periodically and familiarize him with developing activities. Mitchum, in one of his early formative roles, impresses with his quiet credibility. One can sense the wheels turning within him as he sits and reflects. Due to his shrewd reflection, when he speaks it is with meaning and purpose and listeners are likely to pay close attention. Mitchum's persona as Sergeant Keeley is reminiscent of an early line in *Out of the Past* when he tells Kirk Douglas during their first meeting that he never learned anything listening to himself. Keeley is also shrewd enough to know what Mitchell needs at a critical crossroad, the wife he loves, and so she is summoned. She renders strong moral support when the disconsolate young soldier needs it most.

4) An interesting character ensemble. As earlier mentioned, one of the major reasons why John Huston scored such a big success in his first directorial assignment in *The Maltese Falcon* was due to the interest generated by casting offbeat types such as Sydney Greenstreet, Peter Lorre and Elisha Cook, Jr., *Murder, My Sweet* had the likes of Mike Mazurki, Otto Kruger and others whose paths crossed with wisecracking detective Dick Powell. In *Crossfire*, two fascinating offbeat characters generate great interest and curiosity, Gloria Grahame and Paul Kelly. Grahame alternates between a sensitive melancholia and a desire to mother the morose soldier to a steely obstinance when she refuses to vouch for his presence in her apartment at the time the murder was committed. Kelly, a self-admitted liar whose life is askew, overhears the conversation and willingly supplies the needed alibi for the tormented soldier. Curiosity abounds over what type of relationship Grahame and Kelly could forge. A driving natural curiosity on the part of film viewers is a major reason for casting offbeat types and providing them with enigmatic screen personas. The technique provides a perfect mix and seasoning for effective film noir.

The same year that *Crossfire* was released, 1947, and the identical year that the term film noir was first used, an epic brilliantly evoking the darkness of the human spirit in the most absorbingly ingenious manner was released by the RKO noir factory. With appropriate symbolism, the director of that film was French. The young lady who skyrocketed to stardom was in her early twenties. Her co-star would become the ultimate film noir male lead.

FIVE

Jane Greer: Hollywood's Unforgettable Femme Fatale

In the manner of vintage wine, the 1947 film noir masterpiece *Out of the Past* improves with age, specifically with increased viewing. Much has been written about the earlier RKO triumvirate of Scott, Dmytryk and Paxton. *Out of the Past* embodied the finest efforts of a quintet of unique talents, the directorial skills of Jacques Tourneur creatively shaping a Daniel Mainwaring script utilizing three ideal performers. Robert Mitchum exemplified the definitive noir male lead, an intelligent victim powerless to distance himself from equally perfect femme fatale Jane Greer, caught in an obsessive triangle completed by ruthless syndicate operator Kirk Douglas. All three performers were beginning promising careers and none would be more convincing than in *Out of the Past.*

These promising newcomers convey the impression of being much older than their actual ages. Jane Greer was a youthful 22 when the film was shot while the two rivals for her affections, Robert Mitchum and Kirk Douglas, were also both in their twenties. The trio appears as timeless as age itself due to the clever dialogue, which reveals the performers as voices of experience well beyond what would be expected from individuals of their ages, as well as the adroit use of lighting. An existential moodiness prevails. Mitchum and Greer are forced to live by night after crossing syndicate boss Douglas. The biting Mainwaring dialogue carries a strong dose of fatalism. Mitchum emerges as an existential victim, someone who knows he is ultimately doomed but is determined to extend the conflict as long as possible.

The story components fall into the following pattern:

1) Private detective Jeff Markham is hired by mob boss Whit Sterling to find Kathie Moffett, who has shot him, almost costing him his life, and stolen $40,000. He indicates he is not interested in punishing her or retrieving his money, only in

getting her back. Sterling tells Markham that when he sees Moffett, he will understand why his interest is only in seeing her again.

2) Shrewd bloodhound Markham tracks Kathie down in Acapulco. He remembers Sterling's words about understanding his need for desiring Moffett's return once he sees her. He falls hard for Kathie, who convinces him that Sterling epitomizes evil and all she wanted was to be rid of him. He believes her emphatic declaration that she never stole any money from the syndicate boss. Together they go back to San Francisco, where Markham starts a detective agency, making just enough money to survive. He states in narration that they were scraping the bottom of the barrel but that it was all right with him as long as he had Kathie.

3) Markham's old detective partner from New York, Jack Fisher, spots the lovers at a San Francisco racetrack. Sterling has hired him to find his old partner. The two former partners have a bitter confrontation at a rural cabin hideaway being used by Markham and Moffett. They come to blows over Kathie, with the femme fatale shooting Fisher fatally. As a stunned Markham prepares to bury Fisher, Kathie disappears into the night, driving away. Markham finds her checkbook with the amount of $40,000 written inside, revealing that she lied to him.

4) The second phase of the film begins with Markham taking the name of Jeff Bailey and running his own gas station in the tranquil Northern California town of Bridgeport. He romances Ann, a sweet local girl who knows nothing of his past. The pattern is disrupted when longtime Sterling associate Joe Stefanos finds him. He tells Markham-Bailey how anxious Whit is to see him. Hoping that seeing Sterling at his Lake Tahoe mansion one last time will terminate their relationship and enable him to put his past behind him, Jeff agrees. He has Ann drive him that evening, enabling him to tell her about his past.

5) The double cross by Sterling. Never having forgiven Markham-Bailey for double crossing him, Whit plans a clever revenge by asking Jeff to perform one last assignment, obtaining tax documents from a San Francisco attorney, Leonard Eels, who is intent on blackmailing the syndicate boss. Turning him into the Internal Revenue Service would ultimately cost Sterling ten years in a federal prison. Stefanos kills the attorney with Sterling set to frame Jeff for the murders of Eels as well as the detective's former partner, Fisher, with Markham-Bailey learning that Kathie, who has returned to Sterling, has signed an affidavit implicating the detective.

The pattern of double crosses generates tension involving the three characters. The twists and turns of the story reveal Kathie alternately seeking to ruin and even, on one occasion, kill Jeff, then throw herself into his arms. At one point he states with bitter admiration how Kathie is able to shift sides with such quick adroitness. Yet, all the same, like Sterling before him, Markham-Bailey remains her victim. Eventually they die together, seemingly the fitting end to an existential drama with the hapless Jeff caught in the vise-like grip of a cold fate.

The femme fatale role of Kathie Moffett, played with superb conviction and a requisite coolness under fire by Jane Greer, was a case of a gifted young performer surmounting a major dramatic challenge. While the role of Kathie was a star maker, it also could have been a star breaker had it been entrusted to someone lacking the superb dramatic instincts of Greer, who invested the amoral Kathie with the unique ability and charismatic fascination to break two normally strong-willed men who sought to retain romantic links to her in the face of repeated treachery.

RKO, a Hollywood dream factory on Melrose Avenue, became the accomplished creators of "lean and mean" suspense vehicles, providing crisply written, taut mystery films to America and the rest of the world. Shooting schedules were short and scrupulously maintained with all eyes focused on achieving maximum quality at minimal costs, enabling a steady level of productivity to be maintained.

Jane Greer emerged in timely fashion at RKO as a definitive femme fatale combining beauty with brains, turning raw sensuality on and off like a spigot as she wove her magic opposite Robert Mitchum and Kirk Douglas. Greer is the film's glamorous centerpiece, using her charms with skillful cunning, a predator whose warm exterior masks her cold designs.

The dynamic presence etched by a young actress able to convey the experience of a woman well beyond her years, using her considerable charm for personal gain, skyrocketed Greer to impressive stardom in *Out of the Past*. Her popularity with fans and critics continues to increase with each showing of the film as more people are introduced to the special blend of magic woven into the film noir classic. A great painting demands intense focus and study, but Greer in *Out of the Past* is more than a painting, requiring even more intense concentration. Greer in *Out of the Past* is an actress who received a rare opportunity to portray a female Svengali with the strategically ruthless mind of a Dr. Moriarity beneath an often soft-as-silk exterior. Even the sensuality was fine-tuned between a powerful eroticism and the come hither glances of a sweet girl next door. The Kathie Moffett character, featuring more character nuances than a sports car has gears, required a special kind of actress to portray her, and Jane Greer possessed that special kind of ability.

Early Career Beginnings

In order to convey the level of sophistication Kathie Moffett displayed at the tender age of 22 required a unique maturity. Jane Greer was benefited by her early roots in the entertainment industry, in which she developed invaluable experience that aided her in *Out of the Past* as well as other challenging RKO vehicles undertaken in the same period.

Jane grew up in Washington, D.C., born Bettejane Greer on September 9, 1924. Her mother recognized early in Bettejane's life her daughter's performing potentials, encouraging her participation in many beauty and talent contests. By 12, young Bettejane was modeling professionally. She was also an avid movie fan, responding with the kind of total empathy expected from someone who had acting in her blood.

"My favorite actress was Irene Dunne," Jane recalled with fondness. "I absolutely

The grim expression on Robert Mitchum's face reflects his latest keen disappointment over being double crossed by femme fatale Jane Greer in the 1947 film noir masterpiece, *Out of the Past*, directed by Jacques Tourneur. Greer shifted between Mitchum and Kirk Douglas in the film, ultimately destroying them both.

adored her. I reacted so intensely to her starring performance in *Love Affair* that my mother waited with me until everyone had left so I could finish crying. She was a great performer capable of bringing an emotional reaction out of me. Another actress of my youth that I just loved was Jeanette MacDonald."

It came as no surprise that Bettejean's high school days were highlighted by her involvement in dramatics. Her performing instincts and sense of adventure prompted Greer to drop out of high school in her senior year to accept a singing spot with a top local band.

"I was a singer with the Enrique Madriguera Orchestra at the Del Rio Club in Washington," she revealed. "Enrique was a popular bandleader of the period who wrote the song *Adios*."

Greer's career was beginning just as the United States was becoming involved in World War II. The conflict abroad had a definite link to launching her acting career, another of the many footnotes of how famous performers received their breaks. Posing prettily in a WAC uniform, Greer's picture was spotted in Hollywood and one of filmdom's most fascinating enigmas, Howard Hughes, offered her a contract in 1943.

"I'll never forget the first time I met him," Jane recollected. "Here I was a young girl who had just come to Hollywood from D.C., and I was very nervous. He had a man pick me up in a limousine and drive me to his office at Goldwyn Studios. Howard was a night person and invited me to his office for a midnight meeting. It was six months after he signed me to my contract that I met him. One of his assistants gave me something to read for him, a scene from *The Awful Truth*. I was nervous enough already and became even more nervous at the idea of reading something my first meeting with him without any preparation. The assistant told me not to worry and to just go ahead and read the scene naturally. Well, Howard was hard of hearing, and here I was, very nervous, so I read the scene in a very low voice. I don't know how much he was able to hear but he appeared to be satisfied and everything seemed to go all right."

During that same year Greer, who had begun her professional entertainment career as a nightclub singer, married one of the singing legends of the twentieth century. It was Rudy Vallee who had begun the crooning generation embraced later by singers such as Frank Sinatra, Russ Columbo and Perry Como. Jane's acting career was beginning at a point when Vallee's film endeavors had reached a significant point with his memorable performance acting and singing in one of director Preston Sturges' greatest films, *The Palm Beach Story*. When her brief marriage to Vallee reached its end, the man who had brought her out to Hollywood to embark on an acting career emerged.

Fudge, Kewpie Dolls and Howard Hughes

"After Rudy and I had reunited for the last time and split up, I began to see Howard Hughes," Greer revealed. "He took me out on dates to the then popular

It took little time for Washington, D.C., singer-model Jane Greer to rise to stardom after being signed by RKO. After initially starring in the brilliant 1947 drama *They Won't Believe Me* with Robert Young and Susan Hayward, she achieved a film noir milestone in the unforgettable role of the resourceful, ruthless femme fatale Kathie Moffett in *Out of the Past*. She would round out the forties by starring again with Mitchum in her third memorable RKO movie of the decade, *The Big Steal*, a fast-moving, engaging caper film directed by Don Siegel. Greer had to survive a temporary blacklisting by studio boss Howard Hughes to reteam with her *Out of the Past* co-star Mitchum.

Ocean Park amusement park next to the Pacific. Howard had a passion for fudge. He just loved it. He also loved throwing baseballs and knocking down pins. He used to rejoice whenever he would win a kewpie doll. He'd give them to me to give to my mother."

The famous billionaire who spent some of the most fascinating years of his storied life on the Hollywood scene would later resurface in Jane Greer's career, but her next big break was being signed by RKO in 1945 and being put immediately to work. In view of the fact that she would have two starring roles in RKO films shot in 1946, one of which was *Out of the Past*, it is easy to see how quickly the young brunette contract player impressed studio executives and was propelled up the ladder to stardom.

The Year the Screen Magic Fell into Place

Since her signing by RKO, Greer had benefited from frequent activity, the process of moving a performer through the ranks as experience and confidence are secured. In 1946, Greer entered the ranks of stardom. In addition to her famous role as Kathie Moffett in *Out of the Past*, she appeared in two other major productions with impressive casts.

Sinbad the Sailor was a swashbuckling sea adventure in which Douglas Fairbanks, Jr., starred in the same kind of role his father performed with gusto in such silent films as *The Thief of Baghdad* and *The Black Pirate*. Director Richard Wallace kept the action at a brisk pace as the ornate sets and lavish Arab costumes were emphasized. Jane performed in a cast of notables that, in addition to Fairbanks, included Maureen O'Hara, Anthony Quinn, Walter Slezak, Mike Mazurki, George Tobias and Sheldon Leonard.

Lighten the Hair, Surge to Stardom

Joan Harrison was a legend of her time. She grew up in the idyllic town of Guildford, a short half-hour's ride by British Rail from London's Waterloo Station. It is now a popular city for trying out plays destined for London's West End. Joan received an impressive education that included stops at both the Sorbonne in Paris and Oxford University in her own country. The master Alfred Hitchcock recognized her creative talents, utilizing her as a screenwriter. Her impressive Hitchcock credits included *Rebecca, Foreign Correspondent, Suspicion* and *Saboteur*. Harrison was one of the pioneering women who achieved significance in a non-acting capacity as she moved from writing to producing.

As a top RKO producer of the '40s, Harrison broke ground at the Melrose studio just as Virginia Van Upp was producing *Gilda* at nearby Columbia on Gower Street. Harrison debuted as a producer with the noir classic *Phantom Lady* in 1944, starring Franchot Tone and Ella Raines. She subsequently produced *Uncle Harry* in 1945 and the George Raft detective film *Nocturne* in 1946. The highly respected Harrison thought she spotted a gem in Jane Greer and asked her to visit her in her office.

"Joan had me in mind for a part and wanted to talk to me," Greer recalled. "She told me she thought my hair was too dark and that this gave me an older look. Rudy [Vallee] liked my hair dark. I guess he wanted a Hedy Lamarr look from me. Anyhow, Joan believed that if my hair was lightened and more highlight was put into it that I would have a more natural look. She told me that as things stood I had a Gale Sondergard look, which suited me for more exotic roles playing an older woman than I was. So when my hair color was lightened and I had the look that Joan wanted, she cast me in a film she was producing that gave my career a great boost."

The film was *They Won't Believe Me* and the positive notices Jane received for her performance had a domino effect, providing her with her golden opportunity to portray the ruthless but fascinating Kathie Moffett in *Out of the Past* as her next assignment.

The combination of producer Joan Harrison and director Irving Pichel in *They Won't Believe Me* was as impressively educated a tandem as ever pooled forces at a Hollywood studio. While Harrison was educated at the Sorbonne and Oxford, the multi-talented Pichel was a Harvard graduate. Greer was cast in a sympathetic role unlike that of Kathie Moffett. She was romantically linked to Robert Young, cast against type as a selfish Cassanova who lived by the credo, "I never saw an attractive woman to whom I wouldn't succumb." Susan Hayward plays another Young love interest, while Rita Johnson is cast as the wealthy and long-suffering wife who foolishly refuses to let her faithless husband go, instead living by the precept that her fat assets will provide an eventual restraining leash.

The narrative technique employed in *They Won't Believe Me* was a successful film noir method used effectively in *Out of the Past* and *Double Indemnity*. Young, after taking the stand on his own behalf in his trial for the murder of Hayward, fills in the essential details of his life, beginning with his days as a Wall Street broker, when he falls in love with intelligent and sophisticated magazine writer Janice Bell (Greer). In distinct contrast to the character she would play in her next film, the predatory Kathie Moffett, Janice Bell was a sincere, decent person who refused to allow her relationship with Larry Ballentine to continue while he remained married and accepted the largesse of his wealthy wife.

A Voice of Calm Reason

While Greer's character in *They Won't Believe Me* is poles removed from Kathie Moffett in *Out of the Past*, there are significant links between the two roles to prompt a discerning analyst to see why the first film could serve as a prelude to the second.

It is understandable after carefully analyzing *They Won't Believe Me* why RKO personnel would be motivated to offer Greer the plum female lead in *Out of the Past* in that, when the moral distinctions are removed, both women possessed great strength and an ability to take charge. In *Out of the Past,* a casehardened Robert Mitchum is willing to battle syndicate boss Kirk Douglas and his minions without backing off, but can be reduced to putty in the manipulative hands of Kathie Moffett. Robert Young's character of Larry Ballentine, like so many habitual philanderers, was a man of vacillating weakness. Of all the characters in the film, male and female, Greer exhibits the greatest strength and sturdiness of character.

The post–World War II cinema era marked a noted change in the female in film. While Barbara Stanwyck had broken significant ground playing a powerful femme fatale role in *Double Indemnity*, Joan Crawford had won an Academy Award in her debut film for Warner Bros., *Mildred Pierce*, following her well-publicized departure from MGM. The 1945 release was about a strong career woman who, after a divorce, builds up a chain of successful Southern California restaurants. These were significant historical antecedents for Jane Greer, who in 1946 appeared in two major film noir efforts, playing strong female characters in each.

Greer received star billing alongside Robert Young and Susan Hayward in *They Won't Believe Me.* Producer Warren Duff and RKO then tapped the talented brunette for a lead role in another film. She took one look at the script, and was enchanted.

A Classic to Endure for the Ages

As characteristic of vintage wine and literature, masterpieces are shaped over a long period. *Out of the Past* gains in artistic significance and attracts additional fans with each passing year. Did she realize just how enduring a classic she was about to appear in at RKO?

"No, I never thought about that, but I certainly was impressed by the script," she said with enthusiasm about her great *Out of the Past* role. "This was the kind of part that an actress would absolutely die for! I mean, it was like those parts that Alan Ladd played at Paramount in those days. He wouldn't appear on the screen until he had received a big buildup that made him appear to be eight or nine feet tall. I could see that the *Out of the Past* script was the same kind of story. Here is this detective, Bob Mitchum, who is contacted by Kirk Douglas. He describes Kathie Moffett as someone so special that he tells Bob he will recognize her when he sees her. Then there's this mystique about Kathie having shot Kirk and stolen $40,000 from him, but he isn't concerned about the money and just wants her back. You just couldn't hope for a better buildup as a performer."

Kathie Moffett is presented with an air of mystique, but with this careful buildup having been provided, it is essential for the performer to display the necessary charisma and interest on screen. Greer's initial appearance was so convincing that it has been accorded the same distinction in film noir circles as Lana Turner's electrifying entry in the memorable 1946 MGM drama *The Postman Always Rings Twice*, when she drops her lipstick on the floor and John Garfield observes her in a breathtaking upward sweep.

Mitchum, cast in the role of New York detective Jeff Markham, has been hired by syndicate boss Kirk Douglas to locate and bring back the woman who attempted to kill him and left with $40,000 of his money. He traces her to hot, sun-drenched Acapulco, where he sits and waits for the seemingly inevitable meeting with her. It occurs one lazy afternoon in a dark cantina, La Mar Azul. With the camera stationed behind Mitchum, providing film viewers with the actor's perspective, the stunning Greer emerges from the sunshine into the darkness, wearing a white dress and matching white hat. Director Jacques Tourneur and cinematographer Nicholas Musuraca shrewdly interspersed forces of light and darkness, the judicious mixture that embodies film noir epics. She sits down at a table not far from Mitchum's. The actor responds by getting up and walking to her table. Mitchum reveals that he is lonely and would like to talk to someone, after which they become acquainted. As Greer prepares to leave, she tells him about a drinking spot that, if you close your eyes, reminds one "of a little spot on 56th Street." She concludes with some well-chosen words, "I go there sometimes."

The brief, dramatically convincing first scene for Jane Greer evokes a response as Mitchum, after walking to the telegraph office to wire Douglas that he has found the elusive brunette, is elated to learn that it is siesta time and he cannot notify the syndicate boss. She then shows up at the bar she mentioned, but on the second rather than the first night.

Tourneur and the Search for Mood

With *Out of the Past* destined to ultimately become a film noir classic, it was poetic justice that the 1947 epic was directed by an individual with authentic French lineage. Jacques Tourneur was born in Paris, the son of film director Maurice Thomas, better known as Maurice Tourneur. Jacques traveled to America with his father when the elder Tourneur was in demand there as a director. In 1919, at the age of 15, he became an American citizen, finished high school and went to work at MGM as a script clerk. It was during his MGM days, when he was working under David O. Selznick on a unit filming French Revolution scenes in the screen adaptation of Charles Dickens's *A Tale of Two Cities*, that Tourneur was introduced to writer Val Lewton, who collaborated with him. They had a rapport which found them collaborating on two horror classics at RKO, *Cat People* in 1942 and *I Walked with a Zombie* one year later.

The RKO hierarchy eventually broke up the duo, to the disappointment of both men, believing that the studio could realize greater productivity by having them work independently. Tourneur turned out convincing output at RKO. *Experiment Perilous* in 1944 was similar in content to *Gaslight*, which won a Best Actress

Academy Award for Ingrid Bergman. Paul Lukas, a Best Actor Oscar recipient for *Watch on the Rhine*, psychologically dominated and obsessed Hedy Lamarr in *Experiment Perilous* in the same manner that Charles Boyer played Svengali to Bergman. George Brent plays the doctor whose genuine love for Lamarr rescues her from the murderous designs of a vengeful Lukas. Tourneur also directed *Easy Living* (1949), a drama with Victor Mature as a professional football player nearing the end of his career with added domestic pressures via a crumbling marriage to Lizabeth Scott.

Tourneur posted a winning effort in a stellar Western released by Universal in 1946, one year before *Out of the Past: Canyon Passage*, which starred Dana Andrews as a rugged frontiersman intent on building a mule freight line in mid-nineteenth century Oregon. Susan Hayward was Andrews' co-star.

Greer retains a clear recollection of Tourneur as well as the impact the director had on the film:

"When I met this little Frenchman, he spoke with such a pronounced accent that at first I wondered if he spoke English at all. He was very interested in mood from the very beginning. He told me how he wanted me to play my part. At the beginning of the film he looked at me and said, 'Do you know the word *impassive*?,' giving it the French pronunciation. I told him that I had studied French in high school and knew exactly what he meant. 'Well, that is how I want you to be,' he told me."

Tourneur's idea of impassivity was a projection of coolness under fire that gave Kathie Moffett the air of a quick thinking iceberg. Her shrewd stoicism provides her with an advantage over the two men she is able to manipulate through seizing control over their emotions, Mitchum as the detective and Douglas, in one of his earliest roles cast as Whit Sterling, the mob boss who, try as he might, cannot get the image of Greer's Kathie out of his mind.

A director from the French tradition of thematic mood emphasis, Tourneur embraced the definitive noir concept of interspersing light with darkness. The characters are creatures of night, and even interior scenes are cast in shadows. The best example of light interspersed with shadows is the scene in the cabin that Mitchum and Greer have selected to escape the detective's former New York partner, Steve Brodie, who by then is on the payroll of a highly suspicious Douglas. Brodie appears at the cabin just when they begin to falsely believe that they have eluded him. In the fight that begins after Brodie calls Greer "cheap baggage," the shadows of the battling men are cast against the walls. Greer pulls a gun and fires on Brodie, killing him instantly. At the scene's conclusion, the headlights of her car are observed reflecting against the walls as Mitchum crouches down to observe his former partner's lifeless form. Greer has run out on her detective lover as he locates the bankbook revealing the $40,000 deposit.

"Jacques Tourneur spoke to me early in the film about the idea he had to make the best use of light for effect," Jane revealed. "He said that in the beginning he wanted me to be dressed in white along with other white colors. As the story and my character emerged, he wanted to dress me in dark colors to reflect fundamental character changes, with me eventually dressed in black. It was impossible to carry out the color scheme he had in mind because of costuming considerations and the changes needed, but he was able to achieve the basic idea he had about color and mood."

Tourneur, working in close concert with cinematographer Musuraca, kept the accent on the moody darkness associated with film noir. In Robert Mitchum, RKO had cast a player who appeared to jump out of the pages of a Raymond Chandler or James Cain novel. His physical demeanor was ideal for the kind of existentialist survivor he portrayed in *Out of the Past* and a host of other films throughout his lengthy career. The sleepy-eyed look and hooded eyes that marked him as a survivor in the noir netherworld stemmed from a combination of astigmatism (the result of an injury during his professional boxing days) along with insomnia that plagued him during his entire adult life. The broken nose, sustained during his early years as a roustabout and boxer, accented the natural persona of the tough detective. An articulate man capable of repeatedly delivering shrewd one-liners, Mitchum provided a ready answer to the question of why he did not get his nose fixed through cosmetic surgery. "They used to say to me, did you ever think about getting your nose fixed," Mitchum told an interviewer in 1993. "I had it fixed three or four times—by a straight left!"

Mitchum lived the life of a character out of a Chandler or Cain novel along with looking the part. He left his home of Bridgeport, Connecticut, at the age of 15 and undertook a young man's odyssey around Depression America. His freight-hopping excursions saw him work at such jobs as laborer, coal miner, a professional boxer with a 27-bout career, ditch digger and aircraft assembler. In Georgia he was arrested for vagrancy and placed in a chain gang. The treatment he and other prisoners received was so harsh that he quickly managed to escape. In 1940 he married his high school sweetheart, Dorothy Spence, and eventually set down his restless feet in Long Beach, California, where he joined his sister, Julie, who had begun acting with the Players Guild of Long Beach. He wrote material for her nightclub act, wrote plays in which he appeared with the Players Guild and was hired as an assistant by noted astrologer Carroll Righter. After registering with an actor friend for the Screen Extras Guild, he began obtaining work in low-budget Hopalong Cassidy Westerns. When he thought he was in danger of being stuck permanently in that mold, he quipped that he got out of low-budget Westerns by "blinking my eyes every time a gun went off in the scenes."

As an RKO contractee it took little time for this American natural to display his dramatic skills in major roles. There was a Best Supporting Actor Oscar nomination for *The Story of G.I. Joe*, the only one bestowed on him by the Academy during his 100-plus film career.

Just when Mitchum's career was in high gear, an event occurred which almost deprived RKO of casting the ideal actor as Jeff Markham-Bailey in *Out of the Past*. The actor discovered that his business manager had embezzled almost all of his money. Dorothy Mitchum insisted that the family return to the East Coast and that he give up his film career. RKO, undoubtedly recognizing what a nugget it had, insisted that Mitchum honor his contract. He then returned to Hollywood, initially by himself, ultimately carving out an indelible chapter of movie history.

"Robert Mitchum was a great friend and such a great man," Jane Greer lauded her co-star. "He had a superb eye for detail and was always looking out for me. If he saw that my dress was crooked at the shoulders he would ask someone in costuming, 'Do you suppose you could get a couple of pins and straighten her dress?' He was wonderful throughout the picture."

The Mitchum-Greer team ignited screen explosives as the Jeff Markham-Bailey character demonstrated capability in dealing with others, including mobster Whit Sterling, but displayed an Achilles heel when it came to the shrewd feminine wiles of Kathie. It was a weakness shared by Sterling as the captivating brunette juggled their emotions by moving from one man to another, repeating the process with dizzying rapidity. "I played the character of Kathie Moffett at the stoic level that Jacques Tourneur wanted," Greer said, "but every now and then I would vary things a little by changing expressions."

A Successful Adaptation

Often a novelist will express disappointment, dismay or worse at the adaptation of the author's work to the screen. Ernest Hemingway was one author who expressed frequent disappointment over adaptations of his stories to film. In the case of *Out of the Past*, veteran screenwriter Daniel Mainwaring was adapting *Build My Gallows High*, a novel by Geoffrey Homes. This marked one of those rare instances of a novelist adapting his own material since Mainwaring used the name Homes at various stages of his literary and film careers. Mainwaring-Homes specialized in adventure in each realm of writing.

Born in Oakland, Mainwaring graduated from Fresno State College, working his way into the screenwriting ranks from journalism (he was a reporter for the *San Francisco Chronicle*). He began his cinema career in the Publicity Department of Paramount in the early '40s before ultimately becoming a screenwriter and novelist. Among his film credits were *Dangerous Passage, Scared Stiff, Hot Cargo, They Made Me a Killer* and *Big Town*.

Proficient in the mystery realm, Mainwaring also received assistance from two established veterans of the genre for *Out of the Past*. Suspense master James M. Cain was involved in the project, though the extent of his effort will probably never be known. This was a period in which collaboration on film scripts was the accepted norm, with the industry's largest studio, MGM, serving as the major example. It was done at all studios to varying degrees, RKO as well. Cain biographer Roy Hoopes interviewed the great mystery writer repeatedly in the '70s, the last phase of the writer's life, after Cain returned home to his Baltimore roots. Cain was unable to recall at that point having been involved in the *Out of the Past* project. The character

Jeff Markham-Bailey bears close thematic resemblance to those two classic Cain victims of rapacious women, Fred MacMurray with Barbara Stanwyck in *Double Indemnity* and John Garfield opposite Lana Turner in *The Postman Always Rings Twice*, two other film noir classics from the '40s.

The other writer involved in *Out of the Past* was Frank Fenton, a Georgetown University graduate who divided a colorful career between acting and screenwriting. Fenton established himself on both the New York and London stage. His Broadway credits included *Susan and God* and *The Philadelphia Story*. His first screen acting assignment was in the 1943 murder mystery, *Lady of Burlesque*, starring Barbara Stanwyck based on a novel by Gypsy Rose Lee, in which he played seedy burlesque tenor and murder suspect Russell Rogers. He also acted in Billy Wilder's *A Foreign Affair* and starred with John Carradine in the 1943 release, *Isle of Forgotten Sins*, in which they played deep sea divers. His screenwriting career began at Fox in 1935. Fenton was noted for his involvement in two famous mystery series, the Saint and the Falcon, while in the '50s he was involved in both *River of No Return* and *The Wings of Eagles*.

"Recently in the RKO files some pages have turned up," Jane Greer revealed. "A lot of the pages have to do with the narration scenes in *Out of the Past* and they have the initials FF on them, standing for Frank Fenton, so it looks like Fenton had a bigger involvement with the film than what was earlier thought." The Fenton contribution was said to be heaviest in the narrative of Mitchum during the ride with his new love Virginia Huston en route to Douglas's Lake Tahoe mansion. The narrative is some of the most memorable ever written, revealing the plight of a detective caught in an existentialist fate from which he is powerless to extricate himself.

From Novel to Screenplay

The recent republication of the previously long out-of-print novel *Build My Gallows High* has provided an opportunity for interested devotees of *Out of the Past* to enjoy the suspenseful writing of Daniel Mainwaring as well as observe the adaptation process from book to film. Prion Books Limited of London specializes in making available literary works later translated to the screen as part of its Film Ink Series, which also includes such film classics as *The Asphalt Jungle* by W.C. Burnett and *Dr. Strangelove* by Peter George, as well as another literary work adapted to the screen by Mainwaring, *Invasion of the Body Snatchers* by Jack Finney.

It is historically understandable that a British company would seek to perpetuate great suspense films through the stories from which they were adapted. A major reason why Raymond Chandler was able to propel himself from the ranks of magazine pulp writer to international mystery author stemmed from the manner in which British readers purchased and devoured his Philip Marlowe detective novels at a time when sales of those books were considerably smaller in the United States.

After reading *Build My Gallows High*, which would be retained as the title in the film in England, one observes a familiar pattern at work in the adaptive process. The narrative process with its accent on character development in print encourages the inclusion of a greater number of principal characters than is the case in film, where condensation aids the story's development by focusing on a smaller number, but more concentrated series of images manifested through the characters they portray. In the Mainwaring novel, which was initially published in 1946, the same year that *Out of the Past* was filmed at RKO, the Kathie Moffett character has a reduced role as well as a different name, Mumsie McGonigle. The earlier name carries the ring of a tough gun moll lacking the degree of sophistication and elegance borne by the character with the elegant name of Kathie Moffett. While Mumsie McGonigle possesses a street toughness, it falls short of the slick expertise of smooth seductress Kathie of the film, whose sweeter portrayals to Mitchum as Jeff Markham-Bailey and Douglas as Whit Sterling ultimately render them as her victims against their own better judgment.

The McGonigle character in the novel becomes less of an influence while Meta Carson, the second femme fatale in the book (played in the film by Rhonda Fleming), occupies an expanded role. In the film, Carson and the boss she betrays, Lloyd Eels, known as Leonard in the movie, are both killed by Joe Stefanos, who fatally shoots only the lawyer in *Out of the Past.* The film script invests Kathie Moffett with directional control of the double- and triple-dealing. Also, the action involving Eels's murder occurs in San Francisco, while in the book it occurs in New York.

Another character situation integrated from two-to-one status, in the manner of Kathie Moffett and Meta Carson, is that of Whit Sterling and a major figure in the book who is totally eliminated in the film in the interest of conciseness. Guy Parker is a former small town Nevada police chief who takes over a gambling casino. He is the person who refers Markham to Whit Sterling in the attempt to track down Mugsy McGonigle, later falling for her charms as had Bailey and Sterling.

The Mitchum character of the film is referred to repeatedly as Red Bailey in *Build My Gallows High.* As in the case of Mumsie McGonigle, the Markham-Bailey character in the novel is rougher hewn in conformity with more typified hard-boiled pulp fiction. The characters revealed on screen by Mitchum and Greer are slicker and more glamorous. While clearly able to handle himself physically, the Mitchum screen personality is one of a man who is primarily a thinking detective who resorts to violence only when necessary. The Red Bailey of the book version is described as big and ugly, prompting his rival for the affections of Bailey's Bridgeport girlfriend Ann Miller, forest ranger Jim Caldwell, to be angered by the fact that the other man, at 42, is old enough to be the father of the 20-year-old small town girl (in addition to being unattractive). Red Bailey's rugged machismo is what makes him fascinating to women. His muscles are called upon to bail him out of difficulty. The film persona of Mitchum as Markham-Bailey, on the other hand, is one of a tough, honest detective of admirable brainpower possessing charm. Both qualities are acknowledged by rival Kirk Douglas as Whit Sterling.

The somber existentialist mood established in the film is also present in the book. Every area where Red Bailey pulls up stakes has difficulties. Despite the rural beauty of Bridgeport and the regular availability of fish and game for the sportsman, Mainwaring's narrative refers to the long periods of cold temperatures and the presence of snow, along with the busy body nature of a community where people are too well aware of each other. While it is acknowledged that in L.A., a larger community, it is easier to achieve privacy, Mainwaring refers to the city in an uncomplimentary light as "the hot, dispirited mediocrity that was Los Angeles." New York, if anything, fares even worse. When Bailey goes there on assignment for Whit Sterling to see Meta Carson and attorney Lloyd Eels, his cab driver stops when two youngsters who had been playing hockey in the street with makeshift wooden sticks begin fighting tenaciously. When Bailey looks at the neighborhood and observes what he perceives to be a dog-eat-dog existence in the big city, he is happy he does not live there. The film contains one tart comment from Mitchum made while living in San Francisco indicating that his New York experience made him eager to live elsewhere. The novel reveals an observant, street-wise figure in Red Bailey, who sees shortcomings everywhere. What his main character does not reflect on, Mainwaring as omniscient narrator does. The world clearly exists in a shaky form which makes the observant all the more morose as pessimistic participants in what is seen as a vicious cycle life process in which there are no ultimate winners, only temporary survivors.

As reflective of a noir screenwriter, Daniel Mainwaring in *Build My Gallows High* is preoccupied with the darkness of night, the position of the Moon, intrusion of fog and the disappearance of the Sun. He is a man immersed in mood, as reflected early in the novel (page 3) when he writes, "Red lay back. A weary bit of moon was almost lost in the waste of pale sky." One paragraph later Mainwaring reveals, "[Red] turned his head a little and then he could see the mountains he loved—not red any more because the sun was gone. Up there were pine-fringed lakes and brawling streams and deep drifts of snow."

In the film, Mitchum is more of a pure victim of Jane Greer than was Red Bailey in his relationship with Mumsie McGonigle in the book. When Jack Fisher, Bailey's former business partner played by Steve Brodie in the film, confronts the lovers at their country cabin retreat, the same scenario evolves as in *Out of the Past*. The men fight after Bailey is angered by Fisher's reference to Mumsie as a "dirty, lying little bitch." In the book the amount that was taken by the femme fatale is $60,000 as opposed to $40,000 in the film. The big difference, however, was Bailey's involvement in Fisher's death. In the book, Fisher pulls a gun after Bailey has hit him:

"Fisher backed up against the wall and his little eyes were black with fear. He licked his fat lips and pointed the gun at Red. Suddenly they were fighting for the gun. When Fisher pulled the trigger the muzzle was pointed the wrong way."

The major distinction separating the book and film versions is that in the novel Fisher accidentally kills himself rather than Bailey during their struggle. Red decides that Mumsie, who later went to live with Guy Parker, should take the fall for Fisher's death so he can live in peace with Ann Miller. He reasons that since Mumsie had betrayed both Sterling and himself and was a catalyst in the events leading up to and concluding with the death of Fisher, she should pay the price for his demise with a prison term.

The noir aspect of the story is more starkly drawn in *Out of the Past* with Jane Greer fatally shooting Jack Fisher in the cabin to prevent him from going to Whit Sterling with the news that he had found the couple together. Kathie's cold-blooded makeup was never on better display than when Bailey looks at her and says, "You didn't need to kill him." A steely-edged Kathie insists that she needed to kill Bailey's former partner. Before Bailey even has time to bury Fisher, Kathie jumps into her car and leaves. The film version presents Bailey as more of a victim and Kathie as a ruthless predator who will do anything to protect her interests.

Build My Gallows High ends with Mumsie killing Red to save herself from a prison term. Red is determined to make a deal with Sterling in exchange for the incriminating tax documents once in Eels's possession.

Author Mainwaring provides a note of bitter irony at the book's conclusion. A dying Bailey walks away after being shot by Mumsie in her bedroom after Joe Stefanos has killed Whit Sterling and is then killed by Mumsie. As he steps outside into the darkness with the briefcase containing the tax information he hopes will clear him of suspicion and allow him to live happily thereafter in Bridgeport with Ann Miller, Mainwaring's story concludes with the fateful words: "He didn't hear the gun when Guy [Parker] shot him because he was dead."

Out of the Past is a film divisible into two distinct parts. Part one is dominated by narrative supplied by detective Markham, who explains what prompted him to seek to bury his past and adopt a new identity as Jeff Bailey in the small town of Bridgeport, California. It is abundantly clear, however, that trouble lurks nearby. The clue is revealed when, in the film's opening sequence, a sign posting reveals that Lake Tahoe lies only 79 miles to the north. This is where crime boss Whit Sterling's mansion is located. The narration occurs on a trip to Lake Tahoe, where Bailey is heading with his new girlfriend, Ann Miller, a wholesome, small town girl played by Virginia Huston, who affords a stark contrast to the wily, world-wise, predatory Kathie Moffett. This occurs after Sterling handyman Joe Stefanos locates Jeff. The narration helps piece the story of Jeff's former life together, along with introducing riveting scenes involving his meeting and period together with Kathie.

Part Two and Its Plot Complications

The second part of the film is the resolution of Jeff Markham-Bailey's short but discernibly event-filled life. No sooner does sweet small town girl Ann drop the man she loves off in front of the Sterling mansion overlooking a lake, a deceptively misleading tranquil ambience, than Jeff is back in the hypnotic clutches of Kathie.

He rebuffs her initially, concentrating on preparing for what he hopes will be his final assignment for a man he loathes.

Jeff's assignment for Sterling takes him to San Francisco, where he is to retrieve potentially damaging documents from former mob lawyer turned enemy Leonard Eels. The documents, if turned over to the Internal Revenue Service, could result in a ten-year stretch in a federal penitentiary for Sterling. Jeff learns soon enough that he is a victim of a Sterling-Moffett double cross, and is the designated fall guy for the murder of Eels, after Joe Stefanos actually pulls the trigger.

It is during the second part of the film that the plot becomes complicated. The intricacies of the script with its numerous double, triple and multiple dealings have left many a reviewer wondering if something has been left unexplained. Jane Greer responded to the subject of plot complications by explaining laughingly, "Bob was always talking about the three pages of the script that got lost in the Mimeograph Department."

A careful analysis of the film reveals that the plot structure was consistently in place, the work of three superb story craftsmen. The film's complications resulted in many reviewers denouncing *Out of the Past* for not making sense. In the manner of a great work of fiction by Tolstoy, Joyce or Melville, it took time for the film's essential greatness to be widely recognized. The same phenomenon occurred in the case of what many now call Alfred Hitchcock's crowning cinematic achievement, *Vertigo*.

A Stinging Slap and a Temptation to Retaliate

The most dramatic scene of a film containing more fireworks than an explosives factory is set in the Sterling mansion, when Jeff emerges to tell the cynical mobster that his longstanding cohort, Joe Stefanos, played by Paul Valentine, has died after an attempt to kill the former detective turned gas station operator. Just as Stefanos is preparing to fire on Bailey, who has his back turned, his friend, a young deaf mute called The Kid, played by Dickie Moore, hooks Stefanos's arm with his fishing rod, causing Sterling's henchman to plummet from his mountain perch to his death. After having sworn her eternal love to Bailey in San Francisco, an all-too-typical Kathie convinces Stefanos of the wisdom of killing Jeff.

The scene at Sterling's Lake Tahoe residence provides Greer with another acting challenge, and she skillfully rises to the occasion. She had performed with convincing depth in earlier scenes in which she confidently manipulates Mitchum and Douglas, sometimes pitting them against each other. Her generally unflagging confidence suddenly leaves her as Mitchum, the man she thought had been disposed of, returns from the presumed dead to tell Douglas about her double dealing in his absence. When Mitchum mentions that Greer should take the rap for Douglas's legal misfortunes, referring to her doing a prison stretch for Steve Brodie's murder, she becomes noticeably rattled.

Douglas becomes so obsessed over Greer's decision making in his absence that he asks Mitchum to wait outside so that he can speak with her in private. The ensuing fireworks result in a scene of dazzling credibility that Jane Greer will never forget. A furious Douglas slaps her for her treachery.

"When Kirk Douglas slapped me, he did it so hard that it really hurt and made me feel like slapping him back," Greer recollected, after which she chuckled, "but I couldn't afford to do that because I couldn't risk ruining the take. If I had slapped him back we would have had to do it all over again."

Despite Mitchum's determination to make a deal for his own freedom, using incriminating tax documents as leverage over crime boss Douglas, he learns soon that his life is inextricably linked to Greer's. The treacherous Kathie Moffett, who came close to killing the mobster earlier, finally finishes the job. Mitchum discovers Douglas's prostrate body when he arrives to discuss final plans to secure what he hopes will be his freedom and a new life with Huston. Greer coolly informs a crestfallen Mitchum that she is the only person left with whom to make deals.

The tautly written screenplay shrewdly plays on the predatory Kathie Moffett's sociopathic tendencies at that juncture. Greer is up to the job, stating the case with the same level of casualness as saying "Good morning" to a next door neighbor. She proposes a partnership arrangement with Mitchum, suggesting that they begin anew in Mexico, where they met.

"We deserve a break," Greer tells her victim Mitchum breezily. This is quite a statement in view of the chilling reality that the only reason Mitchum survived a murder attempt by Paul Valentine was through the speedy intercession of Dickie Moore.

"We deserve each other," Mitchum replies in a macabre, death-like tone. A totally defeated look surfaces in Mitchum's eyes. He recognizes he is a dead man walking, with no options other than to follow the coldly calculating Greer to mutual oblivion. His fatal acceptance is underscored when Greer pours a toast to their future. She is cool and bubbly, while Mitchum is the personification of doom. His status is symbolically underscored when, after finishing his drink, he shatters the glass against the fireplace. The broken glass represents his own impending destruction.

When Greer then walks briskly upstairs to finish packing, Mitchum seizes the moment, making a quick call to local police. They then leave for their looming moment with destiny. Mitchum sits in the manner of a dead man awaiting the final call to execution while the unflappable Greer drives. When they promptly reach a highway roadblock, the coolness of the character vanishes. Fire flashes in the eyes of the femme fatale, she pulls out a revolver, and kills Mitchum. Her final words reflect once more her sociopathic status. "You dirty, double-crossing rat!" she fumes. Not even momentarily would she consider how she had earlier attempted to frame the luckless Jeff Markham-Bailey for a murder he never committed, then use Sterling's hit man, Stefanos, in an attempt to kill her former lover. Her one-track mind instead saw Markham-Bailey as a despicable double crosser.

Fill in the Blanks

This highly sophisticated noir masterpiece ends by providing viewers with an opportunity to fill in the blanks and draw their own conclusion. In the wake of the death of the man she loved, sweet local girl Virginia Huston emerges from the police station with Mitchum's rival for her emotions, Richard Webb, who has grown up with her in Bridgeport and known Huston all her life. At one point, exasperated by the woman he loved going away with a man he was convinced was up to no good, Webb tells Mitchum he might attempt to kill him. "Why not?" Mitchum casually replies. "Everyone else is."

In the film's final scene, Huston steps away from Webb and walks toward Mitchum's gas station and Dickie Moore. Acknowledging that the deaf mute knew Mitchum better than anybody else, Huston explains that she has to know whether the man she loved was planning to go away with Greer. Moore nods affirmatively and Huston walks away.

Moore's nod prompts speculation. Did Moore genuinely believe that Mitchum was going away with Greer? Could he have been mistaken? A conclusion that contains logical weight is that shrewd detective Mitchum, a pragmatist who is always thinking, had prepared for this type of eventuality, when the sincere woman he loved, and with whom he wanted to spend his life, would seek an answer to the ultimate question of whether he was planning on returning to her in Bridgeport or going away with the predatory femme fatale.

A logical conclusion is that Mitchum covered the eventuality by telling his faithful friend Moore to respond to the question posed by Huston for a practical psychological reason. If Huston could be convinced that Mitchum had actually decided to go away with Greer, which he had not, being trapped instead by circumstances following the murder of Douglas, perhaps the sincere small town girl could more easily move on with her life. Perhaps she would find ultimate happiness in the arms of Richard Webb, who conceded that he had loved her from her childhood, and the time he had laced on her first pair of roller skates. That would be the most intelligent plan Mitchum could conceive for Huston to stop imagining what life could have been like with the two of them together, had he only survived. Moore's response provided an opportunity for closure on Huston's part.

The character of The Kid is played adroitly by former child star Dickie Moore, who would years later marry '40s and '50s cinema musical star Jane Powell. The character was a carryover by Mainwaring from his novel. Moore, a former *Our Gang* performer, had the perfect brooding look for the role of Mitchum's faithful companion. His deaf mute status only made him that much more interesting on screen, since such characters engender great empathy and heightened attention on the part of film viewers.

Another element about *Out of the Past* that impresses viewers is the authentic settings, leading many to believe that RKO shot it in the locations revealed in the drama—Lake Tahoe, Bridgeport, San Francisco, Los Angeles, New York, Mexico

City and Acapulco. While the only scene set in New York was an indoor meeting involving Markham and Sterling with associates Stefanos and Fisher, the San Francisco and Acapulco settings look authentic.

"I did all my work on the RKO lot," Jane put the issue into perspective. "There were some scenes filmed at Lake Arrowhead, but I wasn't involved in any of them. The scenes that were supposed to be on Acapulco Beach were all shot in Malibu."

The Lake Arrowhead scenes covered two locations, Lake Tahoe and Bridgeport, saving the studio money since Arrowhead's Southern California location was much closer to the studio. The realistic looking Acapulco cantina was an authentic reproduction made on the RKO lot. What about that realistic depiction of San Francisco's Telegraph Hill?

"The studio actually built a town for the San Francisco settings," Greer revealed. "They built it out at the edge of the Valley in Chatsworth. That was where they also built the cabin where I met with Bob and the murder of Steve Brodie took place."

Chatsworth was a familiar location for film studios of the period. Numerous westerns were shot there, a location made all the more credible due to the surrounding mountains. Chatsworth became the site of the Moors of Yorkshire in Northern England in the 1939 Samuel Goldwyn drama directed by William Wyler, *Wuthering Heights*, while it served the purpose of a small Welsh mining town for John Ford's 1941 classic, *How Green Was My Valley*.

Out of the Past was a milestone American post–World War II film that blended two-fisted noir realism with great performances, along with solid direction and camerawork which projected the dark melancholia sought. The dark, brooding cinematography helped transform three young stars headed for film greatness (Jane Greer, Robert Mitchum and Kirk Douglas) from performers in their twenties—in Greer's case, her early twenties—into brooding, timeless figures of great maturity.

An Oscar-Caliber Performance

The hypnotically fascinating Kathie Moffett has become a model for femme fatales in a period when the genre has enjoyed great interest. Greer's riveting performance has emerged as one of the memorable efforts rendered by a leading lady in the post–World War II era. The fact that it is much more recognizable than numerous Academy Award efforts again sheds light on the selection process, which was marked by bloc voting on the part of giants such as MGM and Fox.

Like vintage wine, *Out of the Past* achieves additional impact and overall value within the lexicon of great American films with increased showings. Such a memorable effort should have solidified Greer's acting career, but in Hollywood the unpredictable is frequently the norm, and ensuing circumstances occurred that were anything but kind to the elegant brunette.

An examination of Greer's career in the late '40s would appear to indicate a pattern at work. Her on-screen chemistry with Mitchum was electrifying and Daniel Mainwaring delivered a brilliant, rapidly paced script for *Out of the Past*, so when one observes that just two short years following the film's release the two stars were re-teamed in another tightly paced drama with the scenario supplied by the identical writer, Mainwaring, for the same studio, RKO, the typical conclusion is that the studio sought to recapture the old magic and achieve another milestone by incorporating the same talent into the product. In the case of the 1949 RKO release, *The Big Steal,* such a conclusion would be totally misleading. That successful effort resulted from a chain of circumstances that almost saw Greer's previously burgeoning career destroyed.

Howard Hughes resurfaced in Greer's life in a totally different way than before. The reclusive billionaire bought RKO Studios, then turned on the actress, seeking to ruin her career.

"He called me into his office one day and told me he was not using me any more," she explained. "Since I was under exclusive contract to Howard at RKO, that meant I would not be able to work for anyone else, either. I told him directly that this meant he was ruining my film career. He replied by saying, 'Yes, that's right.'"

After acquiring RKO, Hughes had loaned Greer out periodically to Fox, but was ultimately intent on destroying her career by contractually enforcing inactivity during a period when the brunette star was in great demand. She ultimately received her liberating breakthrough in the highly received caper film, *The Big Steal*, a part she received under a bizarre twist of circumstances.

"Ketti Frings did the story for *The Big Steal* and told me that she wanted me for the lead opposite Bob," Greer revealed. "I told her I'd love to do it, but that Howard would not let me. When Howard was contacted, he confirmed what I knew in my own mind. He was adamant about me not starring in *The Big Steal.*"

A highly publicized Hollywood controversy of the period ultimately worked to Jane Greer's advantage, enabling her to star in the film and save her career. Fears abounded over how the public would react to the conviction of Robert Mitchum on a marijuana charge. He served two months at the Sheriff's Honor Farm in Castaic, north of the San Fernando Valley, doing his time without complaint. Mitchum was not only far from a whiner; when he was released he unloaded one of his great one-liners. When asked by reporters to describe his experience, Mitchum quipped, "Jail is like Palm Springs without the riffraff. A great place to get in shape, only you meet a better class of people." The drug charge enhanced Mitchum's image as a rebel, but in the Hollywood climate of 1948 it was thought that his career might be over and that Hughes was taking a foolish gamble by putting him back to work in an RKO film. What many still do not realize is that after his release Mitchum's case was reviewed, a plea of not guilty was eventually ordered and his conviction was expunged from the record.

As speculation flourished regarding Mitchum's ultimate fate, one of the individuals expressing concern about his future was Lizabeth Scott, who was slated to star opposite him in *The Big Steal.* Through a twist of fate, Scott's apprehension became Greer's good fortune.

"Lizabeth Scott was set for the role, but she decided she did not want to work with someone who had been declared a felon through a marijuana conviction," Greer recalled. "She bowed out 60 days from the time that filming was slated to begin. Howard tried hard to find someone for the part but couldn't, so he reluctantly sent for me."

Recently it has been revealed that there was a strong influence behind Scott's reluctance to star opposite Mitchum following his incarceration. Paramount producer Hal B. Wallis was apprehensive about having Scott, his leading female star of the early post war period, appear opposite Mitchum, squelching the potential loanout to RKO for *The Big Steal.*

It has been said by many that little occurring in Hollywood escaped Howard Hughes' attention. Greer learned this firsthand when she was summoned to see the eccentric studio boss in connection with the female lead in *The Big Steal.*

"Howard called me in and told me that he would be using me in the film," she said, "but then he really surprised me by asking me if my pregnancy would stand in the way of doing *The Big Steal.* I was shocked that he knew I was pregnant. I didn't think anyone in the industry knew. It turned out that Louella Parsons had somehow found out and had told Howard."

Now that Jane had an opportunity to star again in a major film for RKO, there was an obstacle placed in her path. "When Lizabeth Scott bowed out of the role, all of her wardrobe had been selected by Costuming and Howard told me that I would have to make do with it," Greer explained. She then added with a laugh, "I did my best to hide my pregnant state from the camera, but it was tough to do when I had to wear a bolero top."

A humorous incident occurred during location shooting in Mexico when actor William Bendix saw her taking pills. "That William Bendix was a real character," Jane chuckled. "When he asked me why I was taking pills, I thought fast and replied, 'The *tourista.*' They were for my pregnancy and I didn't want to divulge that. He asked if he could try some so I gave him some pills. He later told me, 'Say, those pills work great. I can even drink the water without any problems. Have you got any more?' I contacted my doctor, who sent some more, so William Bendix and I were both taking pregnancy pills during the rest of the Mexico filming!"

In addition to Bendix, *The Big Steal* cast also included silent era heartthrob Ramon Novarro, who starred with Francis X. Bushman in the MGM silent version of *Ben Hur*. "He was the nicest fellow," Jane recalls. "The first day of shooting he brought this large scrapbook with him. It was so fascinating looking at it and tracing his career during the early period of filmmaking."

Despite Greer's various hurdles, along with the difficulty in obtaining the role, she delivered an excellent performance in a notable chase film in which Mitchum and Greer pursue Patric Knowles across Mexico to recover an Army payroll worth several hundred thousand dollars. Geoffrey Homes and Gerald Drayson adapted the screenplay from *The Road to Carmichael's* by Richard Wormser. The Homes (Daniel Mainwaring) connection established another link to *Out of the Past* along with stars Mitchum and Greer. The film was the second directed by Don Siegel. The rapid-paced nature of the movie presaged more of the same for Siegel, who directed Clint Eastwood in adventure vehicles such as *Coogan's Bluff* and *Dirty Harry* while performing in and assisting Eastwood in the latter's directorial debut, *Play Misty for Me*.

As Jane began to raise a family as the wife of prominent film lawyer Edward Lasker, she worked in films less frequently. When Greer returned to action in the late '50s, she appeared as the wife of James Cagney in the highly acclaimed 1957 release *Man of a Thousand Faces*. Movie critic Leonard Maltin had praise for Greer and the rest of the cast, calling the film a "well-acted biography of silent star Lon Chaney." As for the performances, Maltin wrote that "Cagney as Chaney, [Dorothy] Malone as [his] disturbed first wife, Greer as wife who brings him happiness, are all fine."

The film is one that brought an immediate smile to Greer's face. "Cagney was wonderful to work with and I think that the film holds up so well," she enthused. "It's a film that I can enjoy seeing many times and I was so happy that it was shown so frequently on American Movie Classics."

Jane's appearance in the 1964 drama *Where Love Has Gone* proved to be both a reunion and an opportunity to appear in a film with one of the industry's veteran acting giants, Bette Davis. Two premier RKO figures of the forties, director Edward Dmytryk and Susan Hayward, were involved in the production. "Even though I knew Eddie Dmytryk when I was at RKO, I never had the chance to work with him," she said. "It was nice to work with Susan again also after appearing with her in *They Won't Believe Me*. While Susan had the scenes with Bette, it was great to be in a film with her since she is one of the greats."

Where Love Has Gone was adapted from a best-selling novel by Harold Robbins. The story involved the killing by Joey Heatherton of her mother's (Susan Hayward) lover. Davis plays the domineering grandmother, a wealthy matriarch of one of San Francisco's most prominent families. Jane is cast as a sympathetic probation officer.

Déjà Vu and Jeff Bridges

The 1984 production *Against All Odds* was an inspired tribute motivated at least partially by director Taylor Hackford's reverence for *Out of the Past*. Jane appears as the mother of Rachel Ward, reportedly modeled on the character Kathie Moffett.

Jeff Bridges starred in what was said to be the Robert Mitchum role. After his first day on the set with Greer, there was a humorous incident. "When Jeff went home and told his mother he had worked with Jane Greer, this led to an interesting discussion," Jane laughed.

Mrs. Bridges had an immediate response for her actor son. "You worked with her before," she told him.

"No, I didn't," Jeff insisted.

"Oh yes you did," Mom remained emphatic.

"No I didn't," Jeff was equally adamant. "If I'd worked with Jane Greer, I'd remember it."

"Oh no you wouldn't!" Mom Bridges declared.

Mom turned out to be right. Jeff had worked with Jane Greer, but could hardly be faulted for not remembering. In one of the younger film debuts on record, Jeff appeared in the 1950 drama *The Company She Keeps*, as a baby in Greer's arms. Greer turned in an effective performance as an ex-convict determined to go straight, making a play for Dennis O'Keefe, the friend of her parole officer, Randolph Scott. John Houseman produced *The Company She Keeps.*

On the subject of *Against All Odds*, Greer contends that Taylor Hackford suffered unfairly through unfavorable comparisons on the part of reviewers to *Out of the Past*. "Taylor had a great respect for *Out of the Past* and considered *Against All Odds* to be a tribute rather than a remake," she explained. "There were some basic differences. For instance, in *Against All Odds* the characters played by Jeff Bridges and Rachel Ward become immediately involved in a sexual relationship. In *Out of the Past* it took a while for the relationship I had with Bob to develop into that kind of intimate expression."

Leonard Maltin refers to the 1984 film as a "loose remake" of *Out of the Past*. Bridges plays an unemployed former professional football player hired by a sleazy former teammate to find his girlfriend, who has run off to Mexico, as Mitchum had been hired by unscrupulous crime boss Kirk Douglas to locate Greer.

Jane was cast as a mother of a famous star in another film two years later, *Just Between Friends*, where she played the mother of Mary Tyler Moore. The 1986 film revolved around two women who strike up a friendship, unaware that they share the same man, one as a wife and the other as a lover.

In 1982, Jane worked for six weeks as a regular on the popular television series *Falcon Crest*. She was joined in that series by another Greer, her niece Robin. Robin's father Donn was Jane's twin, who in 1943 was spending his time in the South Pacific during the War while his sister was launching her film career and marrying Rudy Vallee. After the war, Donn married and moved to Newport Beach, producing commercials and writing independent scripts.

A skilled actress who worked hard to perfect her craft, Jane Greer mastered roles ranging from ruthless femme fatale Kathie Moffett to the sweet, supportive wife of James Cagney in *Man of a Thousand Faces*. Hers was a special magic that was captured indelibly in the brooding, brilliantly rapacious femme fatale Kathie Moffett opposite an equally compelling Robert Mitchum in *Out of the Past*. As the film masterpiece continued to enchant new audiences during the emerging years,

Greer became a sought-after figure at film nostalgia conventions and for interviews for film articles and books. She remained a popular figure to the time of her death in 2001.

Jane Greer and Robert Mitchum recorded their own special blend of film magic in *Out of the Past*. It is truly a milestone film noir epic that provides more in the way of insight every time that it is viewed.

SIX

Laura (1944)

The film often resembled a dream, so ethereal was it while at the same time remaining a hard-boiled mystery. For individuals advancing the idea that great musical scores can bear heavily on a film's ultimate success, *Laura* will always remain a definitive case in point.

While *Laura* was released over 50 years ago, its haunting melody continues to be played, generally in sophisticated settings such as five-star restaurants. Composer David Raksin's haunting melody falls into the semi-classical realm, while the song with lyrics by Johnny Mercer served as a favorite of numerous balladeers over the last half century. The lyrical tribute by Mercer to the main character and individual after whom the film was named conveys the haunting mysticism which engendered a slavish devotion for moviegoers during better than a half century.

The lyrics "only a dream" form a central psychological core of the hypnotic mystery adapted from the novel of the same name by Vera Caspary. *Laura* bears an indigenous thematic thread to *Rebecca*, a Gothic mystery deftly directed by Alfred Hitchcock. Both *Rebecca* and *Laura* focused on strong psychological reactions to oil portraits of beautiful women presumably dead. In the case of the mysterious Rebecca, who is never seen but remains a central element of the psychological drama, she is deceased while Laura Hunt supplies the electrical jolt to an intelligently woven drama by astonishing those who have reacted strongly to her presumed death with a sudden re-emergence after a weekend at her Connecticut retreat. The body discovered in her apartment was beyond identification since the head was blown off with a high-powered rifle and was presumed to be that of Laura since other physical characteristics matched. It was located in her apartment by Laura's maid, while she was nowhere to be found. When it is learned that the deceased is one Diane Redfern, a model who worked at the same advertising agency as Laura Hunt, suspicions point toward the previously presumed dead woman along with an interesting trio of characters.

The Feuds Behind the Film

It has been noted that numerous great films were made despite endless difficulties, overcoming often-sharp mutual antagonisms, but *Laura* remains in a class by itself on the subject of multiple friction. The controversies and heated confrontations surrounding the making of one of Hollywood's greatest psychological dramas are so labyrinthian in complexity that they could form the plot nucleus for a Russian novel.

The biggest clash, details of which continue to generate speculation, occurred between two Eastern European emigres who became notable Hollywood directors. One of them had become a giant from the early days of talkies and had a celebrated record of achievement when Twentieth Century–Fox's Darryl F. Zanuck signed him to direct *Laura*. Rouben Mamoulian made his screen debut with *Applause* in 1929. Mamoulian, a product of what was then Armenia, clashed with a newcomer to the ranks of directing and producing from Vienna. Otto Preminger came from a distinguished Viennese family. His father was once chief legal counsel to Emperor Franz Josef. When Preminger arrived in America as part of the great creative migration in the wake of Hitler's Third Reich, his heavy Eastern European accent combined with the ability to project a peremptory stuffiness provided him with an opportunity to portray characters from the regime which prompted him to bolt his native Austria as Hollywood made a wave of anti–Nazi films. Preminger had been brought to America by film mogul Joseph Schenck. He had been a stage director in Europe and it was Schenck's belief that he could make a successful transition into movie directing.

Preminger went to work at Twentieth Century–Fox. Zanuck took an immediate dislike to the Viennese emigre that would remain undiminished, even while they labored in unison to make *Laura*. He assigned the Hollywood newcomer to several low-budget projects before finally handing him the reins to direct *Kidnapped* (1938). The two men became promptly involved in a shouting match over a scene involving child star Freddie Bartholomew speaking to his dog. Zanuck angrily sought its inclusion while Preminger insisted that such a scene had never been written. The fact that the Twentieth studio boss would fire Preminger over such a dispute and replace him as director of *Kidnapped* with Alfred Werker indicated personal dislike for the Austrian rather than seeking to correct the point of dispute. The closer the relationship between Zanuck and Preminger is analyzed, the more obvious it becomes just how antagonistic they were toward each other. Such a wide chasm made it virtually impossible to conduct a successful professional relationship. As hostile as the Zanuck-Preminger relationship was at that point, it was destined to heat up even more with the passage of time.

Post War Storm Clouds

When America became involved in World War II, Zanuck left the studio for duty in the United States Army. The grand irony was that World War II on the Fox front served as the lull before the storm that would register in high decibels after Zanuck returned.

While Zanuck was away, Fox was guided by William Goetz. Twentieth's mercurial chief disliked Goetz at least as much as he abhorred Preminger. When Zanuck returned from the service and learned that Goetz had provided his nemesis Preminger with a seven-year contract, it only antagonized the studio boss into disliking both even more intensely. While Zanuck was away, Goetz had also allowed Preminger to act in and direct the 1943 release *Margin for Error*.

Activities related to Preminger's involvement in *Margin for Error* are dramatic enough to encompass a film. In the pre-war period when Zanuck would provide Twentieth contractee Preminger with no work, his earlier benefactor Schenck refused to even see him; when no other studio would hire him, the frustrated Viennese director decided to return to New York, where he had achieved success on the stage prior to his Hollywood excursion and involvement with Fox.

The period between 1938 and 1941 was creatively productive for Preminger as he directed seven plays in New York, one of which was Laurette Taylor's triumphant comeback in Sutton Vane's classic drama, *Outward Bound*. The most successful of all of his productions turned out to be *Margin for Error*, a play written by Clare Boothe Luce, the socially prominent wife of *Time* magazine publisher Henry Luce. When an actor defected, Preminger felt obligated to take over at the last moment in the role of a bullying Nazi consul. After receiving excellent reviews for his performance, a call came to return to Twentieth from writer-producer Nunnally Johnson. Preminger was signed to play a Nazi officer in *The Pied Piper*.

When Fox demonstrated eagerness for Preminger to repeat his critically celebrated role in *Margin for Error*, the man who badly wished to return to directing scented an opportunity. Zanuck was away in the Army and the man with whom to deal was William Goetz, which certainly buoyed his confidence. Preminger secured an agreement with Goetz to act in and direct *Margin for Error* for his actor's fee alone. He also agreed to step down as director after his first week if Goetz was not personally satisfied. To the interim Fox studio chief, this constituted an offer too good to refuse.

Preminger was dissatisfied with the screenplay of *Margin for Error* and hired a young novelist on Army leave to help him revise the script. The writer was Samuel Fuller, who went on to become a famous director, establishing his top marks for the Richard Widmark crime drama *Pickup on South Street*. *Margin for Error* is a comedy thriller in which a Jewish policeman, played by Milton Berle in one of the master comedian's rare film roles, is given the risky and distasteful task of protecting a tyrannical consul in an American city. Preminger portrays the indivious Nazi, who is eventually murdered. Goetz was so delighted with the first rushes that Preminger was given a contract as actor, director and producer.

Zanuck Returns

Before Preminger had an opportunity to celebrate his newly found success at Twentieth, Zanuck returned from Army duty and the battle was renewed with

Preminger while another was launched on a grand scale against Goetz. A take-no-prisoners confrontation immediately occurred between Fox's interim and returning chiefs. In the ensuing battle for studio control, Zanuck announced that he would not return to the Beverly Hills studio until Goetz resigned.

The resulting drama was reminiscent of a nation in turmoil in which two governments exist simultaneously, one in the national capital and the other in exile. Under the terms of the Twentieth power confrontation, Zanuck ran what could be analogously defined as the government in exile from his luxurious beach house in Santa Monica, to which he summoned Fox's producers and directors. Included in that number was Otto Preminger. Zanuck had made his dislike for Preminger crystal clear in 1936. The interim activities during Zanuck's war stint, when Goetz allowed him to direct and perform in a major film, then signed him to a seven-year contract, served only to infuriate the mercurial studio executive all the more. Preminger recounted his meeting with Zanuck at his Santa Monica beach house in *Otto Preminger: An Autobiography*. He recalled that "a butler escorted me through the house to the garden where Zanuck was sitting in swimming trunks beside his pool. His back was to me. He glanced around briefly and then gave me the back of his head again. He picked up a piece of paper and said: 'I see you are working on a few things. I don't think much of them, except for one, *Laura*. I've read it and it isn't bad. You can produce it but as long as I am at Fox you will never direct.'"

The Zanuck decision made that day in Santa Monica would hold enormous repercussions. The film mogul, his dislike for Preminger unabated, refused to allow his enemy to contribute to a project for which he professed enthusiasm in the area that meant more to him than any other professional endeavor, directing, while seeking to confine him to a job he regarded as secondary to his chief interest, producing. Zanuck had proclaimed that a young director eager to perform his craft would never direct a film as long as he headed the studio. This was a tactical professional blunder that would soon generate calamitous results, from which *Laura* would amazingly rebound with a film classic resulting.

Preminger exercised shrewd professional instincts in soliciting B production chief Bryan Foy for support of the *Laura* project after enthusiastically responding to the Vera Caspary novel. Under the Twentieth power structure, Zanuck only generated personal creative control over major productions. By enlisting Foy's support, Preminger was doubtlessly hoping to tiptoe around Zanuck's control. In addition, perhaps Zanuck would project less opposition against him in a lower budgeted project.

Despite the initial B film designation for *Laura*, the casting of the female lead suggested a major production. The part called for an elegant leading lady. Zanuck had his sights initially trained on Jennifer Jones, fresh from a Best Actress Oscar in *The Song of Bernadette*, to play the enigmatic Laura. Jones turned the role down, as did the next actress sought, another elegant brunette beauty, Hedy Lamarr. Zanuck ultimately hired Gene Tierney, who had been a popular magazine model before launching her acting career.

Like Jones and Lamarr, Tierney was reflective of brunette screen elegance, befitting the title role of Laura Hunt, a young woman who moves into a prominent executive position in the competitive advertising world of Madison Avenue. Lamarr and Tierney bear at least one other common note in addition to *Laura*. In 1960, shortly after Lamarr was divorced from Texas oilman Howard Lee, Lee married Tierney. It is logical that a man with an astute eye for pulchritude would marry two women bearing such type similarity, just as Zanuck had sought each woman at different points to star as Laura Hunt, a glamorous and intelligent woman who had conquered Upper East Side Manhattan society.

Preminger began working on the *Laura* screenplay with Jay Dratler. Seeking to inject the dialogue with more pep, he hired Betty Reinhardt and the poet-scenarist Samuel Hoffenstein to instill life into the script where needed. Preminger later noted that "Hoffenstein practically created the character of Waldo Lydecker for Clifton Webb. He was in the habit of overwriting but after the scenes were edited his dialogue was brilliant."

A refined Eastern intellectual who had won rave notices from Rouben Mamoulian, especially for his work on *Dr. Jekyll and Mr. Hyde*, the sophisticated Hoffenstein was a member of the Algonquin Round Table and a friend of noted critic and author Alexander Woollcott. His relationship with Woollcott was thought to be a catalyst for the expansive egotism demonstrated by Webb in his portrayal of the unforgettable Lydecker. It is more than likely not coincidental that Lydecker's first meeting with Gene Tierney as Laura Hunt occurs at the Algonquin Hotel. While *Laura* was shot in its entirety on Fox sound stages, the film has the feel of an authentic Manhattan story, remaining true to the presentation of novelist Caspary. The characters reflect the social opportunism and professional competitiveness of certain brownstone town house occupants living in the expensive residences east of Central Park.

A Director's Firestorm and a Writer's Chagrin

While the Hollywood film industry has a unique "never say die" mentality in which scores of films that were on the verge of dying in pre-production or production phases ultimately emerged as huge successes, *Laura* is perhaps the principal example of a film containing more lives than the proverbial cat as burning hostilities and seemingly endless warfare were overcome. The film most like it for overcoming numerous reversals was *Casablanca*, which initially wore the same B movie stamp imprinted at the outset on *Laura*. It appeared for awhile that *Casablanca* would never even be cast, much less filmed. In the case of *Laura*, the performers constituted the audience, watching high-pitched confrontations at the executive and creative levels.

Once Preminger went to work with Hoffenstein on the *Laura* script, novelist Caspary became exasperated by the fact that a new plot and additional characters had been added. Another sore point with Caspary was that Zanuck had relegated

Police detective Dana Andrews, left, and New York newspaper columnist and radio commentator Clifton Webb discuss the presumed murder of enigmatic Manhattan advertising executive Gene Tierney in a scene from the 1944 Twentieth Century–Fox release *Laura*, directed by Otto Preminger. Her clinging aura envelopes both of their psyches. This scene is highly symbolic in that, as they speak, Tierney as Laura Hunt appears to be looking down at them from her portrait on the wall. This sophisticated look at New York high society was released the same year as *Double Indemnity* and *Murder, My Sweet*, making 1944 perhaps the best in film noir annals.

the production to the B film category. Production chief Bryan Foy did not like the new turns being taken with the screenplay, voicing his disapproval with Zanuck at a meeting.

While the volatile Zanuck continued to dislike Preminger personally, he sided with him on the creative turns *Laura* was taking. The outspoken criticism of Foy resulted in a change that benefited Preminger in his endeavor to make *Laura* in the best possible way. Zanuck decided to take over the supervision of the film which, *ipso facto*, elevated the production from B to A status. Any project over which the Twentieth boss took direct charge would be provided with a considerable budget. Zanuck, like David O. Selznick, was noted for extending himself to the max on his personal projects. On the film that proved to be the Nebraska-born movie mogul's labor of love, *Wilson*, crew workers who arrived on the sound stages early in the morning observed Zanuck slaving over script changes.

With Zanuck now solidly aboard the good ship *Laura*, he turned his attention to securing a director. He asked Twentieth regulars Walter Lang and Lewis Milestone to assume the position. Each refused out of deference to their friend Preminger, knowing how badly he wanted to direct the film. He finally secured the services of Rouben Mamoulian as the third of a three-film contract the Eastern European director had signed. Mamoulian had earlier scored big with Zanuck on *Blood and Sand*, the great Spanish bullfighting epic starring Tyrone Power, after which he directed the comedy *Rings on Her Fingers*, which starred Henry Fonda along with the leading lady of *Laura*, Gene Tierney. It was at a party at Tierney's home that Mamoulian met his wife, the painter Azadia Newman. Mrs. Mamoulian would soon emerge in the multi-tiered controversies surrounding *Laura*. While her role would be peripheral, her husband occupied a major presence in the ongoing friction.

What was needed in Zanuck's case on the delicate subject of assigning a director to *Laura* was the insight of a chess player, that valuable ability to project several moves into the future. Had Zanuck properly weighed his prospective course of action, he would almost assuredly have concluded that by taking the strategic courses he had chosen of assigning Preminger to produce *Laura* and Mamoulian to direct the film that he would be setting off a time bomb inevitably destined to explode. Mamoulian appeared to recognize the potential dangers in a way that Zanuck apparently did not.

"I knew that Preminger, above all, wanted to direct and I talked to him about this before agreeing to direct *Laura*," Mamoulian revealed in a personal interview conducted in his study. "I asked him if it would be a problem for him to be producer of a film I would be directing. His response was that there would be no such problem. He told me how much he had admired my work as a director. Preminger said he would like the opportunity to watch me direct. 'I want to learn,' he assured me."

As an individual stylist, Mamoulian always insisted on total creative control over the projects he undertook. It was with that understanding that he agreed to direct *Laura*. It is possible that Preminger's original intention was to give Mamoulian wide creative latitude. The brewing firestorm related to the fact that Preminger, who was primarily a director and secondarily a producer, had been placed in an awkward creative position by Zanuck. The prudent action on the studio chief's part would have been to either refuse to work with Preminger at all and allow him to seek employment elsewhere, if his antipathy was so great that he did not want him to pursue projects on the Twentieth lot, or, alternatively, to subordinate his personal feelings in the interest of achieving film success, providing the Viennese director with the opportunity to perform in his preferred capacity. To attempt to split differences in the way that Zanuck had, by allowing Preminger to produce but not fulfill his primary creative urge of directing, was to force him to sit uncomfortably on the sideline, too close to the action. It not only provided the torture of sidelining someone with strong directing urges; it created a potentially explosive situation in the relationship between Preminger and Mamoulian since the former possessed his own ideas of how a film should be made while simultaneously feeling frustrated over not being able to direct.

The Time Bomb Explodes

When the time bomb exploded with the result of open warfare between producer and director, the subject, inevitably, was creative control. Mamoulian believed that Preminger had reneged on a promise to provide him with sole creative control. To Mamoulian, the problem with Preminger related to undermining his control.

"I began to hear from Dana Andrews and some of the others that Preminger was asking them, 'What do you think of Mamoulian's direction?'" Mamoulian explained. "I could not tolerate someone going behind my back like that. I could not properly function as a director with that kind of interference. I sought a meeting in Zanuck's office with Preminger present. I was furious over him going behind my back and talking to the performers. I called him a son of a bitch and did my best to get Preminger angry.

"When I explained everything that had happened and when I did everything I could to get Preminger angry, he just sat there. Finally Zanuck spoke up and said that he was firing Preminger from the picture," Mamoulian contended. "At that point I spoke up and said that I didn't want that to happen. 'I have to work in this town,' I told Zanuck, 'and if this happens I'll get a reputation of being a director who got his producer fired. I don't want this to happen so I will instead step down as director.'"

Preminger has a completely different explanation as to how he ultimately emerged as both producer and director of *Laura*. According to Preminger, Mamoulian never understood what *Laura* was all about. He contended that ultimately he had thrown out all of Mamoulian's sets and costumes while discarding all of the footage that his predecessor had shot. Mamoulian's wife Azadia became a subject of the ongoing dispute in that Preminger did not like the portrait of Gene Tierney that she had painted. According to Tierney, "I am not being modest when I say that people remember me less for my acting job than as the girl in the portrait, which was the movie's key prop."

Preminger, believing that the painting lacked the mystical quality for which he was searching, sent his leading lady to pose for studio photographer Frank Polony, whose pictures of Tierney as a starlet had appeared in many magazines. The famous painting that forms the mystical focus of the haunting film was actually an enlarged photograph taken by Polony that was lightly brushed with paint to create the desired effect, then placed in an expensive frame.

Preminger's steady contention in his autobiography as well as in interviews was that the critical meeting regarding Mamoulian's fate was not that which the film's earlier director described, but one he had alone with Zanuck at the studio commissary. According to many sources, the situation was as Tierney described in her autobiography, in which she stated that "Preminger fired his director, Rouben Mamoulian, and took over the film himself." The Preminger view was that Zanuck, reportedly disturbed over rushes he had seen of Mamoulian footage, was highly dissatisfied. According to Preminger, Zanuck disapproved of Mamoulian's style, shots and setups and asked Preminger, "What do you think? Shall I take Mamoulian off the picture?" Preminger revealed that he agreed and that was how Mamoulian's involvement with *Laura* was terminated.

While Zanuck may have expressed dissatisfaction with some of the footage Mamoulian shot, he would also air complaints later when Preminger took over as director. One pivotal area of disagreement: the film's closing sequences, which will be discussed later.

Was Mamoulian Confused About *Laura*?

Preminger insisted that Zanuck took Mamoulian off the picture because the veteran European director did not understand the story, mood or setting of *Laura*. To anyone who has studied Mamoulian's films, or spoken with him on the subject of film, the statement appears unfathomable. The only friction Mamoulian ever had regarding projects related to the subject of control. As a unique stylist, he unvaryingly insisted on being the untrammeled master of the film's destiny. Mamoulian's innovative mastery gave the early days of the talkies numerous fresh breakthroughs, beginning with the use of the moving camera in the 1929 epic *Applause*. In *City Streets* (1931), Mamoulian became the first director to use the voiceover technique, revealing a character's thoughts in dialogue. His stylistic mastery of film was complete and he was in constant demand once he retired from directing to teach and lecture in film departments of major universities worldwide. As a highly educated man of cosmopolitan tastes, he saw international high society from the inside. To say, ultimately, that he could not conceptually understand Vera Caspary's novel, which dealt

This profile shot from *Laura* reveals the exquisite beauty of Gene Tierney as she places her hands on the shoulders of her fiancé, Vincent Price, while a thoroughly disapproving Clifton Webb flashes him an icy stare. As self-designated Svengali to Tierney, Webb loathes any man to whom she becomes romantically attached, but appears to hate Price even beyond the norm.

with the intricate nuances of Upper East Side Manhattan society, is a broad enough sweep. The contention that he could not understand the developed screenplay concept borders on the preposterous in that the individual Preminger credits most with the successful screenplay adaptation of *Laura* is none other than Samuel Hoffenstein, whom Mamoulian singled out as one of his favorite scenarists, and with whom he enjoyed working and successfully interacted. Hoffenstein scripted three of Mamoulian's proudest cinema triumphs of the director's productive early 30s period, *Dr. Jekyll and Mr. Hyde* (1931), *Love Me Tonight* (1932) and *The Song of Songs* (1933). When the foregoing factors are evaluated, it appears more likely than ever that a personal clash was the determining factor in Mamoulian's departure.

When all factors are evaluated, Mamoulian's account of what transpired appears to be the accurate one. It appears logical that Zanuck would be more likely to take Mamoulian's side in any clash with the film's producer.

Another point to consider: the film industry predilection to defer to seniority as a resolving point in disputes. Mamoulian biographer Tom Milne makes the following observation regarding the disagreement between the film's director and producer: "Since Preminger at the time was a comparative newcomer to Hollywood, the studio offered to fire him; Mamoulian, knowing that he (Mamoulian) already had a reputation for being difficult, preferred to bow out gracefully since he was not particularly involved in the film anyway."

Mamoulian's rock solid individuality was based on the knowledge that his cinema stylization carried a unique ring. Even before the controversy with Preminger, Mamoulian as a young director making his first film, *Applause*, risked his career in appealing to Paramount's high command in the face of a revolt from co-workers over revolutionary camera techniques. He later told Paramount's high command that if he could not cast Fredric March in the lead of *Dr. Jekyll and Mr. Hyde*, considered to be a devastating risk at that time, he did not wish to direct the film. After *Laura* came incidents in the late '50s and early '60s. Even before a studio fire demolished the elaborate sets of *Porgy and Bess*, the film adaptation of the Mamoulian Broadway musical hit, differences between Samuel Goldwyn, in the process of producing his final movie, and his director had reached an irreconcilable point. The supreme moment of irony arrived after Mamoulian's firing by Goldwyn with the arrival of replacement Otto Preminger! In the early '60s, with *Cleopatra*, Mamoulian and Twentieth's high affinity clashed over locale shooting, with the director insisting on Rome and the studio opting for London. That along with other creative differences prompted Mamoulian to resign.

The major mistake regarding the Mamoulian-Preminger dispute was made by Zanuck for putting two such strong-willed directors, individuals with disparate ideas about style, on a potential collision course, one made even more seemingly inevitable by restricting the Viennese filmmaker to producer's activities on a film he eagerly sought to direct. Preminger's stated disagreement with Mamoulian on sets and costuming could well have been a major friction point considering their differences in style. Mamoulian stated repeatedly that film realism had no place in his creative repertoire and that his personal genre was stylization, as evidenced in his *Dr. Jekyll and Mr. Hyde* and *Love Me Tonight*. Contrast Mamoulian's stylization with what critics have termed Preminger's obsession with moral objectivity and uncertainty, reflecting in the mysterious quality of Gene Tierney as Laura Hunt, and it becomes easier to see why Preminger, in observing the disparities in style between sets and costumes between himself and Mamoulian, could well have believed that filmdom's master of stylization did not understand *Laura*. While Preminger aimed toward what critic Molly Haskell called "a disconcertingly autonomous reality," Mamoulian was geared toward using stylization to entertain audiences in theaters. In short, while Preminger's instincts would opt toward more of an austere realism in *Laura*, he would observe costumes and sets utilized by Mamoulian, which fell within his creative framework, as opulent and unrealistic. The difference involved creative preference.

More Fireworks

While World War II raged in European and Pacific theaters, seismic blasts continued to reverberate on the Twentieth Century–Fox battlefield. Once Mamoulian left the scene, more warfare raged involving veteran cameraman Lucien Ballard. Since Ballard had been Mamoulian's choice, it is quite possible that he was resentful over the course of events. According to Preminger, Ballard ignored him on the set, smoking cigars and reading the paper when he was supposed to be setting up shots, in hopes of being fired so he could do a film at MGM with the actress to whom he was engaged, Merle Oberon. Preminger ultimately fired Ballard, but Zanuck insisted on the veteran cinematographer honoring his contract. He was demoted to the cameraman's lowest level, the test stage, while Joseph LaShelle was brought in to replace him. LaShelle ended up earning the lone Academy Award garnered by *Laura* (for Black and White Cinematography).

With battles raging on other fronts, Preminger and Zanuck, two individuals seemingly destined to disagree, were at odds on the subject of casting. The studio head sought to cast Laird Cregar, heavy, offbeat character actor and a Twentieth contractee, to play Waldo Lydecker. Cregar had performed impressively for Zanuck as the nasty and hypocritical bullfight critic loathed by Tyrone Power in *Blood and Sand* and as the psychopathic policeman with an obsession for Carole Landis in Bruce Humberstone's *I Wake Up Screaming* with Betty Grable. Preminger strongly believed that the actor who fit the role of Lydecker to perfection was veteran stage actor Clifton Webb. When the casting possibility was posed to Zanuck, he reportedly became furious, rejecting Webb because "he flies." This statement reportedly puzzled Preminger, who learned that Zanuck's adamance stemmed from Webb's perceived flighty homosexuality.

Preminger proved to be as persistent in Webb's favor as was Zanuck's adamant opposition. Webb was performing locally at the Biltmore Theater in Noel Coward's *Blithe Spirit* and Preminger did his best to inveigle Twentieth's boss to attend a performance. When Zanuck refused, an undaunted Preminger filmed what he considered to be the actor's best scene of the play, which he then played for him. Ultimately Zanuck yielded to Preminger's persistence while clinging to the demand that Webb's close-ups be kept to a minimum. Zanuck reputedly hoped that Webb would prove to be a failure, but later admitted his excellence in the role of the stuffy killer with the superiority complex.

While on a New York business trip, Zanuck viewed rushes sent to him by Preminger, and disparaged the performance of Dana Andrews. Tierney had described Preminger's choices of Andrews and Webb as "gambles." She explained, "Andrews was unproven as a leading man. Webb had never made a movie, but had spent his career on Broadway and had an image that was, well, prissy." Zanuck had resented the prissy image of Webb enough to remark that "he flies" and acceded to Preminger's insistent wish with the greatest reluctance. While in New York, watching the latest rushes of *Laura*, Zanuck registered anger over Andrews' reserved performance, disparagingly referring to him as an "agreeable schoolboy." Twentieth's studio head believed that Andrews was not tough enough to play Detective McPherson, lamenting, "I was afraid of this all along and this is why I wanted John Hodiak but stupidly listened to Preminger."

Andrews' performance contained a notable level of reserve, but with good reason. Here was a detective who, realizing he was dealing with a social class known for its shrewdness, but not generally linked to homicide investigations, recognized the importance of finesse in solving the murder. Andrews was also playing a man coming apart at the emotional seams after identifying so closely with the presumed victim, Laura Hunt. The shrewd and always combative Lydecker observed McPherson's dilemma and responded to this erotic fixation with a presumably dead woman by hurling some of his prototypically succinct and acidic invective.

The Andrews performance, as characteristic as Tierney's portrayal of Laura, represented the moral ambiguity Preminger sought to represent on screen. A film realist, Preminger *would* clash with the different approach of Mamoulian, an innovative stylist. One trait that Preminger held in common with Mamoulian, however, was in his exercise of daring casting instincts. By holding his ground against Zanuck's disapproval of Andrews and Webb, who comprised fascinating on-screen contrasts and played against each other brilliantly, Preminger's creative impulses were vindicated.

More Zanuck Opposition

If after completing the shooting of *Laura*, Preminger emitted a sigh of relief and believed that his problems were over, he was destined to suffer disappointment. After viewing his work, Zanuck had misgivings about the film's ending. He insisted that the final 15 minutes be reshot from Tierney's viewpoint. Preminger was understandably thunderstruck. To tamper with the end of a film at that point was disconcerting enough; in the case of a mystery such as *Laura*, the careful weaving of a consistent continuity pattern was severely jeopardized. Zanuck was insistent enough in his belief that he compelled Preminger to either reshoot the ending or be replaced by another director.

Preminger's account of what transpired represents yet another chapter of the unpredictable holding sway with the topsy–*Laura* project. After Preminger had finished reshooting the end of the film, Zanuck decided to preview *Laura* in the Twentieth screening room for Walter Winchell, at that time the most powerful and widely read newspaper columnist in the nation. As Winchell and a female companion sat in the deep leather chairs behind Zanuck and watched the film, the columnist and companion laughed at Webb's lines, which caused him to turn around and eye them in bewilderment. At the finish, according to Preminger, an enthusiastic Winchell yelled, "Bigtime! Bigtime! Congratulations, Darryl. Except for the ending. I didn't get it."

The Winchell comment about the end of the film prompted Zanuck to reimpose the original footage. At that point, Preminger could breathe a sigh of relief without any more surprises from Zanuck.

Zanuck Memo Input

While Hollywood's unrivaled champion in the arcane art of memo production was David O. Selznick, Zanuck contributed significant input in that direction. While many of his ideas, particularly in the realm of casting, came to naught, in no small measure due to the determination of Preminger, some of his comments in memoranda demonstrated analytical astuteness in the story realm.

In an October 30, 1943, communication Preminger and executive producer Bryan Foy, Zanuck expressed satisfaction concerning the first draft of the *Laura* script regarding continuity while finding the dialogue "ordinary." A major irony emerges regarding proposed script changes in the fascinating Waldo Lydecker character. The intelligent recommendations in effect drew a blueprint of the very actor Preminger sought to secure, Clifton Webb, accepted by Zanuck only after formidable arm-twisting. Zanuck liked the Lydecker character, exclaiming that "Waldo is the only well-drawn character throughout, and even his lines can be punched up with more sarcastic humor and ironic, sadistic wisecracks."

Zanuck at that point revealed dissatisfaction with the character portrait of Laura, describing her as "a mess" and stating pessimistically that "I doubt if any first-rate actress would ever play her." Mark McPherson, on the other hand, is described as "generally well drawn, but I think needs work." He states that Detective McPherson ought to be more like James Cagney. Zanuck emphasized John Huston's great film noir epic as a model to be emulated, writing, "All of the people, Mark included, should seem as if they stepped out of *The Maltese Falcon*—everyone a distinct, different personality. This is what made *The Maltese Falcon*. It wasn't the plot, it was the amazing characters."

The Zanuck references to *The Maltese Falcon* along with his belief that Detective McPherson should have more of the James Cagney in him presages the studio head's later disapproval of Dana Andrews' performance in rushes as he hungered for more overt toughness on the actor's part. Here again Preminger was ahead of his boss on the professional persona of McPherson. Humphrey Bogart, portraying tough San Francisco detective Sam Spade, demonstrated a more combative demeanor in *The Maltese Falcon* than did Andrews as McPherson in *Laura*. Two important elements demonstrate the differences in the two characters and why they should have been played in disparate fashions. Sam Spade was an old school San Francisco detective accustomed to solving cases by roughing up characters (especially gunsel Elisha Cook, Jr.) from the city's low life. McPherson, in seeking to solve a grisly shooting death among the champagne-swilling and limousine-riding social elite of Upper East Side Manhattan, was dealing with people who, if a misstep is made, could exert pressure on city officials to fire him. Lydecker was an influential columnist and commentator with a penchant for character destruction. The other reason why Andrews needed to portray his character with greater reserve than Bogart in *The Maltese Falcon* stemmed from the tortured ambiguity the detective felt in initially falling in love with the portrait and memory of a dead woman, followed by the shock of her sudden materialization and recognition that the object of his lustful fascination was a suspect in the death of the woman actually killed, model Diane Redfern.

Zanuck was directly on point in his quest for colorful individuality of characterization in *Laura*. Despite the aforementioned differences between *Laura* and *The Maltese Falcon*, particularly in the area of social milieu, the studio boss was accurate in stating that what made John Huston's film great was not the plot, but the fascinating array of characters. In that context, the earlier film provided an impressive standard to be emulated.

A March 20, 1944, Zanuck memo to Preminger indicated he was "pleased with the present script of *Laura*." On the subject of the female lead, he stated that "Laura's charm should be in her frankness and honesty. Where the others are Park Avenue cutthroats, she should be as fresh as a child." He still sought improvement in Waldo's dialogue, striving for witty sarcasm at times, but making him overall "likable and charming." He sought to incorporate into Waldo's character the biting flavor of *The Man Who Came to Dinner* starring Monty Woolley, a successful screen adaptation of the George S. Kaufman–Moss Hart comedy. The columnist and commentator Sheridan Whiteside, portrayed with such vibrance by Woolley, was inherently comedic in a way that Webb's Lydecker never was. Woolley's sardonic comments were those of a blowhard who could be brought down to earth, the grist for comedy, while Webb's portrayal captured the essence and spirit of a man whose cutting humor was exercised to demolish its targets, who was egomaniacal and pathologically domineering, and who was ultimately a murderer. Zanuck, as in the manner of his comparison of *Laura* with *The Maltese Falcon*, was immersed in an apples-and-oranges contrast in evaluating a noir drama, *Laura*, with a wittily satirical comedy, *The Man Who Came to Dinner*.

Two Men Hypnotized by Different Love Obsessions

Like so many great films, *Laura* is divisible into two dramatic features. The first half of the bill is the segment in which Laura Hunt is thought to be the victim of a fatal shooting so grisly that the deceased woman's features are unrecognizable. The first half of the film presents two men obsessed by Laura. One knew her in real life; to the other, she exists only in spirit.

Prominent New York columnist and radio commentator Waldo Lydecker carries a permanent opinion of his worth taller than even the Empire State Building. While proclaiming love for Laura, his fixation is that of a cold manipulator. He is what Professor Henry Higgins would have been to Liza Doolittle in George Bernard Shaw's *Pygmalion* or the musical adaptation of that famous play, *My Fair Lady*, if the distinguished linguist had been a humorless, egomaniacal tyrant who sees others as automatons far beneath him. By taking on Laura Hunt as a protégée and serving as her sponsor in the higher echelons of upper crust Manhattan society, he insists on total fealty. Laura is entitled to no life beyond Waldo's unyielding control.

McPherson, a New York detective of superior skill whose past exploits have been written up by Lydecker, falls under the mystical spell of Laura almost from the beginning. The story commences on a steamy New York summer afternoon as McPherson arrives at Lydecker's poshly appointed apartment. Lydecker is sitting in the bathtub writing a column. He describes his first meeting with Laura as he was eating lunch at the Algonquin Hotel. The columnist takes umbrage at the interruption, promptly turning the young woman down when she approaches him with an offer to endorse a pen her advertising agency was seeking to market.

McPherson finds a way to tease the affected columnist-commentator. A popular past time for youngsters as well as adults of the period was pocket pinball games, in which the player seeks to angle tiny steel balls into holes. The investigating detective annoys Lydecker by playing a pinball baseball game while they communicate. This disgusts Lydecker for two reasons, the first being his insistence on undivided attention from the mere mortals with whom he is barely willing to communicate at all, along with his revulsion over a grown man like McPherson playing what he considers to be a child's game reserved for society's commoners. When he indignantly asks McPherson why he must play such a game, the detective realizes he has gotten his goat, something he enjoys to the point that he repeats the activity on a future occasion. A clever detective, he realizes that the game is a device capable of letting Lydecker know he will do things his own way, unruffled by his imperious ways.

The world of Laura Hunt opens up to McPherson as he interrogates those closest to her. In addition to Lydecker looming as a person of suspicion, the contrasting duo of Ann Treadwell and Shelby Carpenter also commands his attention. Treadwell, the wealthy aunt of Laura, is played by Judith Anderson, removed from the ghoulishness of her Mrs. Danvers portrait in *Rebecca*. In *Laura* she assumes the role of a selfish and restless woman with more money than she knows how to spend. Carpenter, played by Vincent Price, is an opportunistic playboy devoid of purpose and character who manages to summon motivation to assist the wealthy woman in the expenditure department. Price, removed from his own later sinister persona in countless horror films, delivered one of his finest screen efforts portraying the Kentucky-bred Carpenter. McPherson soon observes the cross currents flowing from the directions of Lydecker, Treadwell and Carpenter toward the presumed murder victim, Laura.

While Carpenter was engaged to marry Laura (prompting Lydecker to thoroughly detest him whereas he would otherwise have only profoundly disliked him), he admitted to seeing Ann as well. He investigates the Kentucky playboy and, after compiling his dossier, informs Laura about his skill at extracting money from women and that he has written checks with insufficient funds. Clifton Webb delivers one of his most priceless verbal body slams early in the film when, at an Upper East Side cocktail soiree, he is introduced to Carpenter by a middle-aged matron who proclaims that the Carpenters are an "old Kentucky family." As Webb walks away, he hisses over his shoulder, "Sharecroppers, no doubt."

Lydecker follows Carpenter's trail carefully, seeking to display his feckless opportunism and faithlessness during their engagement by taking Laura to her aunt's apartment after dining with her. Shelby attempts to explain away their meeting, revealing that he was using the occasion to inform Ann of his engagement to Laura. This prompted another cutting one-liner from master of sarcasm Lydecker, who states, "In a moment of supreme disaster, he's trite." The opportunistic playboy is in the perpetual position of explaining his conduct. McPherson's investigation reveals that, while being engaged to Laura and seeing Ann Treadwell, he was also dating Diane Redfern, a beautiful model employed by the same advertising firm where his fiancee works. At one point in the film, Ann explains why she is drawn toward Carpenter, revealing that they are well matched because neither one has any character and both are weak, mating rationale of a damnable order.

Music as Obsession Symbolism

Never was beautiful music used to convey mood and project symbolism in the effectively elegant way that the haunting David Raksin *Laura* theme was employed in the first half of the film. The developing obsession of Detective McPherson, enhanced as he learns more about the presumed murder victim and spends much time in her apartment seeking clues, is revealed by the frequent playing of the haunting *Laura* theme on the radio and by string quartets in restaurants. Andrews internalizes his own frustration and ambiguity through his facial expressions on these occasions, letting the audience know that he is gradually losing control and falling in love with a dead woman.

The obsession element enhancing the portrait of a troubled police detective losing a grip on himself as he spirals headlong into an emotional attachment he cannot understand was one area where the seemingly inevitable antagonists, Zanuck and Preminger, were in accord. Zanuck's October 30, 1943, memo to Preminger and Bryan Foy recommends that Andrews, in his acutely mounting fascination with the dead woman, not only stare longingly at the oil painting of her hanging over the fireplace, but that he also spend time staring at her clothes and inhaling the fragrance of her perfume. Zanuck stated, "When he examines her apartment I would like to see him look at her lingerie, among other things. He looks at her shoes, her clothes, and he keeps looking back at the picture. He tries to reconstruct her. She begins to get under his skin."

Twentieth's boss found the obsession element so dramatically intriguing that he supplied more creative input on the subject in his March 20, 1944, memo to Preminger, suggesting the use of dissolves while Detective McPherson was in a newsreel movie theater to demonstrate his preoccupation with Laura. The newsreel theaters served the function in pre-television days of all-news networks today, providing the opportunity for interested individuals to inform themselves on various aspects of the news by providing theaters that showed nothing else. Zanuck suggested that Mark go inside a newsreel theater, then become so preoccupied with Laura that he sees her face everywhere, suggesting that "the woman in the newsreel dissolves into Laura. Madame Chiang Kai-shek dissolves into Laura. A girl on a surfboard dissolves into Laura, and finally the scene is filled with Laura." While the sequence of McPherson in the newsreel theater was not used, the suggestion demonstrated a recognition on Zanuck's part of the dramatic potential of the obsession theme.

The psychologically revealing scene in which a taut Mark visits Laura's bedroom, inspecting her closets, closely observing her clothes, then sniffing her perfume, is followed by returning to the living room and pouring himself a drink. The astute observer Lydecker delivered a crisp observation concerning Mark's dangerous visit to at least the precipice of necrophilia: "You'll end up in a psychiatric ward. I don't think they've ever had a patient who fell in love with a corpse."

Gene Tierney's Gilda

The picture enters part two as a presumed dead Laura Hunt emerges from a weekend spent at her Connecticut retreat. McPherson responds to her sudden presence in the manner of someone convinced he is staring at a ghost. Laura, shocked by the presence of a stranger in her apartment, threatens to call the police. Mark explains that he is the police.

While the first half of the film displayed Laura as woman and mystique, focusing on her climb to success as an advertising executive and fashion designer, the second part is divided into a search for a brutal killer along with a psychological portrait of a beautiful woman. McPherson, who finds himself every bit as much in love with the real woman as the presumably dead mystique so capable of dominating his thoughts and imagination, learns that as he seeks to apprehend a killer, the ongoing investigation reveals the nature of the real Laura. His detective work sees the two areas of inquiry interlap. When he ultimately learns that the dead woman is actually model Diane Redfern, with whom Laura's fiancee, Shelby Carpenter, was also involved, Laura joins the list of suspects. At one point Mark tells Laura that he "suspects nobody and everybody." This line found a place in film detective lexicon, and was employed to great comedic benefit by Peter Sellers portraying Inspector

Clouseau in the masterfully done series of Pink Panther films directed by Blake Edwards.

The portrayal of Laura accomplished a comparable result for Gene Tierney in establishing a signature role with which she would always be linked in the same way that two years later the stamp of Gilda would be imprinted lastingly on Rita Hayworth. Just as Hayworth would insist that in real life she was nothing like the fiery nightclub singer she played in *Gilda*, remarking that men had thought they were marrying Gilda and ended up with Rita Hayworth, Tierney also denied any personal connection to the New York advertising executive she played in *Laura*. Like Hayworth, she realized she was playing a screen character that fascinated audiences and maximized her opportunity.

"The role most often identified with my career was that of the title character in *Laura*," Tierney acknowledged. "The part was unusual in that Laura dominated the story as a presence, felt but unseen, for half the movie. She was the victim of events she had not created and could not control. Laura was a woman of mystery and glamour, unattainable, the kind of woman I admired in the pages of *Vogue* as a young girl."

A great curiosity was created for audiences by having Laura as an unseen presence, a glamorous mystique omnipresent through the oil painting above the fireplace of her apartment. This device accomplished two effective dramatic points: 1) creating a mystique around a beautiful young woman, and 2) enhancing the mystery element by teasing the audience. The first half of the classic drama involved learning about Laura and her interactions with the fascinating New York social types in her life while the second segment began with an introduction to the woman behind the painting on the wall, followed by the resolution of the mystery behind the killing of Diane Redfern, who had been murdered by mistake as a victim of circumstance with Laura Hunt the intended target.

A Different Kind of Noir

With the shadowy hues cast upon its characters, and the mood setting accented by the mystique of a beautiful young woman presumed dead for the first half of the film, many critics have invested *Laura* with the label of "classic noir." Despite its unmistakable noir ingredients, *Laura* must inevitably be defined as a different kind of noir functioning outside the mainstream of that traditional genre. Classic noir productions generally focus on an intended or actual male victim, usually a detective, pursued by a beautiful, predator, amoral femme fatale. *Out of the Past* fell into that traditional category. Both *The Maltese Falcon* and *Murder, My Sweet* focus on street tough detectives who are able to distance themselves from the temptations generated by femmes fatales. In order to solve murders and restore order, it is necessary for both detectives to walk through minefields populated by subterranean levels of San Francisco and Los Angeles society. Powell can never shake the cretinous presence of Mike Mazurki in his unforgettable role of Moose Malloy.

Laura signifies a reversal of traditional film noir story structure. Laura Hunt's woman of mystery is a polar opposite from the traditional film noir images of Jane Greer, Claire Trevor or Barbara Stanwyck. Rather than a femme fatale, as female leads generally are in film noir classics, Tierney plays a young woman of accomplishment who, through the combination of beauty, talent, intelligence and charisma enters Manhattan's Park Avenue aristocracy. In depicting her as an accomplished young executive in the highly competitive New York advertising world, Tierney's professional uniqueness is showcased. While the depiction of a young woman of the same milieu in a contemporary framework would be nonetheless impressive, it must be remembered that the film was set two generations earlier during World War II, at a point when female executive accomplishment in the male-dominated Park Avenue advertising environment was exceedingly rare. The traditional noir portrayal of detectives dealing with lower echelon toughs is also reversed, replaced by the martini-swilling set—ardent partygoers and partygivers with sweeping views of Central Park.

Obsession and a Man of the People

While Lydecker continues to attempt to control Laura's life, his obsession undiminished, Detective McPherson falls into an awkward position. His heart tells him he has fallen deeply in love with Laura while his professional detective's instincts force him to recognize that she is a murder suspect. When McPherson interrogates the perpetually vacillating, forever opportunistic Carpenter, the roaming lothario admits that he had taken Diane Redfern to Laura's apartment when the woman to whom he was engaged was out of the city. He explains that when the doorbell rang, he hid in the closet while the lovely model answered the door. Carpenter heard a shot and returned to the living room to find her dead. Fearful that he would be accused of murder, Shelby fled.

As the film moves toward its conclusion, a battle of wits develops between Detective McPherson, an unpretentious man of the people seeking to solve crimes with common sense, and Lydecker, who enjoys confrontation. As befits the egomaniacal, he believes he can toy with the detective and outwit him at game's end. The smugly confident killer with the superiority complex is pitted against "Man of the People" McPherson. The detective engages in a shrewd ploy that threatens to drive Laura, who has begun to reciprocate his feelings toward her, away from him. He arrests her for the murder of Diane Redfern, then later informs her that his ploy is meant to bring the real killer into the open.

Lydecker's chief enemy, his overwhelming ego, soon begins to do him in as he engages in an argument with Mark after the detective has released Laura from custody and taken her home. The attention she is displaying toward the detective draws the ire of the egocentric columnist. Eventually Mark stumbles on the murder weapon, a shotgun, hidden inside the grandfather clock in Laura's living room.

The Ultimate Possession

After Mark finds the murder weapon, he concludes that Lydecker is Diane Redfern's killer. Laura was his pathological possession, a creation rather than a flesh and blood human being for him to parade before Park Avenue society in the manner of a grand trophy. Control was his unstinting objective and his prize possession was considered to be his sole property. When his proprietary control was threatened by an impending marriage to Carpenter, an enraged Lydecker, feeling betrayed by his beautiful brunette protégée, decided that if he could not have her then nobody would. Mark concludes that when Diane Redfern opened the door to her killer, Lydecker, observing her in the darkness, mistook the svelte brunette for Laura, who was of comparable height, weight and hair color as the model. The logical conclusion McPherson reaches is that, having attempted to kill Laura for her engagement to Carpenter, he would be presently disposed to murder her for the currently blossoming relationship with the detective.

Lydecker almost succeeds in his murder attempt by convincing Mark that he has left her apartment to deliver his weekly radio broadcast. On this occasion he substitutes a tape from an earlier program. When the officer assigned to watch the building does not see Lydecker leave, Mark becomes immediately aware that Laura's life is in danger. The shrewdly sinister Lydecker quickly retrieves his shotgun, loads it and confronts Laura in her bedroom as she is about to retire.

The domineering Lydecker confirms McPherson's belief that he will seek to kill Laura a second time due to the attention displayed toward him as he had earlier attempted to destroy her for her then impending marriage to Carpenter. Rather than truly loving Laura, the warped Lydecker's obsession resulted from seeing her as a carefully constructed extension of himself. Since he perceives himself as her creator, he is unwilling to allow her to exist apart from his straitjacket control. As he stands on the threshold of taking her life, Lydecker provides what he considers logical justification for an act of destruction:

"The best part of myself. That's what you are. Do you think I'm going to leave it to the vulgar pawings of a second-rate detective?"

Mark and his detective consorts arrive just as Lydecker is prepared to kill Laura. As he breaks down the door and runs into the room, Laura rushes toward him, throwing herself into his arms. A wild and furious Waldo wheels and fires, destroying the grandfather clock that has served as a hiding place for his weapon of destruction. He is promptly killed in a rain of gunfire from Mark and the other detectives. As he slumps to the ground, one word tumbles from the dying man's lips: "Laura."

A Unique Heavy

After seeing and evaluating the fascinating plot of *Laura*, it becomes more understandable why Preminger fought so tenaciously with Zanuck to invest Clifton Webb with the key role of Waldo Lydecker. The highly sophisticated, thoroughly cosmopolitan, eternally witty, all-star New York socialite with the sharp tongue and rapier-sharp pen provided one of the most unique heavies in cinema annals along with Gavin Elster, played by Tom Helmore in Alfred Hitchcock's *Vertigo*. The fascinating element behind the nattily attired aristocrat was that, beneath the trappings, he was every bit as ruthless as the psychopathic, perpetually laughing early Richard Widmark or the hulking, take-no-prisoners presence of Mike Mazurki. Webb's character substituted cunning for brute force, and the street smart Andrews detective realized that the only way to apprehend such a formidable adversary was through patient shrewdness rather than the forceful action employed against street ruffians.

Laura broke new ground in allowing the killer to serve as narrator, describing in the most glowing terms a woman he has attempted to kill once and will seek to do so again. He relishes his savage propensity for barbs, revealing that "I don't use a pen. I write with a goose quill dipped in venom." He revels in his egotism with the explanation: "In my case, self-absorption is justified." Lydecker possesses a basic trait of intelligent and egomaniacal serial killers such as the Unabomber and Zodiac Killer of taunting and toying with investigating authorities. He revels in following Mark around in his investigative pursuits, always willing to supply input, particularly when it involves nasty comments about Carpenter.

The cunning Lydecker enjoys his volunteer role of alter ego investigator under McPherson in showering himself with grandiose attributes realized through his relationship with Laura. "How singularly innocent I look this morning," he remarks to the detective. "Have you ever seen such candid eyes?" He credits his association with Laura as molding him into "the kindest, gentlest, the most sympathetic man in the world." Lydecker's self-serving puffery does not stop there as he proclaims that the new post–Laura Waldo "should be sincerely sorry to see my neighbors' children devoured by wolves."

Zanuck, Preminger and More Controversy

While Zanuck and Preminger were never destined to become the best of friends, once that their mutual success of *Laura* was behind them they decided to jointly build on that achievement. They attempted to promptly recapture the magic of the 1944 sensation with another noir entry, *Fallen Angel*, bringing back Dana Andrews to star. Preminger was back in his familiar territory of moral ambiguity, using an appropriate leading man in Andrews who personified uncertainty in the common man with a touch of the suave hurled in for good measure. When Andrews arrives in a small California town as a down-on-his-luck con artist, he immediately develops a fondness for sexy restaurant waitress Linda Darnell.

The bad girl-good girl scenario was utilized in the Harry Kleiner adaptation of Marty Holland's novel as con man Andrews and streetwise Darnell decide that the best way for the sexy brunette to leave a town she loathes with the same negative intensity she feels toward her waitress job is to quickly secure a large chunk of money. Andrews and Darnell agree that the most feasible way to meet that objective is for him to woo town rich girl Alice Faye. When he succeeds in making Faye fall in love with him and marries her as a prelude to a quick divorce and anticipated cash settlement, the plot goes awry when Darnell is found murdered and Andrews emerges as the leading suspect. During that period of strife, Andrews falls in love with Faye, who believes his proclamations of innocence and fights for him. Buoyed by her example, Andrews abandons his old con artist's ways and reforms, emulating the sincerity of his spouse. He even manages through using his cunning more positively to identify and lead the police to the killer, bad cop Charles Bickford.

The major difficulty of *Fallen Angel* was that critics were mindful of the attempt of the Zanuck-Preminger team to achieve another *Laura* blockbuster with a stirring sequel. *Laura* was one of the most unique of films and could not be duplicated. Its success was equally difficult to match. As a result, many are inclined to consider *Fallen Angel* a flop when it possessed solid entertainment values more readily discernible but for the high expectations of another *Laura* delivered one year later.

While controversy raged during the filming of *Laura* and resurfaced with *Fallen Angel*, this time Preminger was not a major player. Alice Faye, one of Zanuck's two premier female musical stars, along with Betty Grable, was using *Fallen Angel* as a transition from glitzy musicals to solid drama. Faye received her big career boost by starring in the spectacular 1937 release, *In Old Chicago*, replacing recently deceased blonde bombshell Jean Harlow. Faye delighted Zanuck and Twentieth stockholders with her gold-studded track record resulting from her blonde good looks, stunning figure and sincere girl-next-door demeanor. These assets proved the perfect blend of ingredients for successful musical entertainment.

Now approaching 30, Faye anxiously undertook the challenge of propelling herself into a new dramatic sphere. She became disappointed over several events on the *Fallen Angel* project, for which Zanuck rather than director Preminger was blamed. Faye believed that by cutting selective scenes in which she was featured that Zanuck was purposely building up studio newcomer Linda Darnell at her expense while seeking to exploit her proven audience drawing power. The blonde star was also disappointed over the cutting of a song for which she had prepared for two weeks. It was sung during a romantic beach sequence with Andrews.

Ultimately Faye became so incensed at the studio boss that she made one of the more dramatic and well-publicized studio exits in film history by hurling her dressing room keys when she reached the main gate, an emotional severing of ties with Zanuck and the only studio with which she was associated in her storied career. Faye would not return to Twentieth Century–Fox for 17 years, to star in the remake of *State Fair* (1962) during a period when Darryl F. Zanuck was no longer in charge.

Preminger's Leading Man

Dana Andrews had starred in two Otto Preminger Twentieth Century–Fox films in as many years with *Laura* and *Fallen Angel* in the mid–40s and would be tapped by the Austrian director for two more performances. While some critics found fault with what they saw as rigid stolidity in Andrews performances, to Preminger his human vulnerability in demonstrating the problems besetting the common man amid social tensions as evidenced by Detective McPherson entering the world of Manhattan's rich and famous and drifter Eric Stanton groping for identity and ultimately finding himself at odds with his own corrupt behavior in *Fallen Angel* made him believable. In Andrews' next appearance in a Preminger vehicle, *Daisy Kenyon* (1947), he portrays a successful and dynamic New York attorney beset by human vulnerability as he strays from his wife to pursue Joan Crawford. The ensuing triangle is completed by Henry Fonda, Crawford's offbeat and reclusive husband, who ultimately hangs onto his wife. The premier Preminger-Andrews creative association apart from *Laura* came in the probing 1950 release, *Where the Sidewalk Ends*, a reunion with Gene Tierney. The Preminger penchant for exploring human vulnerability was again present as Andrews, portraying a brutal New York police detective, inadvertently kills a man, then seeks to conceal his guilt while continuing his search for a killer on whom to pin the murder.

Laura marked a significant directional turn for film noir, which began taking turns outside the original shadowy confines of street wise detectives, deadly but colorful low-life characters and ruthless femmes fatales who would stop at nothing to get their way. Moral ambiguity and victimization became increasingly pervasive elements as the genre continued to be shaped and reshaped during a period of intense competition for audiences.

SEVEN

An Obsession in White and a Final Reckoning: *The Postman Always Rings Twice* (1946)

The captivating brunette Jane Greer was one of a triumvirate of great screen femmes fatales who seized the attention of a movie hungry public during the halcyon 1946-47 period, when the major studios were producing an average of 90 new films per year. The hypnotic performance of Greer as a woman who will stop at nothing to get her way in the 1947 RKO release *Out of the Past* had been preceded by two bonanza successes at Columbia and MGM the preceding year, in which two of the world's most beautiful women, a ravishing redhead and captivating blonde, were provided with the ultimate buildup and support in what became the two most memorable roles of their careers. Harry Cohn at Columbia pulled out all stops to provide his greatest-ever star, Rita Hayworth, with her maximal showcase in *Gilda*. The MGM release has become one of the enduring film noir classics, and the most memorable role of the beautiful blonde discovered by Mervyn LeRoy as a teenager while attending Hollywood High, Lana Turner.

TV Guide in its review of *The Postman Always Rings Twice* referred to the film as "a torrid, hard-hitting romance [which] comes to startling life under [Tay] Garnett's shrewd direction, surprisingly at MGM." A good point was raised with the "surprisingly at MGM" phraseology, a reference to the basic "don't rock the boat" commercialism attributed to studio boss Louis B. Mayer. While Mayer's rule of thumb was that an occasional film could be made basically for the sake of art with questionable commercial value, this rubric was less applicable when related to certain box office personalities, of whom Lana Turner was at the top of the list. A star of great popularity, before her solid dramatic triumph in *Postman* the studio was content to use her in safer vehicles designed to reveal her beauty in comfortable settings geared toward making her popular to both men and women. In *Ziegfeld Girl* she portrayed the flashy blonde showgirl in tandem with the dark-haired Viennese beauty of Hedy Lamarr. Mervyn LeRoy's *Johnny Eager* utilized two of the most physically captivating stars ever to appear together on screen as Turner was cast opposite the adonis from Nebraska, Robert Taylor. It was LeRoy who was credited with discovering the radiant Hollywood High beauty. LeRoy launched her career in *They Won't Forget*. Looking fetching in a sweater, the sexy teenager was immediately christened "the sweater girl."

While captivating good looks such as Turner and Taylor possessed make the films in which they appear more potentially salable, a career downside almost inevitably arises. With basic emphasis on the star's photogenic gifts, which serve to achieve commercial results, the challenge associated with taking chances on roles and enhancing acting skills are often de-emphasized or become a non-factor.

Lana's director in *Postman*, Tay Garnett, as an MGM director under the same studio where both Turner and Taylor were under contract, explained:

> The temptation is great for a gal of that beauty of face and body—she had everything—to coast on that. The same holds true for actors. Bob Taylor had the same problem – to avoid being just a pretty face. Lana was a little late starting [as an actress]. She was rather ga-ga when she was picked up at a soda fountain and suddenly she was a movie star. It was almost that fast. She couldn't believe it. So for a long time Lana was inclined to do whatever the studio said.

Garnett's comment displays the level of sensitivity needed to successfully relate to a star in a major vehicle. An on-the-set cohesion was a happy characteristic of the shooting of *Postman*. Garnett's familiarity with Lana as a performer in her various films for the studio prompted his belief that she was ripe for the dramatic challenge of *The Postman Always Rings Twice*. The studio wanted Lana in the film, having been convinced by producer Carey Wilson that it was the perfect property to stimulate the blonde star's career at a time when the studio believed that her career had leveled off.

"I had a very insistent voice in choosing her," Tay Garnett revealed. "I didn't have the final say because at Metro at that time almost everything was done by committee. Producer Wilson and I were good friends and both agreed on Lana. Actually, it was a question of convincing Lana." The resulting sequence is reminiscent of Rouben Mamoulian's realization that Fred Astaire was the perfect lead for another highly touted MGM musical production, *Silk Stockings*. When the dancing great needed convincing, Mamoulian took him to lunch at the studio commissary and successfully made his case. Garnett took Lana to lunch at the then-popular Hollywood hangout, Romanoff's, and told her, "This is the best acting opportunity you've had."

While Garnett was doing the blonde beauty a gigantic favor by convincing her to take the lead role in *The Postman Always Rings Twice*, a residual benefit flowed in his direction. It turned out to be the capstone of his long directing career as well as the most impressive credit in the career of the blonde star.

James Cain's Hat Trick

The resounding triumph of *The Postman Always Rings Twice* resulted in what in sports parlance is termed a "hat trick" by the Baltimore-born mystery author James Cain. Never in Hollywood suspense film annals or in any other category would any author ever enjoy three such huge successes apportioned over a three-year period as did Cain with the culmination of *Postman*.

It so happened that *Postman*, Cain's first novella, was the last of his famous cinema trio to be filmed and released. MGM, a studio noted for exercising caution, was doubtlessly influenced by the tremendous commercial and artistic acclaim generated by Cain's two preceding successes, Paramount's *Double Indemnity* and, one year later, *Mildred Pierce*, an adaptation of another emotion-packed novella that garnered an Oscar for a famous actress who used the vehicle to spectacularly jumpstart a sagging career.

Joan Crawford, one of MGM's most prominent stars in its lustrous history, was unceremoniously dropped after 18 years when studio boss Louis Mayer believed that her box office appeal had dried up. She signed with Warner Bros. and spent a year nervously waiting for an opportunity to prove that the magnetism was still there and that Mayer had been wrong. At that point of tenuous uncertainty producer Jerry Wald brought her the script of *Mildred Pierce*. Barbara Stanwyck and Bette Davis had earlier turned it down, but Crawford found the script based on the Cain novella a heavensent opportunity to resuscitate her career.

Crawford would eventually secure an Oscar for her brilliant portrayal of a long-suffering mother determined to give her daughter (Ann Blyth) the good things in life that had been denied to her. The result was that Veda Pierce became an incorrigibly spoiled brat who, as soon as one favor had been granted by mother Mildred, would promptly and huffily up the ante.

Crawford's dramatic instincts told her that the thematic ingredients were present for a major success, but before she would have an opportunity to go before the cameras she had to prove herself to the film's director. The tempestuous Hungarian Michael Curtiz had become Jack L. Warner's top director on the Burbank lot with his Academy Award effort in the brilliant *Casablanca* two years earlier. His reluctance to put her in the role resulted in an extraordinary request from an established star as Crawford agreed to do a test to convince him of her worthiness to play Mildred Pierce. After Crawford was approved, the temperamental director rejected 16-year-old Universal contract player Ann Blyth for the key role of Mildred's strong-willed and spoiled daughter. Once more Crawford made an extraordinary gesture for a major star, agreeing to work with the teenager on her lines, then do a screen test with her. Crawford proceeded to do screen tests with most of the other character actors, demonstrating an attitude of unencumbered teamwork in the pursuit of success.

Mildred Pierce is characteristic of so many Hollywood classics for the number of potential mine fields successfully skirted so that ultimate triumph could be realized.

The first day on the set saw fireworks emanate from the mercurial Michael Curtiz as he became livid in the belief that Crawford had defied his order not to wear shoulder pads. He tore at her dress and, upon inspection, learned that the shoulder pads existed only in his imagination. She proceeded to endure the director's abuse until Curtiz realized the level of her professionalism and determination to succeed in *Mildred Pierce*, winning his respect. Crawford even injected some humor into the situation at the post-production party by presenting the Hungarian with a huge pair of shoulder pads made for her by Adrian, the famous dress designer.

After observing Crawford's professionalism and her determination to deliver the ultimate in cooperation and performing skill to each scene, a strong lobbying effort commenced on the Burbank lot to secure an Academy Award for the veteran actress. It culminated on Oscar night with her selection, even though she had a 104 degree temperature and could not attend the ceremonies, listening with a crowd of well wishers on the radio at home. When the announcement was made, cheers filled the room. Crawford's career had soared back into high gear.

As for Cain, he was ecstatic over the feeling and conviction Crawford put into the lead character of his novel. The year before, it had been a bravado performance from Barbara Stanwyck, who should have learned from that success not to look another Cain gift horse in the mouth, but her refusal along with that of Bette Davis had provided Crawford's opportunity to garner a major triumph at a new studio. A grateful Cain sent Crawford a leather-bound copy of *Mildred Pierce*, which he inscribed: "To Joan Crawford, who brought Mildred to life as I had always hoped she would be, and who has my lifelong gratitude." Theater patrons appreciably agreed as the film raked in $5 million in 1945, returning Crawford to the ranks of the popular moneymaking stars.

While *Mildred Pierce* has been classified as brilliant film noir, it is of a different variety from the basic story model within the genre. In most instances, the tension and obsessive element of the story relates to the relationship between a greedy and grasping femme fatale and the men who fall vulnerable to their seductive charms, often graphically aware of the emotional quicksand in which they are ensconced. The relationships involving Barbara Stanwyck and Fred MacMurray in *Double Indemnity* as well as that of Jane Greer and Robert Mitchum in *Out of the Past* epitomize that classic dramatic thread. Crawford as *Mildred Pierce* is a definitive survivor who, after her marriage to Bruce Bennett crumbles, accelerates her career from a woman who begins by baking and selling pies to the proprietor of a string of restaurants. Rather than including a traditional femme fatale, *Mildred Pierce* instead has a daughter fatale played with the appropriate degree of self-centered smugness by Ann Blyth as Veda, the girl who will stop at nothing, not even two-timing her mother by romantically pursuing Mildred's faithless husband, Zachary Scott. As film historian David Thomson noted, "The family and mother love are undermined. Suburbia inextricably confuses happiness and the dollar."

Films involving opportunistic females sometimes include a shrewd and worldwise woman capable of seeing through the veneer of superficiality, making barbed comments to display dissatisfaction. Thelma Ritter, the faithful personal assistant of Bette Davis in *All About Eve*, makes her displeasure evident in biting comments directed at Anne Baxter, who plays the opportunistic aspiring actress, Eve Harrington. In *Mildred Pierce* the savvy friend of Crawford, bitingly witty Eve Arden, directs barbs at young Veda. One of the most brilliantly acidic lines in film history was Arden's trenchant summation of the selfish daughter: "Personally Veda's convinced me that alligators have the right idea. They eat their young." Both Arden and Blyth would receive Best Supporting Actress nominations for *Mildred Pierce*, an honor ultimately bestowed on Anne Revere, who portrayed Elizabeth Taylor's mother in *National Velvet*.

Mildred Pierce demonstrated Curtiz's familiarity with the dangerous and often melancholy world of evening, while screenwriter Ranald MacDougall robustly adapted Cain's novel with fidelity. The opening sequence, when Zachary Scott is gunned down but his murderer is not seen, provided a captivating mystery thread that is not resolved until it is revealed that long-suffering mother Mildred is willing to pay the ultimate price for her daughter Veda of confessing to a murder her offspring committed.

The impressive Cain hat trick would be achieved in 1946 with *Postman*, completing the string of top performances by Hollywood actresses in their signature roles—Stanwyck in 1944 in *Double Indemnity,* Crawford in 1945 in *Mildred Pierce* and blonde bombshell Turner completing the cycle in 1946 in *The Postman Always Rings Twice*. Cain was so impressed with Turner's performance that she received a leather-bound first edition of the novel, as had Crawford for *Mildred Pierce*, with a comparable dedication: "For my dear Lana, thank you for giving a performance that was even finer than I expected."

Cain's first mystery book, preceded only by a scholarly tome entitled *Our Government*, was published in 1934. Due to censorship fears, it took better than a decade for the film to be made and released. France and Italy, two liberal European nations outside the scope of influence of the feared Breen and later Johnston Office, tackled *Postman* long before the Cain novella was filmed in the author's home nation. A French version of *Postman* was released in 1939, *Le Dernier Tournant*, starring Michel Simon, Fernand Gravet and Cortinne Luchaire. Italian filmmaker Luchino Visconti ignored the copyright on *Postman* and made his own film from Cain's story, the 1942 release, *Ossessione,* starring Clara Calamai, Massimo Girotti and Elio Marcuzzo. Livid MGM studio executives reacted immediately, blocking all prints from American release. *Ossessione* would not be seen in the United States until 1977, and only then in a truncated art house run.

The fact that it took 12 years between the time that *Postman* was published in 1934 and released to the public in 1946 results in a failure to grasp a fundamental point in the novella written by Cain, that of the linkage to the Great Depression. *Postman* was both written and published during the period following the bank failure and accession to office in March 1933 of President Franklin Delano Roosevelt, who exhorted Americans not to lose their confidence or faith with the famous words uttered in his inaugural address: "We have nothing to fear but fear itself."

The character of Frank Chambers etched indelibly in print by James Cain and adapted to the screen by scenarists Harry Ruskin and Niven Busch looms in his own way as every bit the definitive Depression creature as the unforgettable image of Tom Joad cemented into public consciousness by John Steinbeck in Twentieth Century–Fox's *The Grapes of Wrath*, brought to the screen with convincing fidelity through a brilliant portrayal by Henry Fonda and empathic direction from John Ford.

Garfield the Depression Survivor

Lana Turner and director Garnett received their most notable film opportunities from *Postman*, while the blonde siren's love interest made it one of his greatest-ever screen showcases of a memorable career ended all too prematurely by death. John Garfield, born Jacob Julius Garfinkel on March 4, 1913, experienced the type of life growing up in a slum neighborhood of America's largest city that groomed him for the roles he would play with such dynamic feeling. Plagued by a bad heart, he would die in 1952 before reaching his fortieth birthday. Garfield was a busy as well as disciplined dramatic craftsman who left a body of work behind more prolifically commensurate with an older performer.

A member of the distinguished Group Theater, Garfield received valuable training at the Ouspenskaya Drama School in New York run by the great Russian character actress Maria Ouspenskaya. His lower middle class background shaped the performer he would become as he invested his roles as a Depression survivor and uncompromising rebel with energetic conviction. Garfield co-founded Enterprise Productions for the purpose of encouraging left-leaning artists. Two socially conscious dramas symbolized his thematic thinking, *Body and Soul* (1947), and *Force of Evil* (1948). The latter film was written and directed by Abraham Polansky, who ultimately outlasted a lengthy blacklist period by directing the 1969 film *Tell Them Willie Boy Was Here,* starring Robert Redford and Robert Blake. The heart attack which caused Garfield's ultimate death was considered to have been at least partially triggered by political problems during the '50s.

The role of drifter Frank Chambers was familiar to Garfield, who had demonstrated himself to be every bit as much as a Depression wanderer, survivor and rebel as Tom Joad of *The Grapes of Wrath*. The basic difference separating the two men was that Joad was a sturdy Oklahoman determined to surmount the considerable obstacles confronting him, while Garfield was the classic city boy who employs every measure of his street smartness to survive Depression rigors.

A quick perusal of the titles of Garfield films underscores the degree to which the stocky battler with the New York accent was pitted against the hands of fate. He starred as a battling survivor confronting hostile forces in such social message films as *Dust Be My Destiny, They Made Me a Criminal, Castle on the Hudson, Saturday's Children, The Sea Wolf, Dangerously They Live, Nobody Lives Forever, Body and Soul* and *Force of Evil.*

From an artistic standpoint, Garfield could be classified as a stepfather of the film characters of the definitive period in which survival often required exceptional tenacity and wit. James Dean typified rebellion during the '50s as a young man blossoming into adulthood amid the uncertainties of the atomic age and the awareness that, for the first time, humankind possessed the potential to destroy life as we know it.

From thematic example, Dean could be called the stepson of Garfield. Dean's screen persona was that of a young man attempting to come to grips with a world around him that makes little if any sense. Garfield also sought to make sense of a world he was seeking to understand, but within the confines of a Depression period in which the first order of business was that of surviving in a society immersed in economic and social conflict.

Garfield's dramatic persona made him as ideal a choice for drifter Frank Chambers as was Lana Turner a perfect Cora Smith. In the Cain novella, the action begins with Chambers being thrown off a hay truck. The screen version shows him being let out in front of the luncheonette–gas station Twin Oaks run by Cora's husband Nick by Kyle Sackett, the County District Attorney, who had picked him up while hitchhiking. Garfield's motivation in stopping there was the "HELP WANTED" sign posted by Nick Smith. This alteration from the Cain novella made thematic sense in that continuity was established as Sackett, skillfully played by veteran character actor Leon Ames, appears in the first scene, and at the close of the film when, awaiting execution, Chambers is informed by him that his request for a stay of execution has been denied by the governor.

An Obsession in White

Another deviation from the Cain story surfaces early in the film, but one that neither the author nor anyone else would question. Cain's novella has first person narrator Chambers revealing his first glimpse of the tempestuous Cora after her husband, a Greek called Nick Papadakis in the novella, had walked in from the kitchen after he had been talking to the proprietor about working for him.

"Then I saw her. She had been out back, in the kitchen, but she came in to gather up my dishes. Except for the shape, she really wasn't any raving beauty, but she had a sulky look to her, and her lips stuck out in a way that made me want to mash them in for her."

No one has ever described Lana Turner as anything but a raving beauty. Cain had been attempting to write as realistic and hard-hitting suspense story with a Depression setting as possible. There was a stirring reality to the woman for whom Chambers would stoop to murdering a man who had befriended him possessing a cheap and commonplace sensuality. For screen visuality, however, it was advantageous to present a woman of smoldering passion with the face and figure capable of driving a man to the kind of soaring sensuality wherein he would stop at nothing, even killing a kind man who had given him a job.

Cecil Kellaway, front left, sings in glorious drunken bliss, unaware that John Garfield, bottle in hand, is preparing to land a fatal blow in the MGM classic, *The Postman Always Rings Twice* (1946), directed by Tay Garnett. Kellaway's wife Lana Turner looks on nervously. The film was adapted from a best seller by James M. Cain, who had two other works adapted into forties screen blockbusters, *Double Indemnity* and *Mildred Pierce*.

When John Garfield sees Lana Turner for the first time, her luncheonette uniform is white, the only contrast the black "TWIN OAKS" inscribed on it. When Garfield, who is waiting for a hamburger Nick Smith (Cecil Kellaway) is preparing for him (sizzling on a nearby stove), gets his first look at Lana Turner, she becomes for him an instant obsession in white.

Most scenes involving men and women fated to be lovers concentrate on the faces involved. By pursuing a different tactic, the result was a scene for the ages. While the hamburger is frying and Garfield looks after it as Nick is pumping gas for a customer, the camera reveals a lipstick container falling to the floor. A unique panning shot produces immediate high level voltage so stark and convincing in its natural sensuality and visual imaginativeness that film enthusiasts have not stopped talking and writing about it better than 50 years later. In place of tilting from the leading lady's face downward to her seductive body, the reverse occurs as the camera's eye presents the scene from Garfield's viewpoint. Startled by the sight and sound of the lipstick dropping, then rolling across the floor, his first view is of the dropped object. The camera then moves slowly upward, in the same manner as Garfield's eyes. Slowly but surely he takes in Lana's curvaceous body as she is appropriately attired in snugly fitting white shorts and halter, until his eyes ultimately register on her flawless face. The white accent is consistently followed to the top of her head and to the turban she wears. A closeup of Garfield reveals an hypnotic stare accompanied by an inaudible gulp. Turner slinks away like a prowling jungle cat and Garfield learns that he has burned his hamburger. But at a time like that, with body temperature accelerating to the boiling point, who cares about one ruined hamburger?

This intensely erotic scene demonstrates a significant point about sensuality at its rawest being demonstrated in its most advanced form through imagination rather than comprehensive graphic design. *The Postman Always Rings Twice* affords a classic example illustrating each technique. When director Bob Rafelson remade *Postman,* his 1980 production sought to take advantage of liberalized production codes from the old Breen Office days which prevailed when the 1946 version was filmed. The 1980 release included an evening scene in the luncheonette when a hungry Jack Nicholson ravished Jessica Lange on a table. While that graphic scene was quickly forgotten by most, the blazing eroticism of the 1946 release remains fervently imprinted in the minds of all who viewed it.

Tay Garnett was concerned about censors during the production, later commenting, "It was a real chore to do *Postman* under the Breen Office, but I think I managed to get the sex across. I think I like it better that way. I'm not a voyeur, and I don't like all the body display that you get in pictures nowadays. I think that it's just a crutch for untalented directors and writers."

Sustaining Dramatic Heat

Cinematic success is frequently related to flexibility, the ability to shift gears. Producer Carey Wilson's involvement with *Postman* embodied an abrupt subject matter transition since he had earlier achieved recognition at the studio of the roaring lion as a producer and screenwriter of Andy Hardy films. As for Garnett, *Postman* marked an opportunity to execute a career milestone leap, to accomplish the very thing he convinced Lana Turner she could achieve through the film.

Garnett was one of the many local Los Angeles products to obtain success as a director in the formative period of filmmaking. After attending Polytechnic and Los Angeles high schools, he joined the Navy when the United States entered World War I, served as a flight instructor in San Diego and was badly injured in a crash which left him with a permanent limp and the walking stick that became his trademark.

He was asked to put on blackout sketches at the San Diego Naval Base, some of which were seen and enjoyed by Alan Holubar, an independent film producer and director. In 1922, Holubar shot a movie, *Hurricane's Girl*, at the base and recruited Garnett to perform some flying stunts. Holubar was pleased enough with Garnett's work to enlist him as a script doctor for two more of his films.

Like so many of his contemporaries, Garnett moved around a great deal before finding a home at MGM. He worked at Hal Roach Studio, First National and Pathe. It was while he was under contract to Pathe that Garnett directed what many consider to be his best film next to *Postman*, an imaginative drama set on a cruise ship, where two ultimately doomed lovers, Kay Francis, who is dying of heart disease, and William Powell, a condemned murderer awaiting capture and execution, party and try to convince themselves and each other that their love will endure all. The 1932 release *One Way Passage* secured an Academy Award for Best Original Story. Garnett directed a major MGM success with the 1935 release *China Seas*, keeping the adventure stirring as a dynamite cast including Clark Gable, Jean Harlow, Wallace Beery and Rosalind Russell enhanced chances for a robust commercial reception.

Garnett had begun his film career performing Navy stunts. Action continued to be his hallmark in subsequent efforts, commercial vehicles such as *Professional Soldier*, *Trade Winds*, and a John Wayne action film with an East Indies setting, *Seven Sinners*. When Garnett arrived at his new home, MGM, in 1943, studio operatives thought enough of the new director on the lot to provide him with two films starring the Culver City dream factory's number one leading lady, Greer Garson. While the elegant Britisher Garson notched her fourth successive Best Actress Oscar nomination with *Mrs. Parkington* in 1944, the film starring the "Queen of Culver City" the following year, *The Valley of Decision*, was by far the commercially stronger of the two Garnett-directed efforts. While Garson had won an Academy Award for *Mrs. Miniver*, a milestone William Wyler effort, *The Valley of Decision* outgrossed that Oscar winner on its first release with a soaring $5,560,000 figure.

Garnett's next effort after *The Valley of Decision* was *The Postman Always Rings Twice*. His skillful direction bears on a point that has been previously made, that creativity frequently involves a continuation of playing the cards originally dealt. Garnett's earlier commercial films were known for their sustained action. While *Postman* was a film noted for drama, and was far from a formula adventure, Garnett's experience in commercial efforts shot at breakneck pace geared him to dealing with dramatic tension in a quickly paced setting.

The one word that jumps out when evaluating *Postman* is temperature. The room was set at boiling point with Garfield's tensely combustible first meeting with torrid femme fatale Turner. Garnett exercised consummate skill in sustaining the torrid tempo, bolstered by the brilliant on screen chemistry of Garfield and Turner. Had it not been for Garfield's rejection by the Army due to his bad heart, Cameron Mitchell, who had been tested for the Frank Chambers part, would have been given the plum role opposite Turner. When Garfield was released from service duty and the film was in production, a wary Garnett observed the actor playing handball, requesting him to stop. A feisty Garfield replied, "I've got a tricky ticker, so what?" Garnett responded as diplomatically as he knew how: "Don't get me wrong. I don't want to louse up your fun, but I've got to finish this picture."

Forces of Irony and Great Supporting Efforts

Reflective of the best films noir, *Postman* uses irony to significant advantage in developing a suspenseful story. A supreme note of irony, building within the framework of the torrid heat revealed in the developing relationship between Frank and Cora, is the childlike innocence of Cecil Kellaway as Nick Smith. During the evenings he enjoys relaxing in the living quarters of the building that serves by day as a diner with both Frank and Cora. While an often tipsy Nick warbles "She's Funny That Way" on his guitar, Frank and Cora sit in smoldering frustration, wishing they were alone. Nick innocently suggests that Cora dance with his handyman Frank while he sings and strums his guitar. On another occasion, when Frank and Cora are attempting to escape detection from an inebriated Nick after a moonlight interlude at the nearby beach, he spots them on their return and exclaims, "I wasn't expecting you back so early."

In addition to Kellaway's stirring support, excellent efforts were also displayed by the earlier mentioned Leon Ames as District Attorney Kyle Sackett, who pursues Garfield like a stubborn bloodhound until ultimately obtaining his first degree murder conviction, and Hume Cronyn as the slick and wily Arthur Keats, the criminal defense attorney who calls Ames's bluff in court and, so that his rival can save a measure of face, agrees to have Turner plead guilty of manslaughter in exchange for a recommendation of clemency, resulting in her walking out of court with her freedom. The Ames-Cronyn encounter is one of the most imaginative courtroom scenes ever filmed. One can almost literally see the rapidly clicking wheels in Arthur Keats' agile legal brain as he spirits a guilty Cora to freedom, convinced that Sackett is bluffing since the company that insured Nick Smith's life had paid the entire $10,000 proceeds without protest, indicating to the cunning attorney that they lacked information to directly link Cora or Frank to his murder.

While Sackett remains the bloodhound, convinced that Frank and Cora killed Nick Smith, Keats is the all-purpose cynic. He has decided to laugh rather than cry over the corruption he sees in life from his ringside seat as a criminal defense attorney, but the laughter is laced with sneers. After he has arranged a marriage between Turner and Garfield after Nick's murder to avoid possible prosecution by local authorities since they are living under the same roof in an unwed state, Cronyn delivers a biting assessment of the situation with the line, "I can only think of 15 or 20 reasons why you shouldn't be happy."

The casting by MGM and director Tay Garnett of John Garfield and Lana Turner in *The Postman Always Rings Twice* resulted in screen dynamite: the teaming of the street-wise Depression survivor on the run Garfield alongside MGM's sensuous "sweater girl." The scene in the diner when Garfield casts his eyes on Turner for the first time has been called by many the sexiest ever filmed. Since the sensuality was non-verbal and contained not even a kiss, viewer imagination was invited to fill in the details.

Cain's Inner Tension

In *Postman* and *Double Indemnity,* author Cain and his faithful film adapters used dramatic irony in the form of a Catch-22 to shrewdly develop inner tension in each story. The homicidal duos of Barbara Stanwyck and Fred MacMurray in *Double Indemnity* and Lana Turner and John Garfield in *Postman* plot murders against the husbands of the femmes fatales so they can be together. Once the murders are committed, however, the scrutiny imposed by investigating authorities and their own inner-generated tensions relating to the crimes drive them apart and against each other in ways that did not exist prior to their deadly deeds.

After the public notoriety of Lana Turner's trial, business improves so much at the diner that it is expanded into an outdoor as well as indoor facility to accommodate curiosity seekers. Turner's attitude toward Garfield is hostile since, while in the hospital nursing injuries sustained when Kellaway's car spun out of control in the process of attempting to make his death look like an accident, Ames coaxes him into a signed statement pinning the murder entirely on Turner.

While the two live under the same roof, married to satisfy the law, their mutual hostilities continue to grow. Tragedy strikes when Cora's mother sustains a heart attack and ultimately dies, prompting the blonde to travel home to Iowa. Frank takes her to the train station in East Los Angeles, then immediately acquaints himself with Madge Gorland, played by Audrey Totter, helping her cool her automobile's radiator, after which he heats up her temperature, proposing a trip to Tijuana, an offer she promptly accepts.

Ultimate Irony and a Form of Resolution

Cora returns to Los Angeles following her mother's death and funeral with a new resolution to make her relationship with Frank work. Her hopes are dashed when Madge shows up at the restaurant to return a tie Frank left behind which, ironically, was the wedding gift Cora bestowed on him. A furious Cora threatens to turn her husband in to Sackett. She has nothing to lose since she has already been tried in connection with Nick's death and is spared by the double jeopardy provision of the United States Constitution.

Eventually Frank is able to prevail upon her his sincerity to cooperate with her desires and forge a successful marriage. It is revealed that she is bearing his child. Cora maintains that she never intended to turn her husband over to the D.A., but had intended to leave him. Instead they decide to go for another one of their evening beach swims.

The evening beach settings provided the major obstacle to what was an otherwise smoothly paced production schedule. Fog disrupted activity, prompting Garnett and everyone else to become nervous, but eventually it lifted and some of the most dramatic scenes of the film were shot. Lana was again an image in white clad in a stunning one-piece bathing suit.

Compelling irony has been compounded upon irony in this devastating film, leading up to the dramatic conclusion, when the killers are forced to pay for their evil deed. After a long swim, as John and Lana are sharing hope for a new beginning, a distracted Garfield fails to see an oncoming vehicle on the highway. He swerves quickly and smashes into a highway barrier. Lana is killed instantly. The car door flies open and the lipstick container she had been holding drops to the ground, completing another thematic thread. Garfield sees her for the first time when her lipstick drops to the restaurant floor, while it drops to the ground on the highway at the point of her death.

Another film linkage, mentioned earlier, is that Sackett, who picked up Chambers as a hitchhiker and dropped him off in front of the diner, is with him in prison before his execution. After he reveals that the governor has refused to grant the prisoner a stay of execution, Chambers, who has narrated the account of his story to a priest, emphatically declares to Sackett that he loved Cora more than anyone in his life and would never kill her. Sackett then provides the prisoner awaiting execution with information that it would make no difference even if he were found innocent of killing Cora. The police found what was to be a farewell note from Cora in the cash register of the diner. While revealing her great love for Frank, she also reveals enough details to implicate him in Nick's murder. Sackett explains that one way or another he would be executed, if not for Cora's death, then for that of Nick.

This disclosure puts Frank's punishment in a different light. The title idea passed along by accident to Cain by his helpful screenwriter confidante, Vincent Lawrence, to whom he dedicated the book, provided the perfect note on which to end the film. Frank tells Sackett, "You know, there's something about this which is like expecting a letter you're just crazy to get, and you hang around the front door for fear you might not hear 'em ring. You never notice that he always rings twice. The truth is you always hear 'em ring the second time, even if you're way out in the back yard." Now able to accept his ultimate fate, Frank Chambers turns to the priest who has patiently heard him out, saying, "Father, could you send up a prayer for me and Cora and, if you can find it in your heart, make it so we're together—wherever it is."

The gripping drama of *The Postman Always Rings Twice* kept theater audiences glued to their seats. The public response to *Postman* was both emphatic and immediate as more than $4 million soared into the coffers of MGM from the initial box office receipts.

EIGHT

British Noir: *The Third Man* (1949) and *Across the Bridge* (1957)

> In Italy, for 30 years under the Borgias they had warfare, terror, murder, bloodshed; they produced Michelangelo, Leonardo da Vinci and the Renaissance. In Switzerland, they had brotherly love, 500 years of democracy and peace, and what did that produce? The cuckoo clock.
>
> —Orson Welles from *The Third Man* (1949)

The world of film noir holds a natural affinity toward Britain, the brooding world of shadowy images along with the moral dilemmas which emerge in the greatest of drama in a society that took over where Greek tragedians like Sophocles and Aeschylus left off, forging a dynamic new tradition with such masters of human complexities and moral dilemmas as Shakespeare and Marlowe. Nor can it be forgotten that long before either one of them surfaced there was that anonymous classic from the world of darkened bogs, *Beowulf*.

In addition to revealing the darkness of a world often spinning in a turbulent sea of anarchy, film noir also explores the world of the cynic with humor sometimes employed, generally of the sardonic cutting variety. Two transplanted Irish playwrights who took London by storm, Oscar Wilde and George Bernard Shaw, were master word toreadors alternately waving capes and swords at entranced audiences. Wilde and Shaw explored the world of moral dilemmas and human ambiguity, fertile mine fields for scenarists putting words to paper and directors generating mood through darkened shadows and occasional glittering neon signs.

Raymond Chandler, who touched off waves of enthusiasm in France as well as England at the close of the war before attaining a comparable audience in America, came to England as a young boy from Chicago and received an English prep school education.

Two British noir epics to be evaluated involve a baton passing between a London director who hit his stride before the war and gave a break to a young Yorkshireman and world traveler. While working on a documentary, *We Serve*, young veteran and established director Carol Reed provided Ken Annakin, who had been dutifully involved in camera duties, an opportunity to "come over to our side," helping launch the younger man on a brilliant career as a globetrotting director who combined variety and quality. While Reed would achieve the greatest dramatic triumph of his career with the highly acclaimed 1949 noir classic *The Third Man*, Annakin would direct the film he acknowledges as his personal favorite less than a decade after Reed's great achievement. *Across the Bridge* was a 1957 release showcasing Rod Steiger in one of his early brilliant efforts, one that presaged the Best Actor Oscar he would receive a decade later for *In the Heat of the Night*.

One of the most interesting aspects of Britain in general and London in particular is internationalism, the cosmopolitan world center ambience of the society. This is borne out in its films. While both Reed and Annakin were born in Britain and received their film training there, the two films showcased, *The Third Man* and *Across the Bridge*, were not shot mainly in Britain. Post-war Vienna was the setting for Reed's film while Annakin's, though shot in Spain, was supposed to be set in Mexico and in Texas near the Mexican border. Studio interiors for *The Third Man* were shot both in Vienna and at Shepperton Studios near London. The hotel room scenes that were supposed to bear a New York setting in *Across the Bridge* were filmed at Pinewood Studios just outside London. The film begins in London.

The fact that neither *The Third Man* nor *Across the Bridge* bore a London main setting is not surprising for British filmmakers. While many great British directors begin doing films in their own country, often in the country's largest city, London, the world consciousness of the cinema artist frequently results in an expanding of wings. Once David Lean etched a name in the British cinema with typically English films such as *Brief Encounter*, he ultimately became a director with catholic internationalized tastes, as reflected by *Lawrence of Arabia*, *Doctor Zhivago* and *The Bridge on the River Kwai*. Annakin followed a similar career pattern, beginning at the close of the war at Gainsborough Studios in North London, then expanding to such outposts as the island of Tobago, South Africa, New Zealand, Australia, Sweden, Italy, Spain and Malaysia.

Carol Reed: The Man Behind the Third Man

The great brick structure at 213 Kings Road bespeaks of a man and a tradition, the residence of one of Britain's cinema giants. It is situated in one of the busiest sections of that most international of cities, London, that of Chelsea, where so many of history's immortals lived.

At 213 Kings Road, one is impressed by the vastness of what was once one impressive house, which is now divided between second floor flats and businesses on the ground level. Two blue plaques with white lettering encrusted against the brick structure inform passers-by of the identities of two entertainment notables who resided there. The first plaque is in honor of Ellen Terry, one of the leading stage actresses of Victorian England. The house was initially built for her, and holds a familial linkage to the great film director who resided there much later for the better part of three decades.

The second plaque spells out volumes in a few succinctly chosen words:

SIR CAROL REED
FILM DIRECTOR
LIVED HERE
1948–1976

Sir Carol Reed died April 25, 1976. He moved into the large house at the zenith of his powers, the year that his enduring masterpiece, *The Third Man*, was being filmed. British stage aficionados are also aware that the home's original occupant, the celebrated Ellen Terry, performed opposite Reed's father, Sir Herbert Beerbohm Tree, one of Victorian England's most celebrated actors and theater impresarios.

While his legendary father died in 1917, before Carol Reed had reached his teens, Carol was very much his father's son in manner and recognition. His was a playful youth rooted in studying people and reading. These traits would remain with him his entire life. On those few occasions when Reed was not actively engaged in directing a film, he would divide his time between reading books and screenplays, ever on the lookout for a filmable property, and in the pastime of observing people. His son Max recalled that in his youth his father would take him to the Cumberland Hotel, located near London's Marble Arch, to observe the behavior of people in the lobby. Max was told by his father that the way to learn about human nature was to observe how people walked and talked. When Reed purchased a flat on the French Riviera in Cannes, the location was not that of the sumptuous sea view available to someone of his position and wealth, but one situated in the older section of town. Reed's main attraction was the busy bus station observable below. The famous director would sit comfortably on the balcony with a pair of binoculars, carefully studying the activities of people going to and coming from the bus station, resembling the James Stewart character in Alfred Hitchcock's *Rear Window*.

Drifting from Acting to Directing

In the manner of David Lean, young Reed showed a marked disinclination for academic pursuits. The reason was the same: a propensity for creative activity. Whereas Lean spent much of his Croydon youth sneaking into film theaters, even when his parents preferred him spending time elsewhere, young Reed lived in a world of drama, that of human characterization. He saw within himself the potential to become another Sir Herbert Beerbohm Tree. At one point, hoping to find a career for young Reed away from dramatic pursuits, he was sent abroad by his family. Guy Hamilton, who would later become a Reed directing protégé, recounted an anecdote about that period.

"Carol was sent to Canada by his family in hopes that he would become a farmer," Hamilton explained, "but before he ever reached there he was caught up in a mix-up at Ellis Island. He met a young man there at Ellis Island who had been there long enough so that he could provide Carol with helpful advice. That young man was Mike Romanoff, who became well known later by running one of the most famous restaurants in Beverly Hills, and one that was a favorite meeting spot for the film colony."

The plaque at 213 Kings Road in Southwest London's colorful Chelsea area informs passersby that this was where the distinguished director Sir Carol Reed lived during his most productive period, extending to the time of his death. Chelsea has been a popular area for London's creative set. One of Reed's neighbors was Peter Ustinov. Several blocks to the south in Sloane Square is located the Royal Court Theatre, where post–World War II drama history was made with the debut of John Osborne's provocative play, *Look Back in Anger*.

This was the same Mike Romanoff who played himself in *In a Lonely Place.* Humphrey Bogart was a regular patron at his restaurant, as was Alfred Hitchcock. Cinemagoers can be grateful that Reed ultimately returned to England and never pursued a farming career.

In addition to being Sir Herbert Beerbohm Tree's son with his acute dramatic preferences, the young man who blossomed into early manhood resembled him in appearance as well, inheriting his father's tall, upright bearing as well as his aristocratic good looks. By the time he turned 18, his father's acquaintances remarked on their physical similarities. There was one area, though, where he would never prove his father's equal, that of acting.

Reed was philosophical about that period of his earliest contact with London's theatrical scene, recognizing his shortcomings but noting the practical experience he derived from acting as a way station en route to his life's work, film directing. This experience enabled him to interact so empathetically with actors that he became known as an actor's director. It was through those early acting efforts that he would meet his first significant role model, a man with a reputation in the artistic world akin to that of his father.

Edgar Wallace was justifiably a legend in his own time, astounding London by his prolific skills as a mystery novelist. To Wallace, writing came as naturally as talking. He dictated scores of manuscripts to a shorthand secretary, and they rapidly became best sellers. Wallace then sought a new world to conquer, the London stage. He took a liking to the soft-spoken, hard-working Reed, diverting him from acting into stage-managing and, ultimately, an all-purpose protégé. The opportunity enabled Reed to develop the kind of all-encompassing perspective he would need as a director.

The workaholic director was likely to find but one type of person who could relate to his world, which existed exclusively in the realm of films: an actress. He married twice and both wives were famous British performers. Reed married Diana Wynyard in 1943 and Penelope Dudley Ward, better known as "Pempie," in 1948. The second union endured for the rest of Reed's life.

Peter Ustinov, a neighbor of Reed's on King's Road during the 50s, observed that it was impossible to interest the famous director in any topic but films. Reed once asked, during an extended conversation outside his realm, "What's a Cold War?"

Hollywood beckoned the talent of Edgar Wallace as the early talkies period began to bloom. Had Wallace been able to establish a niche in Hollywood it is entirely conceivable that the directing career of Carol Reed would have begun there rather than London. Instead of achieving the anticipated film triumphs in Hollywood, Wallace's stay was short and tragic. Wallace fell ill and died before he could complete the screenplay on which he was then working, *King Kong*.

A New Mentor and a Cinema Launching

Wallace was a link established by the solid work ethic of young Carol Reed. His next major influence was forged by a linkage to his father. While Reed was sad and dismayed over the death of Wallace, an enterprising director provided him with a fresh opportunity.

Basil Dean had been given a chance by Sir Herbert Beerbohm Tree similar to that Reed had received from Edgar Wallace. Dean became a trusted subordinate of Tree. Remembering the good turn provided by Tree, Reed was given an opportunity to learn the film business by Dean. Product was in demand in London as well as Hollywood. While Reed had been trained in the stage, his love of the camera prompted a career turn from which he would never deviate. From that point on, his world would revolve around the cinema.

When Reed was in need of a job following his mentor Wallace's death, Dean hired him. By then Dean was enjoying success in that new cinema craze, "The Talkies," founding in 1932 Associated Talking Pictures. He was head of the film studios at Ealing, a suburb west of London. Success in any area of endeavor involves timing. Just as Reed was the right man at the right time under Edgar Wallace, the same applied to Basil Dean, who was just embarking on a string of musical successes starring George Formby and Gracie Fields. Dean observed that the energetic Reed shared many of his famous father's qualities, which would be of use to him in making talking films.

Reed's valuable stage experience served him well in a new niche of the rapidly developing world of celluloid and sound. Before the evolution of directors who could both select the pictures and direct actors in their lines, silent directors relied on dialogue coaches. Reed became one of the first of a new breed that was not long needed as shrewd directors, such as the young Alfred Hitchcock (the first British director to use sound), made the passage from silent to sound films successfully. This phase provided Reed with a beginning in films.

The first film where Reed directed scenes was Dean's *Autumn Crocus* (1934), which starred West End matinee idol Ivor Novello and Fay Compton. After spending three years learning his craft as a dialogue coach and assistant director, Reed was given his first opportunity to direct a film. He shared activity with another young director, Robert Wyler, in *It Happened in Paris*, a French play adapted by another screen personage destined to ultimately achieve greatness as a director, John Huston. Nicholas Wapshott noted: "Nothing remains of the film, but contemporary reports describe it as the story of a wealthy American who studies painting in Paris and poses as a poor man. It was released on December 9, 1935, and must have been at least a satisfactory debut, for Dean handed Reed a script of *Midshipman Easy* and told him to direct the picture himself. So Reed began his directing career."

During his early period, Reed was in no position to exert the control he later was able to wield concerning material. He was grateful to be given an opportunity, as manifested by his remarks years later in a lecture to film students: "It did not occur to me to wonder if the script was good or bad. I accepted it with gratitude. One can try to pick and choose too much before one has established oneself. I have seen many people fail because they have not realized they were being given an opportunity which would probably never come their way again. Don't wait, therefore, for the ideal thing, but take the chance that comes and make sure that you do everything to make a success of it."

While Reed developed his craft by turning out light and engaging entertainments, he stated his belief that the British cinema would soon be tackling more weighty subject matter. He received his opportunity to contribute to the early development of that trend with his first dramatic blockbuster, the 1939 classic *The Stars Look Down*, an adaptation of an A.J. Cronin best-selling novel about a mining disaster. It starred Michael Redgrave and Margaret Lockwood. Some of the stoutest praise for the film came from film critic Graham Greene, who would be seeing a great deal of Reed after the war. Reed followed up immediately on his great success with his next effort, in many ways a remake of Hitchcock's *The Lady Vanishes*: the 1940 release *Night Train to Munich*, in which Rex Harrison spirits Margaret Lockwood and her scientist father to safety from the pursuing Nazis.

While David Lean and Noel Coward filmed the definitive story about the

British Navy in World War II with the compelling 1942 release, *In Which We Serve*, Reed directed the comparably powerful film about the British Army, *The Way Ahead*, released in 1944. Private Peter Ustinov adapted the screenplay from an Eric Ambler story while also making his debut as an actor in the film, which featured David Niven, Stanley Holloway and the director's future wife, Penelope Dudley Ward.

Making his film debut in *The Way Ahead* along with the aforementioned Ustinov was a young soldier who, hearing that Reed was casting a film and wanting to become an actor, submitted his picture to the director. It was the beginning of a great career for Trevor Howard, who would eventually play a major role in Reed's enduring classic, *The Third Man*.

Guy Green was a talented young cinematographer who also received a solid career boost after being hired by Reed for *The Way Ahead*. The battle sequences at the end of the film are devastating in their close-up realism of the grit of mid–twentieth century combat. Green, who would later go on to a highly successful career as a director, had been recommended to Reed by a film legend to be who was already making a mark in the British cinema.

"I was recommended to Carol Reed for *The Way Ahead* by David Lean," Green revealed. "I had worked with David and I admired them both as directors. David was very much a technician and had everything worked out in advance. With Carol he had a passion for the story and working with the actors."

Green recalled one occasion when Reed's brilliant skill at working with actors enabled him to rescue what could have been a disastrous occasion into one of improvisational triumph. "Carol was having the hardest time to get an actor to do his lines correctly," Green recalled. "Finally he told the actor to go ahead and mumble his lines and it turned out to be effective."

Guy Green worked as camera operator to cinematographer Ronald Neame, another individual later destined to achieve recognition as a director, on *In Which We Serve* and *This Happy Breed*. In the earlier film he photographed the fighting sequences after being sent on a destroyer by Lean to the South Atlantic. His efforts would hold him in good stead when he filmed battle sequences for Reed. Sitting comfortably in his Beverly Hills home, he recalled his experiences during that pivotal moment in his career when he shot the North African battle sequences.

"I remember arriving with Carol along with the cast and crew in Tripoli," Green said. "Gen. Montgomery and his British troops had gone and now the Americans were there. We arrived just before Christmas. I'll never forget seeing Carol and an American colonel running after a turkey which would be our Christmas meal and finally tracking it down."

The Way Ahead shows the progression of the initially growling malcontents ultimately honed to fighting edge for the desert campaign. It was only natural for the film to conclude by showing the soldiers in action. The brilliant battle footage blended the cinematic instincts of Green as a cameraman and Reed as a director.

"We did very little actual shooting at Tripoli, mainly trench action," Green explained. "We moved on to the town of Bizerta and that was where the major action took place. As I said, the Americans were occupying the area there at the time and cooperated with us by blowing up some buildings that had already been substantially damaged. We spent three to four weeks shooting there and did it all with two cameras."

Not only did the American military supply helpful assistance to the film crew; a Scottish colonel also supplied help in a practical manner. "One time when we needed an explosion, we learned that the piece was too large for our purposes," Green said. "The colonel said the piece needed to be cut in half so he asked us to give it to him. I watched as he took it behind a building and broke it in half."

Another incident also stood out in Green's mind from the period. He and the members of the cast and crew had been transported by car from Algiers to Tripoli, upon which things changed for the better. "We had been on British rations all along, but when we reached Tripoli the Americans provided us with breakfasts including bacon, eggs and orange juice," Green said. "We got some luxury once the Americans became involved and we were all thankful for that."

Great craftsmen often have a facility for imparting their successful techniques to young assistants, who go on to achieve later greatness. In Green's case, in addition to his aforementioned directorial success, he secured an Oscar for his camerawork in David Lean's memorable screen rendering of the Charles Dickens novel *Great Expectations*.

Ken Annakin received a golden opportunity under Reed during the filming of *We Serve*, a documentary highlighting the efforts of British women during the war, with a cast of many of the nation's most memorable actresses, including Diana Wynyard and Margaret Rutherford.

"I had been operating my camera and finally Carol told me that I could be of service on the other side," Annakin said. "After that experience, I went on to direct documentaries during the rest of the war, and when I got the chance after the war to direct my first feature, *Holiday Camp*, I took as my model a fine film Carol had directed, *Bank Holiday*."

Annakin, after serving an apprenticeship under Reed, received his opportunity to direct features from producer Sydney Box at Gainsborough Studios. His first feature was so successful that a series was launched. Years later, residing in Beverly Hills near his friend Guy Green, Annakin, like Green, has nothing but fond memories of Reed. In the manner of Green, Annakin lauds Reed for his skills in working with actors as well as for his technical expertise.

"You not only learned a lot from Carol Reed by watching him on the set, but also by talking to him," Annakin explained. "He was completely absorbed in the cinema. Starting out as an actor as Carol did made a good deal of difference in his ability to handle actors. He understood that actors need to work up to a scene and then cool down to get it just right. He believed it was unkind to say 'Stand here and do this' and would run a rehearsal to see how it goes. Carol would give the actor a chance to slide into the naturalness needed for a convincing portrayal."

In addition to citing the sensitivity of Reed in working with actors, Annakin also noted another important element which contributed to his greatness as a director. "Carol believed that if you were going to have a successful film, it was necessary to tell a story," Annakin revealed. "You were making a film for an audience. You must have your characters as believable as possible. I believe that Carol was highly influenced by his association with Edgar Wallace. After all, Wallace was the most prolific fiction writer of his period. Pick up his books and you find wonderful stories. Watch Carol's movies and you find wonderful stories. The early influence of Wallace taught Carol the importance of a good story just as his acting experience as a young man taught him the importance of letting actors work things out in their minds before running the camera. He had a great respect for actors. For instance, Carol had a steadfast rule that you never shouted 'Cut' until the actors had walked out of the scene."

Once the war ended, the established Carol Reed would make the same quantum leap that creative directors and writers were making on both sides of the Atlantic. Now that a great conflict was over, people who had endured suffering, hardship and the deaths of relatives and loved ones were ready to accept a greater realism and variety in filmmaking than ever before. As the term film noir came into increasing vogue, creative artists such as Reed were more than happy to accept the challenge.

For Reed, the period between 1947 to 1949 saw him catapult to new heights of achievement and acceptance with the release of three films. Reed's partner in this endeavor was a colorful Eastern European, someone every bit as fascinating as the most interesting characters to emerge from any film he produced.

The Korda Trio

Reed was the kind of director who liked other details resolved for him so he could concentrate on finding interesting film topics, then provide his deft touch to bring an impressive product to the screen. His partnership with Alexander Korda suited his objectives perfectly.

Korda left his native Hungary and eventually worked his way to England. At one point he was married to the beautiful actress Merle Oberon. Ensconced in a penthouse suite at the Claridges Hotel, eminent figures of society were every bit as disposed to visit him as film figures wishing to discuss projects. While some visitors were rudely disrupted by the steady bomb assaults of Hitler's Luftwaffe during the Battle of Britain, with posh Mayfair in the West End a frequent target, Korda would remain unruffled, going on to sip champagne or discuss details of a film idea through all the commotion.

Guy Hamilton was a young man in his middle twenties working for Korda when he received a major opportunity to work as assistant director with Reed in two of the three masterpieces emanating from the partnership between the cinema giants. "Korda was a marvelous character," Hamilton recalled. "Here was a continental refugee who

Sir Carol Reed, far right, is seen during a rare evening of socializing at Chasen's Restaurant, a favorite of the Hollywood film crowd. Ironically, while most of the great director's work was done in his native England and other parts of Europe, his lone Academy Award as Best Director came for a 1968 musical filmed in the cinema capital, *Oliver!*, which garnered six statuettes, including Best Picture.

overcame adversity. He was an enormously lovable man. He was chased out of his native Hungary. Then he was chased out of Berlin when the political climate became so difficult. Then he went to France and finally to London."

As in the case of so many dynamic achievers, Korda was a man who could profit from adversity, becoming invested with a confidence that was infectious. His worldly knowledge also gave him an enhanced perspective in dealing with international film subject matter, as will be later noted.

The first of the dynamic Reed-Korda trio resulted from the director's constant pursuit of good story material. Reed read a review of an F.L. Green novel, *Odd Man Out*, and was intrigued enough to buy a copy. He was familiar with Green in that Diana Wynyard had appeared in a film based on another Green novel, *On the Night of the Fire*, released at the beginning of the war. Green's authenticity of the political conflict and intrigue of Belfast was based on his having moved to the famous Northern Ireland city from his native England after marrying an Irish wife. Eager to film *Odd Man Out*, Reed located Green in Belfast, seeking to interest him in adapting his novel to the screen. While eager to please, Green, having had no exposure to film writing, was diffident. Reed resolved that potential problem by assigning R.C. Sherriff, a film professional who had scripted *Goodbye Mr. Chips*, to assist the novelist.

According to film historian Ephraim Katz, "Reed, one of Britain's finest directors, made his name with this haunting, lyrical masterpiece about a doomed fugitive. In perhaps the greatest performance of his illustrious career, [James] Mason plays Johnny, an IRA leader who breaks out of jail and then plans a payroll holdup of a mill in Belfast to fund his underground operations."

Mason, with his highly distinctive voice and style, had made his mark two years earlier as the elegant Yorkshire native in the highly acclaimed *The Seventh Veil* with Ann Todd. The paradox of Johnny McQueen's life that tortures him is that, while personally deploring violence, he gets caught up in its ugly clutches and is doomed by it. After accidentally killing a man in the holdup, in which he is critically wounded, Johnny is left behind by the panicky driver of the getaway car.

The unique genius of *Odd Man Out* is that, whereas most suspense films would culminate with the main character being shot and ultimately losing his life, the film focuses almost entirely on the period after that episode, revealing through the dark hues of cinematographer Robert Krasker's camera the agony of a brooding man slowly dying, falling periodically into the clutches of those who seek monetary gain by selling him to British authorities as well as those who wish to help him. Meanwhile his sweetheart Kathleen (Kathleen Ryan) and his IRA compatriots seek to locate him. Mason's *tour de force* is enhanced by the convincing manner in which he portrays a delirious man reacting to rapid loss of blood.

Perhaps the most unforgettable relationship Mason forms, however, involve none of the above, but his encounter with a highly eccentric painter when he enters a pub. Robert Newton etched an arresting character portrait as a man dominated by his own selfish wish to paint a man in the final throes of death. Before the mad and tenacious painter can realize his objective of capturing the final death look in Mason's eyes, the dying fugitive retreats toward the docks in a last desperate attempt to escape from his pursuers. While his faithful lover Ryan is there to meet him, so are the relentlessly pursuing police.

Odd Man Out marked the emergence of Reed into an area with which he would thereafter be known as an accomplished master, that of dark, shadowy photographic hues. Robert Krasker's brilliant cinematography enhanced the image of a world in which one man was trapped helplessly, the perfect mood setting for such photography. Ephraim Katz delivered appropriate tribute: "A great work of art, *Odd Man Out* is a painting on celluloid, evoking the best canvases of Goya and Velazquez." It was accordingly no surprise that Rouben Mamoulian, an acknowledged master of style in film, referred to Reed as a "stylist" for whom he held great admiration.

From a Child's Eyes

Following Reed's triumph with *Odd Man Out* in 1947, he teamed up with internationally renowned novelist and former *Spectator* movie critic Graham Greene. It marked the first of three occasions when Reed and Greene collaborated, two of which were during the Korda period. *The Fallen Idol*, a 1948 release, was perhaps even more unique in its daring originality than *Odd Man Out*.

The Fallen Idol involves the potentially tragic dilemma of Baines, an embassy butler, who is investigated by police after his wife, played by Sonia Dresdel, dies in what was really an accidental fall from a stairway. Police suspicions increase when it is learned that Baines, played by Ralph Richardson, was involved in a loveless marriage and enamored with a Frenchwoman (Michele Morgan) working as an embassy typist. Into this dramatic package emerges eight-year-old Felipe, played by Bobby Henrey. The film's perspective is that of the young boy. In his attempt to save Richardson from being charged with a murder he never committed, his persistent but bungling efforts come close to implicating the man he idolizes. Only when police detective Jack Hawkins discovers dirt on the staircase left from a potted plant dropped by Henrey, which prompted the deceased to slip and plunge to her death, is Richardson finally exonerated. Bernard Lee, later to appear in *The Third Man*, portrays a detective.

Guy Hamilton was working for Korda when Reed interviewed him for an assistant director's position on *The Fallen Idol*. It proved to be an auspicious boost that would eventually see him establish himself as a famous director with *Goldfinger* and three other Bond films to his credit, along with the World War II aerial epic *The Battle of Britain*.

"I would have to say that Carol Reed was my film father," Hamilton acknowledged from his home in picturesque Majorca. "When I was interviewed for *The Fallen Idol* I'd had very little experience, but Carol never focused on that. Instead he focused on ideas, on how I viewed things. He was interested in finding out if we could work successfully together."

Hamilton has definite ideas on what made Reed a brilliant director:

"Carol was an actor in the beginning and not a very good one. He realized this and adjusted by moving over behind the camera. His reverence for actors remained with him and he worked marvelously with them. He also was a wonderful editor and would spend as much time as needed to get just what he wanted. The end result was what mattered to him, so much so that he would actually sacrifice a beautiful photographic scene if he believed that, for the sake of the movie, it should be cut."

Reed's relationship with Henrey in *The Fallen Idol*, along with later successes in *A Kid for Two Farthings* and *Oliver!*, stamped him as a director of consummate skill at working with young actors. "Carol was interested in hiring Henrey not for any natural talent but for his freshness," Hamilton explained. "Carol got Bobby Henrey, an eight-year-old boy, to concentrate on what was happening by keeping him always amused and preoccupied. He had a magician come on the set and do tricks. That would engage the youngster's attention and he would shoot the scene. Sometimes he would have Henrey look over at me. That was how he was able to get him to concentrate."

While Robert Krasker would serve as cinematographer for two films of the great Reed-Korda trio, it was Krasker's mentor, Georges Perinal, who served the director's intentions well in *The Fallen Idol* with expressive angles and stylized lighting. Many scenes were shot from the top of the stairs, with Henrey perched as an observer watching the drama develop.

The Fallen Idol received a British Best Film award while Reed was honored as Best Director by the New York Film Critics. The director also received an Oscar nomination, as did Graham Greene in the Best Screenplay category.

Two great films had been made by the Reed-Korda tandem with *Odd Man Out* in 1947 and *The Fallen Idol* in 1948. A magnificent encore awaited the anxious eyes of critics and world film audiences one year later.

A Film for the Ages

The Third Man (1949)

Only rarely in the world of cinematic art does a film achieve the justifiable stamp of classic, a term earned through the collaborative effort of many, finely attuned to the ultimate object of a work of distinction. *The Third Man* is deserving of such acclaim. In 1999, its fiftieth anniversary since its initial British release, it impressed as the same masterpiece that critics and film professionals labeled it. It was seen during a special run in connection with its golden anniversary. It is a film that impresses on many levels, characteristic of classics, the sharp-eyed storytelling, the superb pacing by the director, skillful acting, and insightful, richly hued photography. Also, as with so many classics, serious roadblocks needed to be surmounted before success was achieved.

The original idea for *The Third Man* was born in the fecund creative mind of Graham Greene, but it was Alexander Korda who gave it an ingenious twist. The magnificent result made it appear that *The Third Man* and the Old World charm mixed with the skullduggery and intrigue of Vienna were a natural blend from day one. Such was not the case.

"Graham Greene discussed his idea with Korda in his office," Guy Hamilton reflected. "He wanted to write a screenplay about a man who was walking down the street on the Strand amid the crowds of London's West End and suddenly saw on the other side of the street a man whose funeral he had attended. Korda liked the intrigue of the story premise but added a new twist. He said that he thought such a discovery would be much more powerful and effective if it happened in Vienna rather than London."

Vienna is situated next door to the border of Hungary, Korda's native country, and the wily producer was aware of the cloak-and-dagger activity occurring there at the end of the war. The active black market activity would ultimately form the story genesis of *The Third Man* with Harry Lime's intense involvement in it. Another intriguing element for a shrewd storyteller like Greene was the division of the city at the end of the war, with sections of control and authority involving Russia, the United States, Great Britain and France.

Greene journeyed to Vienna. According to Reed biographer Nicholas Wapshott, Greene became immersed in problems over just what to write about. Despite the city's obvious intrigue, he searched hard for a story. When he visited the Prater, Vienna's great amusement park, Greene was struck by the fact that while the rest of it lay in World War II ruins, the Great Wheel had survived. Greene's impression put to paper would form the backdrop for one of the most memorable scenes in film annals. He visited backstage at the old Josefstadt Theatre, which he later would use as the place where Joseph Cotten and Alida Valli met. Despite his fascinating discoveries, Greene was stumped after ten days as an observer.

According to Nicholas Wapshott, Greene's luck suddenly changed and his story began falling into place after Greene was steered to a knowledgeable young British Intelligence officer, Charles Beauclerk, who provided him with two important information sources that would ultimately fire the British writer's imagination. Greene was particularly fascinated when told by Beauclerk about the Underground Police, who had the responsibility of patrolling Vienna's vast underground sewer network. In a partitioned city, divisions could be overcome by stealthily moving from one power's area of authority to another in the darkness of this labyrinthian underground.

Greene discovered that the main sewer flowed like an underground river and that the air was actually sweet smelling. According to Greene's recollection: "The main sewer, half as wide as the Thames, rushes by under a huge arch, fed by tributary streams: these streams have fallen in waterfalls from higher levels and have been purified in their fall, so that only in the side channels is the air foul. The main stream smells sweet and fresh with a faint tang of ozone, and everywhere in the darkness is the sound of falling and rushing water."

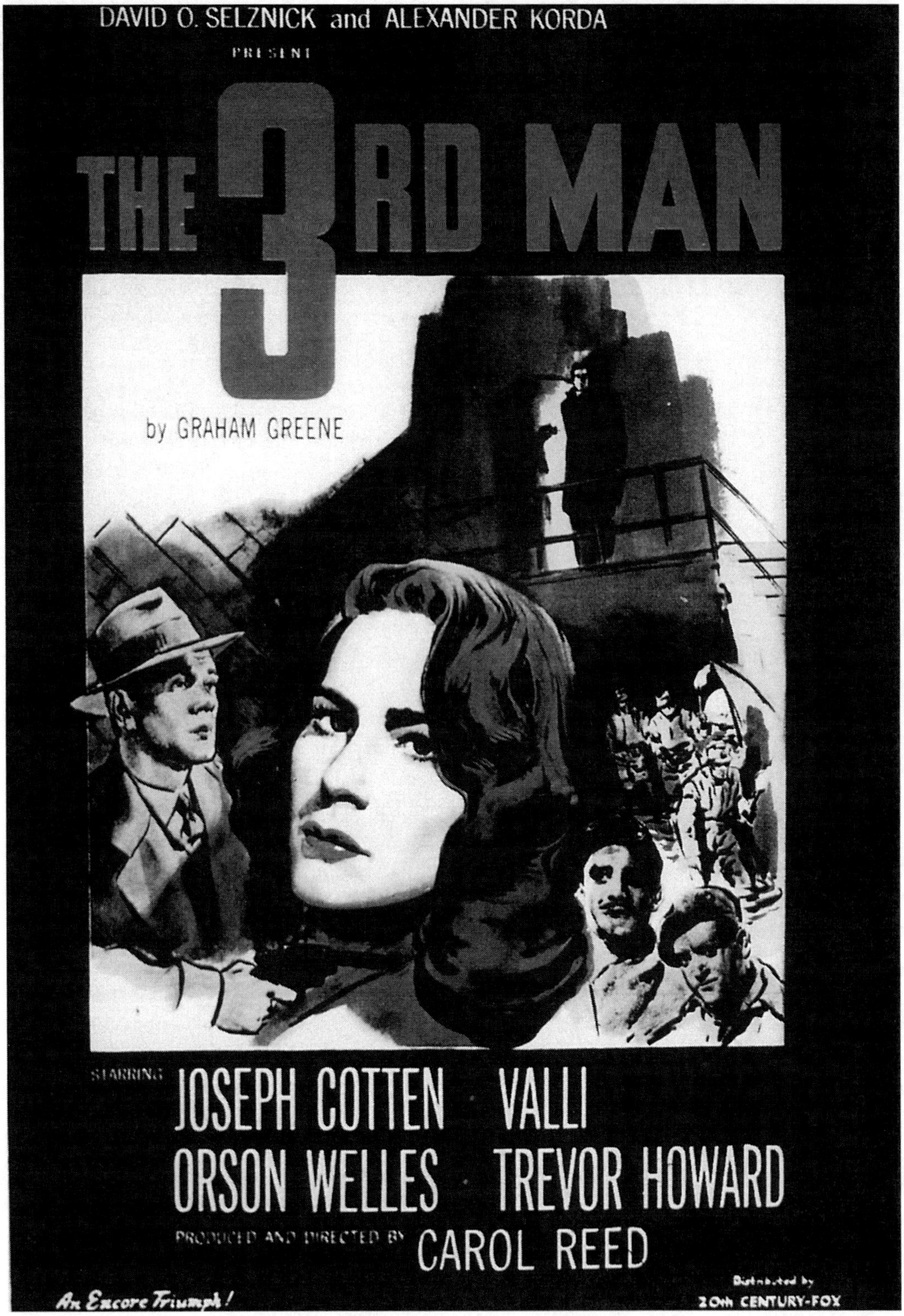
DAVID O. SELZNICK and ALEXANDER KORDA
PRESENT
THE 3RD MAN
by GRAHAM GREENE
STARRING
JOSEPH COTTEN · VALLI
ORSON WELLES · TREVOR HOWARD
PRODUCED AND DIRECTED BY CAROL REED
An Encore Triumph!
Distributed by
20th CENTURY-FOX

While the idea of photographing the Vienna sewers and involving the Underground Police would certainly appeal to the imagination of Reed, this was not enough to constitute a story. Another element needed to be added. According to Wapshott, Beauclerk once more came to the rescue by telling Greene about a sordid racket plaguing Vienna in the post-war period, that of illegally purchasing penicillin from corrupt military personnel, then reselling it on the black market after diluting it.

In the recent account of the making of the great film *In Search of "The Third Man,"* published to coincide with its fiftieth year anniversary, Charles Drazin provides another source for Greene's script subject matter. Korda operative Elizabeth Montagu had preceded the writer to Vienna. According to Drazin, Montagu provided a repository of information for Greene on contemporary Vienna when she provided the writer shortly after his arrival with stories by London *Times* journalist Peter Smollet, who also met the noted author. A few months later, Montagu discovered that Greene's script had drawn heavily on situations and background details of Smollet's stories. Smollet had indicated a willingness to help him, hoping that Greene would assist him in locating a publisher for his Vienna stories.

Initially, after discovering how many details Greene had drawn upon from Smollet's stories, particularly the significant *Third Man* plot information about diluting antibiotics at a children's hospital, Montagu became upset that Smollet's contribution had not been acknowledged by Greene. In the words of Drazin, "the evidence suggests there was nothing underhand in Greene's conduct, and that in the end Greene did help Smollet even if it was not to get his stories published. For in June 1948 Smollet was duly hired by London Film Productions to give 'advice on the film script at present entitled *The Third Man* and to provide assistance in Vienna in connection with the production of a film to be based there.' His fee was 200 guineas, which was probably a good deal more than most publishers of the time would have been prepared to offer for a book of short stories by an unknown writer."

Now Greene was on his way. With his strong writer's propensity for amassing helpful research, Greene likely used both Beauclerk and Smollet as information sources. There was nothing like a sewer chase to bring a dramatic climax to a story in which a ruthless criminal, no matter how charming Harry Lime was on the surface, received his just end. He was eventually tracked down with the aid of his oldest friend, Holly Martins.

Once that Greene and Reed had determined that the story would be built around a friendship involving two men, a major discussion was launched on both

***Opposite:* The land of Shakespeare and Marlowe was the perfect venue for brooding film noir drama. Alexander Korda and David O. Selznick realized this potential, marketing it to astounding international success with the 1949 British production, *The Third Man*, which was distributed by Twentieth Century–Fox. Orson Welles would later regret that he took his entire acting fee up front rather than accepting a percentage since, in his words, the film in Europe "was as popular as *The Sound of Music*."**

sides of the Atlantic over how the film would be cast. Moving into the picture at that moment was someone with definite ideas on casting and story elements. David Selznick, Korda's production partner for *The Third Man,* was responsible for American distribution and determined to move the production slant, at least to some extent, away from its continental European emphasis.

The project was initially perceived by director and scenarist to involve two Englishmen in the top roles. Penciled into the minds of Reed and Greene at one point were Cary Grant and Noel Coward, with the older actor portraying Harry Lime. When Reed and Greene flew across the Atlantic to discuss ideas with Selznick, the producer contributed vital input into one basic area, casting. His producer's eye prompted him to think about the important American market. For a time, James Stewart was considered for the role that eventually went to Selznick contractee Joseph Cotten. As for the ubiquitous Lime, Selznick was high on Robert Mitchum, but when the actor was jailed on his well publicized possession of marijuana conviction attention turned back to a world-famous film figure toward whom Selznick was not eagerly disposed.

"Selznick was against the idea of having Orson Welles play Harry Lime," Guy Hamilton recalled. "He believed he would be box office poison in places like the American Middle West. It was Carol who was always in favor of giving Welles the Lime role."

An Inauspicious Debut

Once Reed's instincts were acted upon and Welles was given the role, it became a waiting game for him to arrive in Vienna. Welles was contracted for two sessions before the camera, one in Vienna, where the famous sewer chase scene would occur, and the other at Shepperton Studios outside London, where the interior of the Prater's Ferris wheel was constructed with the aerial photography of Vienna superimposed. Welles later regretted the deal he struck. "I was given a choice between $100,000 or something like 20 percent of the picture and I took the $100,000," Welles lamented. "Picture grossed, you know, something unbelievable. Because in America it was only a success, but in the rest of the world it was an absolute bombshell—it was *The Sound of Music*, you know. There was never such a hit in 25 years as there was in Europe. I could have retired on that."

Guy Hamilton explained that much of the creativity in extending the scene involving the first meeting between Joseph Cotten and Orson Welles resulted in waiting for the director of *Citizen Kane* to arrive in Vienna. "That was how the sequence with the cat came about," Hamilton said. "We were stretching things out until Orson arrived."

Movie audiences can only be thankful that the delay occurred. The cat sequence invoked the cleverest subtlety as, after the fussy feline refused to cozy up to Cotten, Valli informs him that "he only liked Harry." Once the cat makes his escape out the window and darts across the cobblestoned street in the darkness, he finds some feet belonging to a shadowy figure in a doorway. When the cat begins affectionately licking the man's shoes, the audience is provided with a clue that this is Harry Lime, the man who at that juncture is supposed to be dead.

After Welles ultimately arrived by train and delivered one line in the morning to Cotten in front of the Ferris wheel, he returned for the evening's shooting in the sewer. At that point, the highly-strung Welles became enraged.

"He launched into an immediate tirade about being forced to work in a sewer," Hamilton reflected. "He said that we Europeans might be used to wallowing around like that but that he was an American and Americans even wrapped their food in cellophane. It made for a dramatic speech the way it was delivered but we were nervous when he stormed off. Fortunately Carol was able to bring him under control. Orson's problem may have been that he had just arrived and this was his first exposure to the sewer. We had been shooting there awhile and were used to it by then."

Craftsman Reed was super cool under pressure. After Welles finished delivering his dramatic tirade, Reed calmly exclaimed, "Well, it's his [Welles'] first day, he's nervous, and we've got so many other things to do. We will just have to build a sewer in Shepperton." This is what ultimately happened.

Selznick had cautioned Reed in a memo from America that Cotten and Welles were "frustrated writers" and would seek to alter Greene's screenplay through improvisation. The only alteration Cotten sought was changing his character's name from Rollo to Holly. Welles did some improvising in the famous Ferris wheel scene, with his final comment to Cotten, bristling with sophisticated wit and disdain for society, standing out:

"You know what the fellow said: In Italy, for 30 years under the Borgias they had warfare, terror, murder, bloodshed; they produced Michelangelo, Leonardo da Vinci and the Renaissance. In Switzerland, they had brotherly love, 500 years of democracy and peace, and what did they produce? The cuckoo clock. So long, Holly."

The Karas Story

One of the unique creative gems that Reed devised was using Anton Karas on his zither, opting for solo musical background in place of the traditional symphony orchestra. His unorthodox idea caused early top brass opposition, but the decision has been hailed by film critics and historians as a brilliant innovation.

As a firsthand participant and witness to events, Guy Hamilton unraveled the picture. Karas was first spotted by Reed not, as frequently reported, at a small sausage and beer establishment in a Vienna suburb, but at a dinner party given for Reed by Carl Hartl, the distinguished Austrian film producer, at his home. Hartl was the producer of the original *Sound of Music* in German. Karas was hired to play during the dinner.

"Carol took me aside and asked me the name of the instrument Karas was playing and I told him that I certainly knew," Hamilton chuckled. "Actually I didn't and made it a point to walk over and inquire. I was told that the instrument was called the zither. Carol was so fascinated afterwards that he had me find out the identity of the zither player so he could contact him."

It turned out that Karas was a freelance musician who worked special occasions such as dinner parties and wedding receptions. The zither player was finally located at a *Heurigan*, where he performed in Sievering, near the Vienna studios where many of the film's interiors were shot. A *Heurigen* was a place where winemakers would sell that season's wine. A meeting was arranged on a Sunday, the only day when Reed and crew were not shooting. When Karas arrived for his morning meeting with Reed, they loomed as a Mutt and Jeff combination with the director standing at well over six feet and the diminutive zither player at barely above five feet. After hearing a few chords of the fascinating sounds that had thrilled him weeks earlier, Reed sent his assistant to wake up the sound crew, who assembled in his bedroom with an old Klangfilm recorder, a cheap system used only for tests.

Once Reed broke through one wave of opposition at the production end over his unconventional decision to hire Karas, an influential voice of dissent surfaced when cast and crew reached England for interior shooting at Shepperton Studios. Dr. Hubert Clifford was Musical Director at Shepperton and served in that capacity for Reed on *The Fallen Idol*. "If you want a zither player then I will find you the best zither player in the world!" Clifford enthused. Reed responded that Karas served his purpose. Clifford then asked Reed how he intended to handle the insertions of music into the proper scenes.

"Carol had a ready answer for Dr. Clifford's question," Hamilton explained. "He said he would teach Anton to use the Moviola, and that he could then watch the film and adjust his musical selections to the sequences in the way that a regular musical director would do. It worked out fine."

The acting talent blended superbly as British, American and European influences mixed judiciously into a brilliantly evocative international film noir story about people and forces converging in four power Vienna after the war. Trevor Howard, who was given his first film role by Reed in *The Way Ahead*, was the voice of conscience as Major Calloway, who finally persuaded Cotten to serve as a decoy so Lime could be apprehended. Bernard Lee was convincing as Sergeant Paine, his faithful assistant. The teaming of Cotten with Welles was a reunion of the famed director of *Citizen Kane* and *The Magnificent Ambersons* and his most successful Mercury Theater protégé, who starred in both memorable films. The casting of the hauntingly beautiful Alida Valli was precipitated by Selznick, in that she was his discovery. Two of the most fascinating character performers were Viennese stage greats cast by Reed. Paul Hoerbiger is unforgettable as the porter who, after shunning danger, attempts to help Martins and is killed by Lime's thugs. Hedwig Bleibtreu endures as the crusty landlady of the apartment building where Anna resides; she thunders at the military police for their evening intrusion as they search Anna's premises.

Three units were involved in *The Third Man*. "There was a day crew, a night crew and a unit for the sewer scenes," Hamilton recalled. "Shooting would start at 9:00 and continue until it got dark, which in the Austrian winter was about 4:30. Shooting would then resume at 8:00." Cotten remembered well: "At various hours between midnight and sunrise, we would sit waiting in canvas chairs in the middle of some magnificent square or a mountain of bomb-shattered rubble. Some kind of property man would wrap us in blankets, and we would sit drinking coffee, or, if we were waiting for a mere action scene with no dialogue to twist tongues, there was always nearby a spike for stirring the coffee."

Cotten recalled an incident where Trevor Howard, a colorful actor who enjoyed a good time, decided following a long day of shooting to go out on the town. He did not bother to change his uniform and, when he was confronted by police after indulging of spirits and singing loudly in a saloon, the authorities were astounded to discover that Howard was not a bona fide British Army major and hauled him into jail for impersonating an officer. Reed and his production people used their influence to get Howard released.

"Well, I wanted a change of pace, and I certainly got it," Howard said afterwards.

"Good show, old chap," Reed responded, giving him the day off.

Reed's cinematographer from *Odd Man Out*, Robert Krasker, was provided with more experimental opportunities than in the earlier film shot in Belfast. *The Third Man* was one of the first films in which tilted photographic angles were liberally employed as Reed and Krasker were intent upon capturing a once glorious city desolated by war. The tilted frames caused cartoonists to later joke about the sloping tables and ceilings. The damp cobbled streets helped present a noir image of rain to enhance the brooding mood sought in the film.

Carol Reed later explained the rationale behind Krasker's photography:

> I shot most of the film with a wide-angle lens that distorted the buildings and emphasized the wet cobblestone streets (it cost a good deal to hose them down constantly). But the angle of vision was just to suggest that something crooked was going on. I don't think it's a very good idea. I haven't used it much since—only when I need to shoot someone standing behind another person who's sitting and I don't want to cut off his head.

Reed's response was that of a self-effacing perfectionist always searching for a better result. Look at the magnificent tapestry woven, especially in the evening shots, and what is observable is a stylized cinema presentation of struggling people trapped by fate and corruption in a great city profoundly altered by international conflict, mixing the finest elements of John Le Carre international intrigue and film noir with devastating results.

Another Reed ploy that fell outside the ambit of conventional cinema mode, along with the masterstroke of using Karas and his zither, was the use of a narrator to open the film. The voiceover united with scenes introducing viewers to Vienna, such as money changing hands in black market transactions and displaying check point military stations of Vienna as audiences are informed about the four power post-war status of the city. Veteran *New York Times* critic Bosley Crowther observed: "This voice, which belongs to nobody whom we later see in the film, is glib, shifty, cynical, sardonic—like the voice of a foxy tourist guide." The voice belonged to none other than Carol Reed. Reed had another uncredited performance in the film. When Welles was unavailable when his fingers appear through the grating of the sewer, Reed lowered himself into the culvert and lifted the manhole cover for the camera.

A Finale Inspired by Reed

Graham Greene originally had Holly Martins and Anna Schmidt exiting together through the Vienna Woods following Harry Lime's funeral. Carol Reed backed the view of David Selznick that an ending more appropriate for the fadeout of a typical Hollywood love story, where man and woman were united, was unjustifiable for *The Third Man*. After all, Martins had recently killed the man Anna loved, and Harry's second and real funeral had just concluded. Reed argued that Anna's leaving with the man who had killed her lover would jar audiences, who would see her response as cynical and out of character. Reed preferred a pessimistic ending in which Anna rejected Holly's reconciliation effort. The ultimate ending dovetailed with the prevailing mood of realism of film audiences after a devastating global conflict, the climate in which film noir flourished.

"I was afraid few people would wait in their seats during the girl's long walk from the graveside towards Holly," Greene explained, "and the others would leave the cinema under the impression that the ending was still going to be as conventional as my suggested ending of boy joining girl. I had not given enough credit to the mastery of Reed's direction, and at that stage, of course, we neither of us anticipated Reed's discovery of Anton Karas, the zither player. All I had indicated in my treatment was a kind of signature tune connected with Lime."

Joseph Cotten described the shooting of the film's final scene when, after Valli strolled out of camera view, he anticipated that Reed would shout "Cut" but instead, nothing happened. Reed was waiting to drain every dramatic moment from the film's finale:

"Nobody uttered a word. The camera kept rolling. The special effects men from their high perches continued to drop toasted autumn leaves from above. I continued to puff on my cigarette, and began to get quite panic-stricken. Was there more to the scene? Had I gone blank? What was Carol waiting for me to do? I took one more puff, then in exasperation threw the cigarette to the ground, at which point Carol shouted through his laughter the word I had been waiting desperately to hear—'Cut.'"

In addition to being a hit on both sides of the Atlantic, *The Third Man* secured numerous awards for Reed, while Krasker won an Oscar in the black and white cinematography department. Reed took first prize at the Cannes Film Festival, won Best Director honors from the New York Film Critics and was nominated for an Oscar.

Joseph Cotten is one popular American as he distributes care packages to happy Austrian children during the filming of *The Third Man*. The American producer of the British film, David O. Selznick, was concerned that screenwriter Graham Greene's portrayal of Cotten as a visiting bumbler in Vienna's world of post–World War II black marketers would show America in a bad light.

An Innocent in Vienna

Graham Greene's preoccupation with strong character conflict amid moral ambiguity is epitomized in the relationship between Holly Martins and Harry Lime. Martins has been summoned to Vienna by the man he acknowledges as his oldest friend to write about the medical charities with which Lime is purportedly involved. His child-like innocence heightens drama in that his clumsy and bumbling efforts produce the kind of astonishment wrought by discovery that would never occur in a man of worldly experience.

In the classic manner of master thriller writers such as Greene, the story begins with a shocking twist, the type only the most advanced professionals use since it would appear the end the story before it has begun, begging the question "Where do we go from here?" Holly Martins arrives at Lime's second floor apartment at Stiftgasse 15, only to be informed by the building's porter, played by Viennese veteran stage performer Hoerbiger, that his old friend is dead. Symbolic of war-weary Vienna and the need for reconstruction, the porter is changing a burnt-out light bulb when he sees Martins knocking on the door of Lime's apartment. He demonstrates his awkwardness with English as he explains Lime's death by mentioning that he has gone either to Heaven or Hell, pointing downward for Heaven and upward for Hell.

Cotten as Martins just has time to reach the cemetery for the funeral in progress of what is presumed at the time to be for Harry Lime. The classically beautiful Alida Valli looks hauntingly brooding while Trevor Howard as Major Calloway looks impassive. Lime's two main henchmen, Kurtz and Popescu, are also there. Scenarist Greene has constructed a scene introducing major characters Cotten will encounter in his Viennese adventure. As for the funeral, Cotten's clumsy forays will soon reveal that things are anything but what they seem to be. After the service, Howard, learning that Cotten had come to Vienna to see old friend Welles, offers to buy him a drink. Promptly their respective characters are delineated, an unsuspecting innocent writing hack Western novels on the one hand and a crafty, worldwise British Army officer on the other. These differences are particularly noticeable in a dialogue exchange:

> MARTINS: I guess nobody knew Harry like he did, like I did.... Best friend I ever had.
> CALLOWAY: That sounds like a cheap novelette.
> MARTINS: I write cheap novelettes.

The conversation continues and an inebriated Martins becomes incensed after Calloway reveals that Lime was "the worst racketeer that ever made a dirty living in this city." When Martins takes a clumsy, drunken swing at Calloway, his omnipresent assistant, Sergeant Paine, played by Bernard Lee, punches him with just enough force to thwart him. The scene ends on a note of subtle comedy after the sergeant hears Martin's name and reveals that he is a devoted fan of the American Western novelist. Calloway, remaining coolly professional, tells Paine to take Martins to the Sacher Hotel and get him a room, and that he will secure a ticket on the next day's plane back to America.

The Plot Thickens and a Trip Is Extended

Once more it is made to appear that the story is over rather than just beginning as Martins is supplied with a night's lodging and will receive a scarce ticket out of town and back to America through Calloway and the British Army. Fate quickly intervenes as a proud Paine informs a hotel guest, Crabbin, played by Wilfrid Hyde-White, of Martins's status as an author. The sergeant's pedestrian literary tastes prompt him to inflate the American's professional reputation. Crabbin, who arranges lectures as one of his functions at the local Cultural Re-Education Section, while not having heard of Martins, is impressed enough nonetheless to offer him an opportunity to address the group's next meeting. Martins, unqualified to speak on the current status of the novel, jumps at the opportunity when Crabbin agrees to stake him to lodging at the Sacher and pocket money for that period. This provides an increasingly curious Martins with a chance to investigate details surrounding the death of his friend.

The scene is replete with various twists. No sooner does Crabbin agree to Martins's terms than the telephone rings and the desk clerk reveals that the call is for him. Martins believes it must be a mistake since he does not know anyone in the city. The caller is Baron Kurtz, a friend of Lime's, who suggests that they meet at the Mozart Cafe around the corner from the Sacher Hotel. He tells him that Martins will be able to recognize him since he will be carrying one of the author's books, which had been given to him by Lime.

The meeting with Baron Kurtz, played by Ernst Deutsch, affords a dramatic contrast between the innocent American hack scribbler and the cunningly sleazy Viennese racketeer, revealing Martins as an Inspector Clousseau–style bumbler in over his head in a world he does not vaguely understand. The American's suspicions are enhanced when Kurtz tells him that Lime's final words concerned his longtime friend, and the need to look after him when he arrived in the city. The conversation occurs in the street outside the apartment building where Lime resided. A stunned Martins gestures toward the porter, who is sweeping the sidewalk, and exclaims, "But he said he died instantaneously." An unflappable Kurtz, a master of dissembling, promptly replies: "Well, he died before the ambulance could reach us."

The scene is evocative of the practice of masters of suspense dribbling details with slow shrewdness, holding the audience dramatically captive. Martins is told about a Romanian named Popescu who was also there when Harry Lime was struck down by a truck. When he expresses a desire to talk to him, he is informed that Popescu has left town. Martins inquires about the identity of the beautiful woman at the funeral and is informed that she is an actress at the Josefstadt Theatre. He learns that a Dr. Winkel, Lime's physician, had been quickly summoned to the scene. While far from an astute investigator, Holly Martins is shrewd enough to be suspicious about the events being described.

Unrequited Love

A romantic element is definitely involved in this moody film. It contains the kind of brooding complexity consistent with the finished product, involving a unique triangle. Holly Martins based his actions consistently on his love for Anna Schmidt while she cannot give up loving a man willing to discard and use her for his own benefit. An interesting aspect of this great psychological drama is that Alida Valli as Anna behaves in a manner more consistent with male figures from noir masterpieces. Her continued preoccupation with Harry Lime when he is thought to be dead is comparable to Dana Andrews as Detective Mark McPherson falling in love with Laura Hunt, thought at the time to be deceased. The difference between Valli's and Andrews' characters is that Valli has actually known Orson Welles but cannot give him up. Her obsessiveness in refusing to release her feelings for Welles even after she realizes his evil manner and lack of proper feeling for her is in some ways comparable to the hold that Jane Greer and Barbara Stanwyck held on two intelligent men who logically knew better, Robert Mitchum and Fred MacMurray in *Out of the Past* and *Double Indemnity* respectively.

Cotten's first meeting with Valli in her dressing room at the Josefstadt Theatre, where she is appearing in a costume comedy, reveals problems indigenous to post-war Vienna and throughout Europe. She tells Cotten that the theatrical proprietors are concerned about using the lights too long, a reference to electricity problems and blackouts. Valli reveals that the tea she is offering to Cotten was tossed on stage by an admiring Britisher opening night in place of flowers, a reference to food and drink scarcities. She expresses pleasure when he declines an offer of liquor, explaining that it was also a gift from an admirer and she would prefer selling it.

The woman's distraught condition is immediately manifested in response to a question Cotten asks about whether she loved Welles, to which she replies, "I don't know. How can you know a thing like that afterwards? I don't know anything more except I want to be dead too." The irony of her statement is enhanced by the contrast of her appearing on stage in a light comedy in which she smiles and prances in a carefree manner. She later tells Cotten that she works only in comedies.

The Greene practice of feeding his audience morsels slowly recurs as a new character is introduced to Holly Martins. In recounting Lime's final moments before death, she refers to Dr. Winkel, Harry's doctor, who happened to be passing by and arrived shortly after the accident. Anna further explains that "it was not the driver's fault. Harry had often said what a careful driver he was." The remark about the driver awakens Martins's darkest suspicions. He might be a clumsy investigator, but he is, after all, a writer, albeit a second-rate, formulaic one, and plotting is something he understands. Martins's nostrils observe a foul scent relating to the plot of the death of Harry Lime:

> MARTINS: I don't get it. All of them there—Kurtz, this Romanian Popescu, his own driver knocking him over, his own doctor just passing by? No strangers there at all.
>
> ANNA: I know. I've wondered about it a hundred times, if it really was an accident. What difference does it make? He's dead, isn't he?

When Martins informs her that the porter saw the accident, she goes with him to Harry's apartment, where a heated conversation with the porter develops. The porter becomes rattled by Martins' questioning and finally blurts out, "I was not the only one who did not give evidence." Martins pounces on the revelation in the manner of a hungry prosecuting attorney, asking the porter to explain his comment.

"There was a third man," the porter explains. "He didn't give evidence." A confused Holly asks if the porter means the doctor. The porter reveals that the doctor came later. Becoming increasingly rattled, the porter finally dismisses Martins. While doing so, he retrieves a ball belonging to a young child, who will play a major role in a pivotal scene later. The porter expresses regret that he did not follow his wife's advice and refuse to talk to Martins, adding tartly, "She said you were up to no good." He tells Anna not to bring Martins to the apartment building again.

Rounding Out the Cast of Culprits

Greene was probably the only rival to Somerset Maugham at mid-century in the art of presenting the lowest elements of international criminal society functioning at the most brilliantly orchestrated level. It was no accident that Britain used both writers as secret intelligence operatives during World War II. It was Maugham who summarized Monte Carlo with a pithy comment: "A sunny place for shady people." Greene completes his pastiche of Vienna black market low life by revealing two more characters in rapid sequences. When Martins visits Dr. Winkel in his flat, it is brutally symbolic that he finds him with a carving knife working on a turkey that has just been removed from an oven. This symbolism regarding cutthroat activity will be made abundantly clear later. The wily Greene drops clues and symbols one after another, keeping his viewers on their toes. An uncooperative Winkel stonewalls Martins, letting him know he has guests and cannot spend long talking to him.

The last Harry Lime cohort Martins meets is Popescu, who has returned to town. Kurtz, who plays a violin at the Casanova Club as his ostensible means of livelihood, finishes a number, then introduces Martins to his associate. Lime is in an intoxicated state and has to be calmed down by Anna when he begins loudly berating military police passing through the club. His loosened tongue will prove to be gravely devastating to the porter. After meeting Popescu, played by Siegfried Breuer, who tartly lets Martins know that people in Vienna are better off sticking to their own affairs, by now a highly familiar warning to the writer, the American blurts out that the porter has told him there was a third man who helped carry the dead man to the statue of Franz Josef, where he died. Popescu speaks with acid irony when he comments that it was up to the porter to give evidence at the hearing surrounding Lime's death, adding ironically that it is very difficult to teach Viennese residents to be good citizens.

A Tragic Death and Compounding Problems for Martins

While Holly is observed pacing the street where the alleged accident that took Lime's life occurred, the porter observes him from the upper window of Lime's apartment, calling out to him. His tone is apologetic, an obvious response to his earlier voice-raised conversation with Holly in Lime's apartment, in which he ordered the American to leave. "I am not a bad man," he explains. In recognition of his wife's constant admonition against becoming involved in the mysterious death, the porter explains that his wife will be gone in the evening and that he should return then. He finishes speaking to Martins and turns around, a terrified look on his face.

By the time that Martins arrives with Anna that evening, a crowd has gathered in the darkness. Martins is told by a bystander that the porter has been murdered. The man gestures to his throat, indicating that was how the porter died, linking that act to the symbolic turkey carving by the cold, non-communicative Winkel.

The little boy Hansel takes center stage, still holding the ball the porter retrieved for him. Hansel calls out to his father and begins accusing Martins of the porter's murder, recalling that he had been greatly upset with the American.

An uncomfortable rustling occurs in the crowd on the darkened street as the little boy begins to shout accusingly. Finally Martins runs away with Anna. The little boy, ball in hand, is seen pursuing Martins down the street until they find refuge in a movie theater. Martins and Anna agree to separate. It is the American's objective to see Calloway as soon as possible to report the murder of the porter.

A Great Misunderstanding

A clever writer's ploy was used by Greene to create a gigantic misunderstanding on the part of the audience through identifying with the story's equally confused protagonist. This sharp plot twist occurs when Martins arrives back at the Sacher Hotel after leaving the cinema. He asks the night clerk to secure a cab to take him to International Police Headquarters. The clerk nods knowingly and gestures toward a husky man dressed in black who sits nearby in a chair. The man jumps to his feet. Martins follows him outside to his waiting vehicle.

When Martins informs the man of his intended destination, he receives a swift jolt. The man does not hear him. He is not listening. Instead he starts up quickly and begins racing down the darkened streets of Vienna at a hellish pace. The stylized camerawork of Krasker under Reed's direction is some of the best of the film as the narrow winding streets of the old city are utilized with maximum impact. Also observed are the people of the city as their surprised faces are captured while the speeding van moves at breakneck speed. A terrorized Martins is convinced that he has met his end and will be delivered into the hands of Popescu, Kurtz and their trained minions. The fact that the driver is dressed in black and is a large, hulking man accents the impression that Holly is a doomed man.

The surprise element occurs when the driver screechingly applies his brakes, the vehicle comes to a quick stop, and Holly Martins is delivered into the hands of Crabbit at the Cultural Center. The anticipated famous American novelist is provided with rousing applause from the group, the lone occasion when it will display enthusiasm. Now Martins, who has given the lecture no thought beyond using it as a grubstake opportunity to remain in Vienna to investigate Harry Lime's murder, is on his own, a badly overmatched hack writer unable to answer questions put to him by serious students of literature. He knows nothing about James Joyce or the stream-of-consciousness element of literature. When the highly awkward appearing writer is asked which writer has chiefly influenced his work, he responds "Zane Grey." Crabbin, dabbing his forehead with a handkerchief as he becomes increasingly awkward while greater numbers of disgusted audience members leave the room, attempts to pass off Martins' reference to Western author Grey as "Mr. Martins' little joke."

The American writer's bungling performance provides a note of humor, particularly with Crabbin's increasing nervousness as manifested by his brow wiping. Master craftsman Greene cuts the humor off abruptly, shifting moods instantly as a stern-faced Popescu enters the room, which is by then almost empty of literary patrons. The ensuing dialogue cleverly disguises from the few remaining audience members and Crabbin the urgency of markedly different factual circumstances from the superficial appearance of literary question and answer dialogue:

POPESCU: Can I ask is Mr. Martins engaged in a new book?
MARTINS: Yes, it's called The Third Man.
POPESCU: A novel, Mr. Martins?
MARTINS: It's a murder story. I've just started it. It's based on fact.
POPESCU: Are you a slow writer, Mr. Martins?
MARTINS: Not when I get interested.
POPESCU: I'd say you were doing something pretty dangerous this time.
MARTINS: Yes?
POPESCU: Mixing fact and fiction.
MARTINS: Should I make it all fact?
POPESCU: Why, no, Mr. Martins. I'd stick to fiction, straight fiction.
HOLLY: I'm too far along with the book, Mr. Popescu.
POPESCU: Haven't you ever scrapped a book, Mr. Martins?
HOLLY: Never.

After the meeting is adjourned by a relieved Crabbin, happy that the nightmarish lecture failure is over, Popescu delivers instructions to two grim-faced operatives in the back of the room. Soon they are pursuing Martins, who rushes up a staircase and into a darkened room. As he dashes toward an open window and climbs out, a parrot bites him in the finger. He eludes his pursuers toward rubble, a reminder of the war damage and the current plight of Viennese in a city where corners are being consistently cut and the black market thrives. The chase sequence is also reminiscent of something Martins would write, the differences being cobbled streets and running rather than horseback pursuers in open spaces in the American West.

Welles' Emergence

Welles' role is unique in that, after being discussed repeatedly, the object of Cotten's bungling albeit sincere efforts, Valli's torment and Calloway's disdain, he emerges a full hour into the film. In his first scene he is seen but not heard. Anything but a rock solid opening scene with Welles would be a let down in view of 1) the large buildup of his character, and 2) the long period before his emergence. The Ferris wheel scene, which occurs after Martins has called out to Kurtz and Winkel at ground level below Winkel's apartment and stated that he wished to see Lime, is highly memorable.

A great deal occurs within a brief scene on Vienna's Great Wheel. At one point, Lime considers killing his friend, relating that the authorities would not bother looking for a bullet wound after such a long fall. Martins reveals the time that he was caught in a gambling raid after Lime had escaped. Martins is thoroughly sickened when he learns that Lime has been using Anna's forged document status, a process he engineered, to create good will with Russian authorities, who in turn allow the police fugitive a safe haven in their zone. The crackling dialogue reveals Lime as a nihilistic hedonist, devoid of conscience, someone concerned only about his own welfare and contemptuous of society. Once more Martins's function as a Western author is brought into play, this time by his old friend, who scoffs, "The world doesn't make any heroes outside of your stories." When Martins asked if Lime has ever seen any of his victims, the black market racketeer's reply is brutally nihilistic:

> LIME: Victims? Don't be melodramatic. [He opens the door.] Look down there. Would you really feel any pity if one of those dots stopped moving forever? If I offered you 20,000 for every dot that stopped, would you really, old man, tell me to keep my money? Or would you calculate how many dots you could afford to spare? Free of income tax, old man, free of income tax. The only way you can save money nowadays.

Lime's dialogue is sweeping, encompassing government and religion. As for government: "They talk about the people and the proletariat. I talk about the suckers and the mugs. It's the same thing. They have their five-year plans. So have I." When reminded by Martins that he used to believe in God, he replies, "Oh, I still do believe in God, old man. I believe in God and mercy and all that. But the dead are happier dead. They don't miss too much here, poor devils."

The scene concludes with the brilliant Welles ad lib about the cuckoo clock. The pithy statement symbolized the nihilism of Harry Lime, someone laughing at a world he holds in contempt. He lets his old friend know that he can be reached if Holly decides to go to work for him.

Discussion continues to abound in film circles about the famous presumed ad lib of Welles. Guy Hamilton exclaimed: "In my heart of hearts, I believe that Orson heard it somewhere." Enter Charles Drazin, whose intensively researched *In Search of 'The Third Man'* covers all aspects of the film. Drazin uncovered a possible source for the famous Welles dialogue: James McNeill Whistler, a famous American transplant who found success in London as a painter and drama critic. Drazin believes that Welles' witty dialogue was inspired by a passage from Whistler's "Ten o'clock Lecture," named for the hour it was delivered on February 20, 1885:

> A whimsical goddess, and as capricious, her strong sense of joy tolerates no dullness, and, live we never so spotlessly, still may she turn her back upon us.

> As, from time immemorial, she has done upon the Swiss in their mountains. What more worthy people! Whose every Alpine gap yawns with tradition, and is stocked with noble story; yet, the perverse and scornful one will none of it, and the sons of patriots are left with the clock that turns the mill, and the sudden cuckoo, with difficulty restrained in its box.

If the Whistler lecture was indeed Welles' source, he must be credited with taking an orotund oration and condensing it into pithy dialogue of clever irony and meaning. Also, Whistler never made the shrewd contrast between Italy's domestic turmoil amid its concurrent cultural flowering and tranquil Switzerland as Welles did.

Holly's Catch-22

While Holly Martins was constantly climbing in and out of danger in seeking to achieve justice in his own clumsy way, he meets with comparable results in his effort to step into the shoes of his old friend Lime and become the romantic interest of Anna Schmidt. While Lime would turn her in to the Russians even if it meant repatriation to Communist Czechoslovakia, Martins acquits himself with genuine unselfishness and concern for Anna. He gets nothing but rebuffs for his efforts as her sympathies and memories cling to Lime and the relationship they once had.

In order to assist Anna with the authorities, he must help bring his old friend to justice. To do so is to incur the wrath of Anna, involving him in a Catch-22. His conversations with her indicate that the major reason she wishes to talk to him is to perpetuate a link to the man she still loves, despite his selfishness and unfaithfulness. She periodically slips and refers to him as Harry rather than Holly. At one point he sadly concedes, "Wouldn't stand a chance." Anna does nothing to disabuse him of his belief.

Dumb Decoy Duck Duty

Martins gives up on Anna and the entire Vienna scene after she hands him the passport he arranged for her to secure her freedom, returning to police headquarters and informing Calloway that at long last he is ready to please him along with the others who are encouraging him to leave the city of intrigue and great danger. Calloway offers to drive him to the airport but makes one stop at a hospital. He proceeds to gradually win Martins over. An expression of empathic concern grips the American's face as he observes children in the final throes of life, unable to receive the penicillin that would save them. Particularly symbolic is a close-up of a Teddy bear on a chair, presumably belonging to a child who has died, one of the victims of Lime—one of the people he referred to contemptuously as "dots."

When they return to Calloway's Jeep, Martins exclaims, "All right, Calloway. You win. I'll be your dumb decoy duck." He contacts Lime and waits for him at

Cafe Marc Aurel. As Martins sits in the cafe awaiting Lime, there is a brilliant visual ploy. One can see the darkened shadow of an approaching figure. The authorities dramatically tense. It turns out to be an old man selling balloons. Determined to make a sale, a frustrated Paine buys a balloon from him to send him away, out of harm's path.

Anna learns about what is happening from Kurtz, arriving at the cafe and informing Martins that Harry's confederates have been arrested. She accuses Martins of being an opportunist, of conspiring against Harry for gain. Anna turns on Martins bitterly: "Honest, sensible, sober, harmless Holly Martins. Holly. What a silly name. You must feel very proud to be a police informer." As the word "informer" is uttered, Harry appears at the door to the cafe. He pulls a gun and asks Anna to move out of the line of fire. Just as he prepares to fire on Holly, Sergeant Paine appears at the back door. Holly is spared as Lime, determined to elude authorities, runs away.

Ultimate Escape from a Dungeon

Perhaps the most definitively symbolic aspect of a film rich in symbolism is the ultimate pursuit of the ubiquitous Harry Lime and his death. The splendid camerawork of Krasker along with Reed's richly sensitive direction reveal Lime's ultimate solitary, haunted nature with graphic clarity. The winding complex of darkened, cavernous, cave-like entities within the labyrinth of Vienna's sewer system registers on audiences in the manner of Dante conducting a private tour through the Inferno. He runs, huffs and puffs, but ultimately there is no escape for Harry Lime.

Symbolic story unity is revealed in the ultimately critical role Sergeant Paine plays in the perpetually endangered Holly Martins' life. At the film's beginning, as a means of preventing a drunken Martins from striking his commanding officer, he hits him with minimal force to knock him down and repel an attack, wounding his lip. Paine is respectful all the while, letting Martins know he is only doing his job, and turns out to be a devoted reader of the Western writer. At the film's conclusion, Paine saves Martins' life by appearing in a timely fashion at Cafe Marc Aurel just as Lime takes dead aim on his former American compatriot. Later, when Martins pursues a fleeing Lime on foot, it is Paine who runs toward him, imploring him to get out of harm's path. At that point he takes a bullet from Lime in the stomach and drops to the ground, dying instantly. Calloway fires a quick shot at Lime, wounding him in the leg, making his escape all the more futile and his fate inevitable.

Provided with a gun by Calloway and cautioned to "be careful," Martins pursues Lime above ground. He finds a sweating, badly wounded Lime peering at him from an open manhole cover. The final moments of their relationship are enveloped by a silent raw power that any dialogue would have sullied. His face revealing a painful final resolution, Lime delivers a single nod toward the man who had earlier idolized him and was willing to follow him to Vienna or anywhere else in the world.

This unspoken communication bears the existential ring of ultimate fate as Martins fires a fatal shot in what, based on Lime's slow, resigned nod, is a mercy killing.

A Royal Performance and a Royal Honor

With a celebrated international triumph behind him, Reed teamed up with Korda for a lush island adventure set in Ceylon, *An Outcast of the Islands*. While the 1950 release was shocking to some critics due to its steamy love scenes between Trevor Howard and exotic island girl Kerima, it was provided with a gala Royal Premiere while in 1951 Reed was accorded another royal honor, a knighthood. For the last 25 years of his life, the celebrated director would be known as Sir Carol Reed.

Guy Hamilton, who worked again as an assistant director with Reed in *Outcast*, met Kerima for the first time. "We met again many years later in Rome," Hamilton revealed, "where she had a distinguished career with Italian directors as well as American directors such as Joseph Mankiewicz and Howard Hawks." Eventually Kerima would become Mrs. Hamilton. Hoping to give her a buildup consistent with the exotic island girl image conveyed in *Outcast*, Korda's publicity outlet created a coinciding persona, asserting that the actress was born in Algeria. "My wife is actually French and the name Kerima and the Algerian bit was invented by Alex Korda for the usual publicity purposes," Hamilton explained.

Reed and His Critics

As so often occurs, one astounding success can bring with it later problems. Just as David Selznick would lament that he produced his enduring classic, *Gone With the Wind*, as a young man and suffered an enduring fate of critics expecting him to match or surpass it, Reed was judged in the rarified orbit of one of the cinema's monumental masterpieces, *The Third Man*. While none could deny his technical brilliance, the rich photographic hues capturing such varied settings as Ceylon in *An Outcast of the Islands*, East London in *A Kid for Two Farthings* and the circus world in *Trapeze*, that very brilliance oddly enough gave rise to the criticism that his film work was all technical genius and no passion. Prominent British director Michael Powell weighed in with the criticism that Sir Carol was "a watchmaker. He was technically perfect, but displayed no passion at all."

The notion that Reed's films were devoid of passion is refuted by the facts. The groundbreaking film that catapulted Reed into the front ranks of British filmmakers, *The Stars Look Down*, was a move away from frothy conventional entertainments. A serious study of the plight of Welsh coal miners was hardly devoid of passion. It was based on a bestseller by A.J. Cronin, who was never accused of passionless writing. Were James Mason and his faithful, tortured girlfriend Kathleen Ryan passionless in *Odd Man Out*? Was Mason's plight as a revolutionary dying a slow and painful death passionless? In *The Third Man*, was Joseph Cotten devoid of passion as a tortured man learning about the true nature of his oldest friend? Were his constant efforts to help Alida Valli in the wake of constant spurnings passionless? Was Valli's reaction to Orson Welles' believed death without passion? What about *An Outcast of the Islands*? If those explosive love scenes involving Trevor Howard and Kerima were passionless, then why did so many of the prudish express such dismay?

Reed's critics even sniped away at his great masterpiece, *The Third Man*, by contending that Orson Welles was the real creative genius behind the film. Welles was the man who made Reed, the argument goes, and without the ingenious director of *Citizen Kane*, *The Magnificent Ambersons* and *Touch of Evil*, the public would have been left with a routine programmer. There is no evidence that Welles directed any part of the film. His contribution to the script was one superb ad lib. One contention of Reed critics is that Welles made the film by his performance, providing a spark to a movie in great need of life.

Film historian David Thomson contended that Welles was in the film only because of Selznick's production status and insistence on him being cast as Harry Lime. Guy Hamilton, the film's assistant director, insists that Selznick considered Welles box office poison in places like the American Midwest and did not want him. Reed's biographer, Nicholas Wapshot, contends that Selznick's first choice was Robert Mitchum and it was the director who lobbied on Welles' behalf. On the subject of the film's authorship, Thomson then asserted that "a good case can be made for attributing the 'authorship' of the film to Welles. That is not simply a matter of arguing whether Welles wrote or directed any scenes. But his presence subverts the film. Lime becomes a mordant hero, the slick cynicism of the 'cuckoo clock' speech is taken at face value, the actual side effects of dilute penicillin are glossed over." Thomson sees the grandeur of Charles Foster Kane strutting with confident dominance once more. As a result of Welles' dominant efforts, "Reed vanishes and Greene retires. *The Third Man* becomes a companion to *Journey into Fear*, drawn helplessly into Welles' appetite for self-dramatization. And a good thing, too, for it would be a righteous anecdote without him."

To approach the claims of Thomson, consistent with those made by others, it is necessary to turn the perspective around and determine what happened before Welles arrived in Vienna to begin work. As Guy Hamilton pointed out, most of the scenes set in the sewer were already completed, with the exception of shots involving Welles. Was Welles responsible for the angles and hauntingly shadowy photography which has gripped theater patrons throughout the world for two generations? In terms of a dominant presence by Welles in his on-camera appearances, his ultimate emergence transpired after a one-hour buildup in which his character was constantly discussed, and other performers brilliantly interacted resulting from pivotal events involving Harry Lime. There was a well-intentioned Holly Martins seeking to find answers in a nest of ruthless black marketeers. Major Calloway was perpetually distracted by seeking to save Martins from an untimely end in the pursuit of Lime's operatives. Martins and Anna talk about Lime nostalgically. Martins tries unsuccessfully to develop a romance with her. He finally cooperates with Calloway to her benefit and she angrily rebukes him for turning on his friend. A porter who knows too much is murdered. Martins barely escapes the clutches of the executioners of Kurtz and Popescu in the midst of being a suspect himself. Medical orderly Harbin is wanted by police but has disappeared. This entire one-hour drama consisting of professional story twists and turns is complemented with shadowy photography of wet, dark, cobbled Vienna streets.

When all is said and done, it must be concluded that Welles was greatly benefited by all of the aforementioned before he made his entrance, and continued to be aided by brilliant story turns, great photography and taut direction after his celebrated emergence. To contend that Welles has saved the film with a bravura performance is to discount 1) the long buildup before his appearance, and 2) the brilliant collaborative efforts of cast and crew.

Another obstacle Reed was forced to overcome was the persistent haggling from across the Atlantic of producer Selznick, who barraged the director with some of his famous memos. "There was a great deal of niggling just before the final script was printed for distribution to the crew from Selnick in the States," Hamilton recalled. "Constant memos, demanding that 'sidewalk' replace 'pavement,' 'truck' to replace 'lorry' to accommodate our Trans-Atlantic cousins."

Hamilton also reflected on another point of major concern regarding Selznick and *The Third Man*. "After the release of the picture in the U.K., Selznick fiddled about with the picture for release in the States," Hamilton noted. "Selznick was always worried that Carol and Graham were making Joe Cotten look too much like an innocent bumbler abroad."

Selznick's fear related to the belief that American audiences would find *The Third Man* anti–American with Cotten as Holly Martins playing a well-intentioned bumbler who needs to be perpetually saved by the astute efforts of the British Major Calloway. While Selznick inserted changes to coincide with his fears, seeking to make Martins look less ineffectual, it was the Reed version which premiered in Britain and throughout Europe which prevails. Joseph Cotten portrays Holly Martins, not all or a large percentage of Americans. Just as Peter Sellers portrayed one French detective, Inspector Clousseau, director Blake Edwards was hardly poking fun at France. It should also be noted that Alec Guinness was notably successful in two films in which he headed teams of British criminal bumblers in *The Lavender Hill Mob* and *The Ladykillers*. Selznick's fears proved unfounded as Americans evaluated Holly Martins as a well-intentioned bumbler who happened to be American and was in no way meant to be a prototypical example.

Proving His Critics Wrong

While numerous critics were beginning to write Reed off, with others even questioning whether he was the guiding genius behind *The Third Man*, opportunity arose and he took swift advantage. By the time the chapter ended, Sir Carol Reed had not only proven his critics wrong: He secured an Academy Award.

It was a delightful musical adventure inhabited by London street urchins that thrust Reed back to the top of the motion picture world, an adaptation of a work by the Victorian era's premier novelist, Charles Dickens. The adaptation of the Lionel Bart London musical, *Oliver!*, a fantasy based on *Oliver Twist*, called attention to Reed's career long pursuit of variety of subject matter.

"The irony is that Carol always wanted to do a musical and *Oliver!* was a big success," Ken Annakin noted, "but Carol also found that by doing a musical he didn't have the amount of control that he normally exercised on a picture."

Annakin's comment reflects on the greater measure of control generally available to a director of a drama rather than a musical, where choreography is such a paramount factor with singers and dancers performing in between dialogue segments. A fresh creative challenge was presented to a director who thrived upon variety and conquering new ground. "This is Dickens. There are problems of a special kind," Reed acknowledged. "You say to yourself: 'Fagin as a character would never dream of singing anything, nor, perhaps, would the Artful Dodger or Bill Sikes.' They would probably get a laugh. The only way we could do justice to these characters was to cast them as well as we know how, and you can only do that in England. We concentrated upon them and made them the center of attraction. I never visualized *Oliver!* as a show dominated by a single big star. In fact, there are seven very good parts."

One area of *Oliver!* in which Reed stood on familiar ground was his ability to work with youngsters as he enticed excellent performances from eight-year-old Mark Lester as Oliver Twist and 15-year-old Jack Wild as the Artful Dodger. Maintaining his sharp instinct for casting, Reed held out over Columbia Studio protests for a name actor for the key role of Fagin. For a time Peter Sellers was mentioned as studio moguls thought about a marquee name to boost box office receipts, but Reed was determined to give the coveted role to Ron Moody, who had dazzled West End audiences with his stage portrayal. As for the key Bill Sikes role, the director hired his nephew, Oliver Reed, whose convincing portrayal assured that his uncle's superb instinct rather than nepotism had been invoked.

Pauline Kael in *The New Yorker* concluded that the film *Oliver!* totally eclipsed the stage musical. She paid tribute to *Oliver!* and its distinguished director by calling the film "a civilized motion picture, not only emotionally satisfying but so satisfyingly crafted that we can sit back and enjoy what is going on, secure in the knowledge that the camera isn't going to attack us and the editor isn't going to give us an electric shock ... Carol Reed is in the tradition of the older movie artists who conceal their art, and don't try to dazzle us with breathtaking shots and razor-sharp cuts. They are there, all right, but we hardly notice them, because there is always a reason for the camera to be where it is."

In addition to Reed securing an Oscar in the Best Director category, *Oliver!* captured Best Picture honors. Four more Academy Awards were bestowed on the musical for Best Art Direction, Best Achievement in Sound, Best Musical Score and Best Choreography. Reed's acceptance speech demonstrated once more his humility and reverence for collaboration: "You can imagine that never having made a musical before I owe a lot of thanks to a lot of people. I don't know how to sing or dance, so it was all a matter of teamwork."

Following *Oliver!* Reed would direct two more films, *The Last Warrior* (U.S. title: *Flap*), a 1969 release, and the 1971 production, *Follow Me* (U.S. title: *The Public Eye*). On April 25, 1976, as he lay in bed reading a newspaper, Sir Carol Reed was stricken with a second heart attack within a brief period of time, this one proving fatal.

Reed's contribution to the international film industry extended well beyond his own personal output. In the manner of a great teacher, he proved to be a patient and brilliant mentor to a new wave of British directors. In addition to names such as Guy Hamilton, Guy Green and Bryan Forbes, there was Ken Annakin. Not only would Annakin emulate Reed's globetrotting ways of flying to wherever the next filmable story might be, he directed the film that critics called Britain's next great thriller after his mentor's *The Third Man.*

The Ken Annakin Story

When Ken Annakin sits in the living room of his Beverly Hills home, he can still hear those unforgettable words from Carol Reed when he was operating a Mitchell camera while a wartime documentary was being filmed, *We Serve*. The great director told his young cameraman to "come over to our side." Annakin took the advice so close to heart that he never turned back, becoming successful initially as a documentary filmmaker, then launching a heralded career as a film director that has taken him to all parts of the globe.

Annakin's internationally successful films have garnered enthusiastic praise as well as tributes. In July 1998, 15 of his movies were showcased in the prestigious setting of London's National Film Theatre on the South Bank of the Thames River.

Interviewed recently in his Beverly Hills home, the veteran director, who was born and spent his boyhood years in a town of the same name with a different spelling, Beverley in the East Yorkshire section of Northern England, revealed himself as a man with a passionate destiny for travel and adventure. His school days culminated in the early 30s. Before long, the world was gripped in great conflict and Annakin became involved with film documentaries to make the British public fully aware of the effort and stakes involved. He received a major career boost when he was operating a Mitchell camera filming a wartime documentary. Annakin found his niche in directing, enjoying the world of film and its unlimited challenges.

In the midst of the Depression, Annakin located a job in the civil service representing the antipathy of what the adventurous man in his late teens sought, a position in the Income Tax Department. After three years the future director found a way out.

"I made a bet on the English Derby and ended up winning what to me at the time amounted to a fortune, the grand sum of 100," he explained. "That enabled me to purchase a ticket by boat that took me to New Zealand and Australia and eventually America. I turned to cycling, just as I had as a boy in my native Yorkshire, and traveled and labored to all kinds of fascinating places, finding spots people wouldn't normally visit. I even panned for gold for a month in New Zealand. You mention it, I probably did it."

Annakin would rival any director in the annals of cinema in variety of subjects as well as locations. To make films dealing with varied subject matter, it is tremendously helpful for a filmmaker to be familiar with different avenues of life. The formative early learning period for Annakin found him, after his brief stint as a tax clerk, working as an auto salesman, journalist and compere of a roadshow publicizing hair styling and products. The thrust propelling him into his lifelong career, however, came about through doing his part in the global struggle to save the world from the ravages of totalitarianism.

War, Carol Reed and the Big Breakthrough

Annakin was in his twenties when the ferocious struggle began in England as a determined nation sought to turn back the onslaught of Adolf Hitler. The major battle was waged in the air above England and was known as the Battle of Britain, pitting the Nazi crack air fighters, the Luftwaffe, against the challenge of the Royal Air Force. Annakin was serving in the RAF when opportunity surfaced on the heels of tragedy.

"I was working as a mechanic near Liverpool with the RAF," Annakin revealed. "I wore glasses then and my eyesight was not good enough for me to become a pilot. I was injured in the great Liverpool bombing and was incapacitated for one year. I suffered from amnesia and there are still three days out of my life that I cannot account for!"

When Annakin recovered he was put to effective use in a new area he mastered with such adroit flexibility that it would soon become his life's work. With Britain and the cause of democracy hanging in the balance, the British Government, recognizing the importance of film as both an inspirational and instructive tool to a nation gripped in the throes of conflict, grabbed whatever talent was available to aid the war effort via celluloid.

"Often help was in short supply," Annakin recalled, "and if the Ministry of Information thought you could handle a camera, they would hand you one and send you off to shoot film. That was what happened to me and this resulted in my opportunity to enter the film world."

Beginning as an assistant cameraman, Annakin was quickly propelled into the documentary realm. While Americans were generating their own effort through the likes of Frank Capra's *Why We Fight* series, the British undertook an herculean documentary activity of their own. As Annakin entered the scene the documentary focus was in North Africa, where there was crucial tank warfare involving two great generals, Britain's Bernard Montgomery and Germany's "Desert Fox," Erwin Rommel.

The British populace knew little of America's struggle against the Japanese in the Pacific. Annakin's first major effort in film was a documentary called *Pacific Thrust*, in which he sifted through over three million feet of war footage to create an impression of the battles admirals Nimitz and Halsey as well as General MacArthur were engaged in and where they were probably heading.

"I learned from that experience that film has a life of its own," Annakin exclaimed, "and that by skillful editing one can create any effect one desires."

This informative presentation of war propaganda led to Annakin being assigned to work under Carol Reed on *We Serve*, not to be confused with the David Lean feature about the British Navy at war, *In Which We Serve*. *We Serve*, with Reed at the helm, was a government documentary focusing on the ongoing efforts of women in the British military and the role they were playing to aid the war effort. The greatest British actresses were recruited at a nominal 5 pounds a day each, among them Edith Evans, Margaret Rutherford, Nora Swinburne and an actress toward whom Annakin had formed an early fan attachment.

"When I was very young, I fell madly in love with Diana Wynyard," Annakin revealed. "I put pinups of her on the walls of my room and even wrote her love letters. I was astounded when I got to work with her on *We Serve*." Wynyard was Reed's first wife.

The story had a happy ending, which Annakin recounted with buoyant laughter. "When she learned how much of an admirer of hers I was, Diana was kind enough to give me an off-camera kiss, which, of course, thrilled me no end," he reminisced.

Reed liked Annakin's work with the camera and made a major decision that would profoundly affect the young Yorkshireman's life. He was being trained by a veteran director under the fires of world combat.

"Carol told me that he liked my work, but felt that it was time for me to become a part of the production scene," Annakin explained. "Carol was my directing model and mentor during my early period. It was marvelous watching him work with actors. I learned so much by watching him. He was a soft-spoken man and did not say a good deal, but he had a way of empathizing with a performer, of talking out a scene until it was able to take shape in the actor's mind, then be performed with success."

Sydney Box and 1 + 1 = 7

As Annakin moved into his early thirties and began blossoming into one of Britain's top documentary filmmakers, one of the period's noted British movie figures began taking an interest in his career. Sydney Box was destined to play the same kind of prominence in assisting Annakin's development that Carol Reed had earlier. "The two major influences on my early career were Carol in the directing sense and Sydney in the field of producing and setting up shows," Annakin smiled nostalgically. "Sydney told me that if I could make a picture with actors instead of real people, he would give me the chance to direct a feature."

Annakin promptly forged his opportunity. He directed a documentary explaining the British criminal justice system, playing out all court scenes with professional actors. The documentary was a success and Box kept his word.

In the West London suburb of Ealing, the famed Ealing Studios were making their mark with what became trademarked as the "Ealing comedies," which gave Alec Guinness's career a mighty thrust. The launching pad for Annakin's debut into feature films was Gainsborough Studios, situated in North London's Islington section. Box had a prominent position as the war ended in both the production and writing areas, as well as through his linkage to one of the most prodigiously talented families in the history of films. Along with Sydney, it included his wife Muriel, his sister Betty and brother-in-law Peter Rogers. It marked an exciting period for Annakin and all concerned since Gainsborough was a "new kid on the block" in British films, taking over what was previously Islington Studios.

At the time that Annakin became associated with Box on his first feature, the dynamic producer-writer and wife Muriel were basking in the glow of an Academy Award triumph as each garnered an Oscar for Best Original Screenplay in 1946 for their collaboration on *The Seventh Veil*, which Sydney also produced. In the film, sensitive concert pianist Ann Todd is rescued from psychological torment generated by her neurotic cousin, James Mason, by psychiatrist Herbert Lom.

Annakin's joint efforts with the talented Box team resulted in an equation of 1 + 1 = 7, which made perfect mathematical success at Gainsborough as two early film contributions by the new feature director turned into a total of seven films in all. Filmgoers resoundingly endorsed the Annakin-directed efforts.

Annakin's initial feature film was *Holiday Camp*, a delightful British comedy set in one of the new Butlin holiday camps. Mr. and Mrs. Joe Huggett were played by Jack Warner and Kathleen Harrison.

The Huggett sagas were Britain's answer to the successful American Ma and Pa Kettle films spawned by *The Egg and I* and, before them, the Andy Hardy series of the '30s. A nation that had preserved its freedom in the wake of ferocious bombings from the fearsome Luftwaffe and Buzz Bombs had endured through a determined cohesive effort, zealously seeking to preserve home and country. It was understandable why British moviegoers would positively respond to light-hearted comedy surrounding a delightful British family after so much sacrifice had been endured to preserve humor, gaiety and family values from an onrushing Nazi tide that had held Europe in its vise-like grip.

With *Holiday Camp* a rousing success and the British film public clamoring to see more of the Huggetts, Gainsborough was only too happy to oblige. The following year, 1948, saw two Huggett films released, *Here Come the Huggetts* and *Vote for Huggett*, while *The Huggetts Abroad* was released in 1949. Annakin directed each vehicle, trying his hand in a variety of ways. In 1948 a delightful Annakin comedy, *Miranda*, starred the director's most frequent leading lady, Glynis Johns. It was a spoof about young doctor Griffith Jones bringing home mermaid Johns, who hides in the bath to the consternation of wife Googie Withers.

The Maugham Connection and More Sequels

Now that Annakin's career had received a dramatic boost by five richly successful films, he followed those triumphs with linkage to one of the great fiction writers of the twentieth century, a collaboration leading to three cinema winners. Annakin was involved in directing segments from the first two entries in the Somerset Maugham trilogy.

Few achievements please creative talents more than achieving success in a project that falls outside the conventional realm, drowning out fearful cries of "It can't be done!" *Quartet* and the two identically structured films that followed in its successful shadow shattered conventional wisdom by operating outside regular continuity standards. Rather than embracing one storyline, it instead presented three well-defined vignettes, adapted short stories by a masterful storyteller noted for operating within that orbit as well as a novelist.

Maugham's novels had been successfully translated to the screen with *Of Human Bondage* starring Leslie Howard and Bette Davis and *The Razor's Edge* featuring Tyrone Power, Gene Tierney, Best Supporting Actress Oscar recipient Anne Baxter and Herbert Marshall portraying the writer himself. Maugham's compelling short story, *The Letter*, became a powerful dramatic vehicle with William Wyler directing Bette Davis and Herbert Marshall. In the early days of talkies, the Maugham short story *Rain* had been a brilliant starring vehicle for a youthful Joan Crawford and a great character molding opportunity for Walter Huston, but unlike *Quartet* and, latterly, *Trio* and *Encore*, the earlier movies were filmed as total story entities. The Maugham trilogy involved segmented stories standing totally on their own.

The 1948 Gainsborough release *Quartet* saw Annakin direct the final of four segments with Arthur Crabtree, Harold French and Ralph Smart overseeing the others. Each story was filmed with a different cast and crew.

Another note of uniqueness was rendered in the case of *Quartet* and its two sequels. For the first time an author was featured at the beginning of the film commenting on the forthcoming production involving his work. Somerset Maugham was then in his seventies and a true legend. Each story held audience interest due to the fascinating array of characters presented and the unforgettable story twists at the close of the episodes. All successful writers need to be adroit students of character, and Maugham's success reveals him as a highly perceptive observer.

"The characteristic that stood out with Somerset Maugham was his incredible powers of observation," Annakin exclaimed. "The man was always watching, always listening, wherever he was. The people he studied ended up as characters in his novels and short stories."

Annakin's segment, the fourth of the film, was a story of immense sensitivity teaming two consummate British performers. *The Colonel's Lady* starred veteran character actor Cecil Parker as Colonel Peregrine and Nora Swinburne as his long-suffering wife. When Swinburne, after suffering neglect and unfaithfulness at the hands of her selfish husband, writes an enormously popular book of poetry featuring a woman deeply in love with a man she places on a pedestal, speculation abounds over the identity of the mysterious and romantic knight in shining armor. Parker becomes humiliated as speculation reaches fever pitch. The surprise twist is employed at story's end when it is learned that the admired man saluted in romantic verse by Swinburne is her husband in his pre-colonel days, long before his selfish and faithless activities commenced, an original ending devised after several tryouts by Annakin and Sydney Box.

The sensitive, richly evocative performance of Nora Swinburne was rewarded with a 1949 New York Film Critics Circle Award for Best Actress. Annakin's segment had resulted in a prestigious international honor for his leading lady. When the next Maugham omnibus, *Trio*, was filmed by Gainsborough, Annakin, due in no small measure to the acclaim received by *The Colonel's Lady*, was selected to direct two of the three episodes. In *Mister Know-All*, another notable British character performer, Nigel Patrick, delivers a virtuoso effort as a pompous passenger on a luxury cruise laying claim to expertise on every subject, particularly fine jewelry. The story concludes on an admirable note when he falsely concedes making a mistake in identifying a piece of jewelry that will otherwise incriminate a beautiful woman of infidelity in front of her husband.

Walt Disney, Phase One

The union between Walt Disney and Ken Annakin proved to be a mutually rewarding one. The relationship contained two phases, the first of which resulted in two historical adventures, *The Story of Robin Hood* in 1952 and *The Sword and the Rose* released one year later.

"My work on *The Story of Robin Hood* marked a first in my career," Annakin recalled. "This was the first time I used a storyboard. Walt Disney was very good about allowing me complete creative freedom, but he insisted that every scene was sketched out so that we both knew what we were aiming for!"

The setting was Nottingham as Robin Hood and his Merry Men confronted the wicked sheriff and his employer, Prince John. It was the second live action feature film ever produced by Disney Studios. The dashing Richard Todd, Annakin's most frequent leading man, played Robin Hood, who had blazed to glory earlier in films starring Errol Flynn.

The Sword and the Rose saw the pairing of Annakin's most frequent leading man and lady, Richard Todd and Glynis Johns. The film was based on the Charles Major novel *When Knighthood Was in Flower*, and had been previously made as a silent starring Marion Davies.

Another film from Annakin's productive 1950s period that stood out in his mind in a *deja vu* context was the 1955 release *Land of Fury*, a Western set in the 1820s in New Zealand with pioneering husband and wife (Jack Hawkins and Glynis Johns) struggling to impose British order amid primitive surroundings. *Land of Fury* marked Annakin's return to the land down under where he had exercised his adventurous traveling spirit for the first time outside his native England.

"It was my first visit back to the country where I enjoyed myself as a youth living joyously as a carefree bum," Annakin laughed. "We spent 17 days shooting in New Zealand and I particularly enjoyed renewing acquaintances with my newspaper friends who had published my articles on my travel adventures that I wrote when I was there before. It was an unforgettable experience."

During the same period, Annakin also directed *Landfall* and *Double Confession*, both 1953 releases, *You Know What Sailors Are* (1954), and *Value for Money* (1956). The five films represent a versatile Annakin blend. The first two were adventures. While *You Know What Sailors Are* and *Value for Money* were comedies.

Graham Greene and a Personal Favorite

In the early phase of Annakin's career, he became linked to one of the most renowned British fiction authors in Somerset Maugham, with the triumphs of *Quartet* and *Trio* resulting. As an experienced director in his early forties, combining craftsmanship and productivity, Annakin was involved in two projects with a towering British fiction writer of the Maugham stripe in Graham Greene. The result of the second project proved to be the Yorkshireman's favorite film.

Once more in the Annakin tradition, the two films fall into the comedy and high adventure categories. *Loser Takes All* (1956) was a romantic comedy with a glamorous Monte Carlo setting. The lure of the world famous casino was too much for newlywed Rosanno Brazzi, who is convinced he has constructed a foolproof system to beat the house. Glynis Johns plays his wife, who rebels against Brazzi's gambling addiction as the marriage shows signs of crumbling.

Since Greene adapted the screenplay of *Loser Takes All* from his novel, the director had an opportunity to work close at hand with the noted author. Annakin was struck by the consistency with which Greene applied his craft.

"Greene was such a fine writer and I learned so much from him," he recalled. "He was very consistent in his approach to his work. He would begin each morning at 7:30 or 8:00 and continue his writing until 11:30, producing strictly 800 words a day. Then he would go out. We would often visit some of the breathtaking sights of the French Riviera. Then Greene would return to his work at 4:30 and spend the period between then and 7:00 polishing or rewriting, when he would stop working. I was fortunate to get to work with Greene during this period. It was right after he'd had a falling out with Alexander Korda, who had produced *The Third Man* and *The Fallen Idol*, and in *Loser Takes All* Greene took a swipe at the faithlessness of Sir Alex, very entertainingly!"

Comedy was a comfortable vehicle for Britisher Glynis Johns, who portrayed the flaming and tempestuous redhead with equal gusto to her counterpart from across the Atlantic, Susan Hayward. Both red-haired performers exuded perpetual energy.

"Glynis was a very lively and a very sexy actress," Annakin exclaimed. "Not only was she physically energetic. Her mind was always devising ways to brighten up the studio's day. She was creatively inventive."

With one successful Greene vehicle in hand, Annakin secured a short story that needed beefing up for a film, but the idea of which held intrigue for him. Annakin felt that it was time for his career to take a new turn and the film that produced the change he sought would become his all-time favorite.

Across the Bridge (1957)

"John Stafford, the producer of *Across the Bridge*, had acquired this Graham Greene short story which had been around for years but was too frail for a movie," Annakin recalled. "It only dealt with Carl Schaffner's degradation after he crossed the bridge into Mexico. You know nothing about the man or his background. John, with Graham's full permission, engaged Guy Elmes to create the whole first part of the story. We created together a much more sexy adventure, but Graham, through John, brought us back to stark facts delineating Schaffner's actions and development of character strictly so they led up to his short story second half."

A director looking for a fresh challenge, Annakin sought to move outside the orbit of doing entertainments by launching a thriller for an international audience on the order of his mentor Reed and *The Third Man*. He believed that the time was right and that *Across the Bridge* provided the proper vehicle. "I dearly wanted to prove I could make a true character-action story instead of comedies and pure entertainment when I jumped at the chance to make *Across the Bridge*," Annakin explained. "Maybe I envied Carol his *Third Man* and inwardly wanted to prove I could make a film of the same type of quality."

To achieve success in filmmaking requires timing. Annakin saw the times changing in England with respect to audience tastes. "The war and the Blitz had been over ten or eleven years," Annakin revealed, "and British and European audiences were not needing so vitally pure escapist entertainment."

In that Annakin was working with a Greene short story that needed fleshing out for film purposes, it was understandable enough for him to create a first half on his own, with the assistance of Guy Elmes and some dialogue assistance from Dennis Freeman. The Greene story from which *Across the Bridge* was adapted dealt only

Rod Steiger's helpless expression reveals his desperation in the 1957 J. Arthur Rank production, *Across the Bridge*. The Steiger role of an international financier finally brought to ultimate degradation in Mexico helped the New York method actor surge to international stardom. A symbolic passing of the baton occurred with this British film noir classic in that its director, Ken Annakin, was a protégé of Sir Carol Reed. Annakin was moved from the ranks of cameraman while shooting a World War II documentary by Reed. *Across the Bridge* was acknowledged as a great British noir drama in the tradition of Reed's *The Third Man*, which debuted eight years earlier.

with Schaffner's degradation after he crossed the bridge from Texas into Mexico. What is truly impressive when viewing the film is the cohesive flow of the story. Unless told otherwise, the film could easily pass as the creation of one writer. This type of adaptation is very difficult and many films have noticeably suffered from the conspicuous presence of two or more minds tugging in disparate directions, particularly in instances of short stories where great expansion is needed. There is a consistent suspense tension that systematically builds from the time that Rod Steiger learns he is in trouble with authorities and is likely to serve a prison term of some ten years, prompting him to escape and form a new identity, to the film's conclusion when his life ends in an escape attempt from authorities with his one and only true friend, the dog Dolores.

Annakin traveled to Texas and Northern Mexico to photograph the kinds of realistic locations he sought to use in the film. The famous British distributor J. Arthur Rank never shot any films in the Americas. According to Annakin, Spain and Europe were generally considered "our territory." The director found perfect locations around Seville, Cordoba and the Rhonda Valley.

"We created the Mexican border village in Lora del Rio about a half hour from Seville," Annakin explained. "The village became ours and the local people participated with gusto. Apart from my regular British crew, I had a great Spanish art director called Julio Molina. We had great days of hot sun, then danced our nights away in the nightclubs of Seville."

Escaping from Authorities

The film is about the total transformation of one man's life from a role of imperious authority as one of the world's financial magnates to one of total degradation in which he sleeps in dusty culverts in a small Mexican border town. At the film's outset, Scotland Yard detectives visit the international headquarters of Carl Schaffner's enterprises. As soon as his operatives are aware that financial irregularities have been found in Schaffner's books, a call is placed to New York.

Steiger's opening sequence as brash multimillionaire Carl Schaffner is the only time when he is viewed at the peak of his power, convinced that the entire world lies at his disposal. He is seen in a penthouse New York hotel suite proudly holding court at a press conference. When one reporter questions proposed Schaffner mergers as possibly violating U.S. anti-trust laws, he tersely responds that this is a matter for his lawyers. Having received the important call from London about the discoveries of Scotland Yard, Schaffner's operatives seek to get his attention to relay this crucial information. His ego clearly enjoying the attention of the press conference, he snaps imperiously twice at his subordinates, asking to be left alone.

When he finally responds and is provided with the crucial information, the press conference no longer holds any interest for him, nor does an American woman who is flattering him; she is promptly dismissed. Knowing he might face a decade in prison, Schaffner makes swift plans to escape the approaching forces of the law.

The Train Sequence

Many a great suspense film has been bolstered by a dramatic train sequence. Annakin's mentor Carol Reed had one of his earliest suspense successes, *Night Train to Munich*, focused on one dramatic train ride. Three great noir classics, Billy Wilder's *Double Indemnity*, Alfred Hitchcock's *Shadow of a Doubt* and *Strangers on a Train*, used train sequences to heighten suspense. In his British phase, Hitchcock directed *The Lady Vanishes*, a suspense adventure set on a train (Reed's *Night Train to Munich* was a sequel).

Across the Bridge had a compelling train sequence of its own. Trains can be interesting vehicles of mystery due to the fact that a cross section of travelers are presented, people from various walks of life who do not know each other. This type of atmosphere provides just the blend to stimulate a creative mind, the meetings of individuals, frequently with one of a sinister bent and the other unaware of dangers lurking ahead. Such was the case with Farley Granger, who was unintentionally caught up in the machinations of psycho Robert Walker in *Strangers on a Train*. At first blush the meeting between Steiger as Schaffner and fellow traveling companion Paul Scarff, played by Canadian actor Bill Nagy, appears to be such an encounter, a meeting between a ruthless fugitive from the law and an innocent victim. Scarff talks about his wife and his new son, appearing to be a model family man whose chief concern is getting back home to his family. The brilliant plot twist is that things are anything other than what they appear to be.

Stepping into a Victim's Shoes

When one steals an identity belonging to another, it is a case of stepping into the victim's shoes. Schaffner finds this out soon enough when exiting the train after throwing his drugged victim off and stealing his Mexican passport and suitcase. He has even darkened his hair and donned glasses to look more like Scarff.

As Schaffner steals off into the darkness, the alert baggage clerk asks tersely if he is attempting to pull a fast one. Not wishing to arouse suspicion, Schaffner walks silently over to him, learning that he is receiving a traveling companion, Dolores, the dog previously belonging to Scarff. When he opens up Scarff's suitcase, he learns he has inherited more than his dog. He reads a clipping from a newspaper showing a picture of Scarff and a story revealing that he is wanted for killing the governor of a Mexican province. A reward has been offered for his capture.

Resolve One Problem, Face a Fresh One

A clever ploy in mystery stories, particularly those with a strong psychological bent, is that of a character resolving one problem, then immediately encountering another. The technique is particularly effective when the problems become more difficult and circumstances increasingly dangerous. If this process occurs long enough and extends far enough, the character's torment will often reach the breaking point. Annakin plays this trump card with repeated success in *Across the Bridge*.

Schaffner's adoption of a new identity provides an immediate problem just after he believes that waylaying Scarff and stealing his identity has solved his own refugee status. Instead he steps into the shoes of another refugee from justice. Johnny, played by David Knight, is a tow truck driver and handyman at Sam's Motel, where Schaffner is staying. He reads about Scarff and decides to turn him into Mexican police across the bridge. When he does so, Schaffner is confronted with a new problem, which he surmounts when he convinces chief of police Noel Willman of his true identity. The wily international financial mogul provided himself with such an out by breaking into the room of Scarff, who was also staying at Sam's Motel, taking back his own passport, which he had earlier placed in the other man's possession before hurling him from the train.

In addition to proving his identity, Schaffner is able to tell the police chief where Scarff is staying, which ultimately leads to a shootout with police in his room, where he is recovering from a broken leg and other wounds at Sam's Motel. Schaffner immediately seeks to leave the border town, seeking help from the police chief. When he splits his reward with the chief, Schaffner believes he will be allowed to leave for Mexico City. By then the chief has heard all about the financier and his great wealth, telling him that a much higher price must be paid before he secures his freedom.

Another ironic story twist is provided when Schaffner encounters another problem he never anticipated. By turning in Scarff and collecting his reward, Schaffner thinks he will be perceived as someone aiding the Mexican system of justice. He soon learns that Scarff was a local hero loved by the poor people of the town as a fighter against an oppressive system. It gets even worse for Schaffner when the haunting presence of the silent and grieving widow, always cradling her infant son in her arms, is seen periodically by him, a haunting reminder of what he has done. Her presence prompts the same townspeople who admired her husband for battling a corrupt system to embrace her with great sensitivity. This results in greater scorn for stranger Schaffner. An arrestingly symbolic moment of the film is reached during the funeral procession through the town, in which she walks with a sad, tortured dignity, a figure in black, mourning her husband's death. During this funeral procession Mary, played by Marla Landi, the girlfriend of Johnny, who had hoped to collect the reward money himself when he instead turned in Schaffner, openly chastises him for his part in the sad debacle resulting in Scarff's death.

A Bitter Clash of Wills

The film enters a powerful phase with the bitter clash of wills between Rod Steiger and Noel Willman. Steiger, playing an intense, self-made man who came from Germany just before the start of World War II to make a fortune and an international reputation in London, provides the proper measure of insolent bravura as the spoiled magnate suffering tortured isolation as Willman ultimately lets him twist like a reed in the wind.

"We were lucky to be able to cast the young Rod Steiger, who had just finished *On the Waterfront*," Annakin said. "He had never been to Europe before. He brought with him a beatnik companion he had casually picked up at Schwab's Drugstore on Sunset Boulevard. Undoubtedly Rod had great inner problems and he was soaked in Method acting. But one way and another he was a great actor to work with, if you knew how to use his talents. I think I learned that very quickly after two weeks of great arguments about our script and the character of Schaffner. These discussions often involved the theories of Jung and Freud. Anyway, we sorted out Rod's approach. And as a young man playing an older man, together with the gradual degradation of the formidable businessman, I think he did a fantastic job. One of his best creations."

Noel Willman was a British actor trained in the classical theater tradition. His Shakespearean acting was what impressed Annakin when he watched him performing with the Royal Shakespeare Company at Stratford, alerting him to the fine potential for film work which shone in his brilliant portrayal of the corrupt Mexican border town police chief.

Schaffner, someone used to buying people off, initially believes that it will take little money or effort to win the police chief to his side, but he proves to be far more stubborn an obstacle than he ever realized, one resulting in the financier's ultimate demise. When Scotland Yard enters the scene, police chief Willman learns just how rich and famous a man he is dealing with. When an increasingly desperate Steiger offers him ten percent of his fortune if he will secure his freedom, Willman tersely snaps, "Not enough." Willman appears to find Steiger so repellent that he is ultimately eager to cut a brusque, wealthy man down to size. Greene was interested in promoting the strong clash of wills between the international financier and the chief of police of the small border town.

"Graham Greene did not care a damn about degrading Schaffner because he was a business magnate," Annakin revealed. "He loved the struggle between Steiger and Willman as two strong characters vying with each other intellectually. Graham and I were absolutely at one in this concept and I think we pulled it off excellently."

Open Spaces Claustrophobia

Rod Steiger as Schaffner enters a new torturous dimension when police chief Willman applies an additional measure of pressure. At a time when Scotland Yard has arrived on the scene and is seeking the extradition of the fugitive back to England, Willman moves more boldly than ever. Bernard Lee is the Scotland Yard detective leading the team that has traveled to Mexico in an effort to apprehend Schaffner. Veteran character actor Lee, who plays Detective Inspector Hadden, is a cast carryover from *The Third Man*, where he played Sergeant Paine and lost his life in an attempt to save that of Holly Martins. Scotland Yard has pressured information on Steiger's whereabouts from his New York operatives, who are told they could otherwise be prosecuted in concert with their employer's alleged crimes as accessories after the fact. Lee explains to Willman that an international magnate like Steiger, by employing the most skilled international lawyers, will be able to defer extradition for some time. He seeks cooperation from Willman in an attempt to get Steiger back across the bridge and into the United States, facilitating the process of extraditing him back to England for trial.

Willman exhibits the kind of icy independence with Lee that he has demonstrated in his relations with Steiger. He informs Lee that he will not allow the financier to leave town and will break him by applying a new strategy. His ploy represents the element of open spaces claustrophobia exercised with effective dramatic results by director Nicholas Ray in *They Live by Night*. The seemingly contradictory term of open spaces claustrophobia involves a psychologically ironic set of circumstances in which a wanted figure lives in an area where open land can be seen on all sides, but yet there is nowhere to go. This was the case with the haunted young married couple in Depression Oklahoma played by Farley Granger and Cathy O'Donnell in *They Live by Night*. Annakin successfully employs this same element in *Across the Bridge* as the ruthless Willman employs his new strategy. Previously Steiger had been free to use his money and local merchants had accepted it. He not only had a room at what appears to be the only nice hotel in town; he had even been able to order champagne. Once that Willman cracks his whip, Steiger enters a new phase of alienation. Willman issues a directive that nobody in town is to accept Steiger's money or cooperate with him in any way. When he returns to his hotel, the woman with whom he has done business has placed his luggage on the street. When he protests, she tells him he is no longer welcome, nor is his money.

The wily Willman knows he possesses a trump card, which he plays with savage wickedness against Steiger. The local popularity of Paul Scarff and wave of sympathy reserved for his widow and infant child are used to advantage in making Steiger a more hated symbol than ever among townfolk. He offers money and is spurned with expressions of hate and adamant head shaking. Steiger ultimately becomes a hated symbol even among the children of the border town. When he seeks to wash his face at the large pool in the town square, children splash water at him tauntingly, then run away. Deprived of the opportunity to use his money or of lodging, Steiger begins to resemble a caged animal. He sleeps under the stars in dusty culverts with nothing but open spaces around him, but he remains imprisoned in an advanced state of psychological claustrophobia.

His Lone Friend and a Scotland Yard Ploy

Bernard Lee continues to ponder a course of action to entice the increasingly rattled Steiger across the border to the United States, where he can then be apprehended by Scotland Yard and cooperating U.S. authorities. One effort is to use David Knight to drive Steiger from the border town ostensibly to a small town in Texas. This ploy is in concert with a bogus communiqué purporting to be sent by Steiger's lawyers, but actually devised by Scotland Yard. Knight is skeptical of the ploy, noting that he had previously turned Steiger in to Willman. Lee replies that an increasingly desperate Steiger has no choice since on the afternoon in question the local festival is being held and there are no other means of transportation out of town. Knight would surprise Steiger by taking the turn in the road leading to the bridge rather than that to the Texas town where he believes his attorneys will be contacting him.

When Knight takes the turn toward the bridge, an alert Steiger attempts to wrest the steering wheel away from the driver. He brings the Sam's Motel truck to a halt next to the bridge. Steiger leaps from the bridge and lands in the river, swimming to shore. Lee implores his cohorts not to fire their weapons at him, explaining that he wishes to take the fugitive alive.

Lee becomes an exasperated figure himself, seeking to construct a plan that will entice Steiger ultimately across the bridge. Opportunity finally looms when Scarff's widow and her child are crossing the bridge into the United States, their ultimate destination Dallas, where they will live with a local family. As Steiger's isolation becomes more acute, he becomes increasingly involved with Dolores, his only friend. While still in his imperious mode, Steiger sought repeatedly to get rid of the dog. As contacts and opportunities vanish, he appreciates the fact that a loyal dog is impervious to the kinds of alterable circumstances and changing loyalties that typify so much human conduct.

The pivotal event prompting Steiger to recognize the value and loyalty of Dolores occurs while he is lying asleep in an open space with a bright sun shining overhead. While Steiger sleeps, a Mexican scorpion appears. Before it is able to sting Steiger, Dolores begins barking loudly, warning him. He awakens in time to move from harm's path as the scorpion scurries away. A grateful Steiger thanks Dolores for a job well done.

While Mrs. Scarff and her infant son cross the bridge into the United States, Dolores (who knew them from her days as the Scarff dog) accompanies them on their journey. Lee shrewdly recognizes that opportunity has surfaced. He takes the dog and pulls it toward a strategic position on the bridge, tying it up, realizing that Dolores is the last earthly link for an otherwise totally isolated Steiger.

As Steiger lies on the ground trying to sleep that night, he hears the loud barks of Dolores, which trigger him into action. Recognizing the risk he is taking, Steiger is nonetheless determined to free Dolores from her fate. He moves quickly across the bridge and promptly unties Dolores, triggering an immediate response from the law. Vehicles quickly proceed toward Steiger from two directions, determined to cut off all access to freedom. In the interim, an excited Dolores breaks free of the restraining leash Steiger holds. Blinding lights from vehicles in two directions flash in the eyes of Steiger and Dolores. As Steiger is convinced that Dolores is in harm's path, he jumps into the middle of the road in the midst of a swiftly approaching vehicle. He is hit and killed instantly.

The ending reveals the validity of the saying that "no man is an island." Once the daring bravado and imperious, bullying manner of Steiger had been stripped from him by a series of demoralizing incidents and his power base as a wealthy international financier has been demolished, he clings to the faithful love and continuing companionship of a dog, his only surviving link to a world in which he has been reduced to the level of an outcast as well as a refugee from justice.

Annakin on *The Third Man* and Film Noir

"I have to admit that I was not consciously thinking about the movement of film noir when I undertook *Across the Bridge*," Annakin revealed, "but I can see now that it does fall into that category because it deals with the justifiable degradation of a powerful human being."

Bernard Lee, seated left, plots strategy with David Knight while the woman he hopes to marry, Marla Landi, carefully listens, in a scene from *Across the Bridge*. Scotland Yard operative Lee seeks to enlist Knight's help in driving Rod Steiger across the bridge which leads from Mexico to the United States, where he could then apprehend the runaway international financier. Lee, who would later gain fame as James Bond's boss in the famous spy series, had earlier received positive notices in his role in *The Third Man* as Trevor Howard's loyal sergeant subordinate , who is ultimately killed by Orson Welles after he saves the life of Joseph Cotten.

As Carol Reed's protégé, Annakin had directed the first great noir thriller to come out of England since his mentor's *The Third Man*. He found similarity between *The Third Man* and *Across the Bridge* in one important area that enhanced suspense:

"*The Third Man* was an unusual story with great characters in a new setting—Vienna, and the zither music made it terrific. I would add that the Spanish guitar music I had in *Across the Bridge* gave it tremendous atmosphere and the feeling of foreboding and loneliness which Rod Steiger was going into a state of."

Annakin concedes that *Across the Bridge* "was not a pure entertainment movie" and that it would today bear the label "Art House Film." Audiences throughout the

United Kingdom and Europe, however, recognized its distinctive quality and it had legs at the box office.

Of all the 50 films that Annakin made, *Across the Bridge* rates as his favorite. When asked why, he promptly replied, "Somehow the story of Schaffner's comeuppance appealed to me—and in his degradation the dog Dolores should become his conscience and his only friend—yet he had no time to recognize her in his power days. After so many comedies and pure entertainment stories, this subject really hooked me ... with its chance for action yet human drama development."

Carol Reed and Graham Greene, the creative tandem from *The Third Man*, both expressed praise for *Across the Bridge*. Eight years after the earlier film had registered big with audiences and critics, Annakin had achieved a major international success in the same suspense noir realm, giving his career the kind of solid boost that Reed's had received after his earlier epic.

The Soaring '60s

Annakin had wanted to do *Across the Bridge* because it represented a career change for him away from safe and relatively solid commercial properties more geared toward family viewing into the challenging field of noir suspense with art house ramifications. The change resulted in positive recognition from his film peers. "Whenever I worked with top American stars after making *Across the Bridge*, they would come to me, usually after a couple of days and say, 'You made *Across the Bridge*,'" Annakin revealed. "People like Henry Fonda, Dana Andrews and Tony Curtis, along with a number of others, all had seen it."

Disney, Phase Two

After succeeding handsomely with two costume dramas set in Britain, *The Story of Robin Hood* and *When Knighthood Was in Flower*, Annakin returned to the Disney fold to direct two of the more memorable movies ever turned out by the studio. In the early '60s, the film industry, facing stiff competition from the living room entertainment alternative of television, sought to present stunning large screen cinema presentations as an alternative to black-and-white television. The combined Annakin penchants for exciting international locations, adventure and comedy made him a valuable entertainment force. The first high-budget road show production assigned to Annakin was *The Third Man on the Mountain*, which combined the lavish scenery of the Swiss Alps along with a riveting story of a young man seeking to surmount a great obstacle, the climbing of a formidable Matterhorn-like mountain known as the Citadel. James MacArthur stars as the determined young climber whose father died in his attempt to be the first to scale the vaunted peak. While MacArthur is the third rather than the first human to scale the Citadel, a happy and satisfying end awaits him following his courageous effort. The camerawork by

Harry Waxman takes full advantage of the scenic potential afforded as breathtaking color shots of the Matterhorn abound.

"*The Third Man on the Mountain* was the favorite film of Walt Disney," Annakin said. "What impressed him was the theme of the film of one man seeking to conquer the elements. Walt spent his holiday in Switzerland during the making of the film and used the opportunity to help design Disneyland, which he was fervently working on at the time. A short distance from where we were shooting the film, there was a man who had one of the world's most impressive model railway systems. Walt Disney visited him regularly and obtained valuable information on how to design the train system he would build at Disneyland."

With one success under their belts, Disney and Annakin teamed up shortly thereafter to do another scenic road show presentation based on the adventures of a Swiss family, but this time, rather than utilizing the snow-capped peaks of the Alps as a backdrop, the action was set on the warm and tropical Caribbean island of Tobago. *The Swiss Family Robinson* was released in 1960, just one year after *The Third Man on the Mountain*, and became one of the year's top grossing movies to the tune of $30 million. As the name clearly implies, the story is built around the Robinsons from Switzerland, who, in the act of fleeing Napoleonic Europe, are shipwrecked, managing to ultimately find safety on a tropical island. While Mrs. Robinson, played by Dorothy McGuire, bemoans her castaway status, John Mills as Mr. Robinson exhorts his sons (James MacArthur, Tommy Kirk and Kevin Corcoran) to respond to the challenge of constructing a new life for themselves.

Annakin had an opportunity to see a great deal of Disney over the course of the late '50s and '60s in connection with making two winning films for the studio. He developed a keen recognition of Disney's special sense of commitment which, along with his natural genius, made him such a unique creative force.

"Walt Disney had no special philosophy or preferences for what he undertook in the way of projects except for one guiding principle, and that was how to move an audience, the ability to entertain," Annakin said. "He was always creating. I would spend hours in his office, in the course of which he would toss out one idea after another. He was one of the great geniuses of the film industry. He was also very lucky to have an elder brother, Roy, who devoted his life to making Walt's dreams come true commercially."

Acquiring a New Partner

The soaring '60s were a boom period for Annakin on a personal as well as professional plain. In 1960, he met someone who registered a profound impact on the director in both the personal and professional realms.

"When I was in South Africa directing *Elephant Gun*, I met a wonderful and talented lady who impressed me both as a production coordinator and personally," Annakin happily reflected. "Pauline became Mrs. Annakin in 1960. She was one of

England's top production coordinators when I met her and I have treasured her assistance and counsel on films I have directed ever since. We lived in St. Paul de Vence in Southern France throughout the '70s. After that we moved to Southern California, first to Malibu, then to Beverly Hills."

The War Spectacle Phase

Annakin's versatile directing career began during World War II with his involvement beginning as an assistant cameraman in British documentaries. In the spectacle-oriented '60s, two decades after the great conflict concluded, filmmakers were keen on dramatically capturing those enduring moments of history. At that point Annakin encountered a cinema giant who was slated to play a major role in his career in the 1962 spectacle about the D-Day invasion, *The Longest Day.*

"Darryl Zanuck and Walt Disney became the important influences of the mature phase of my career just as Carol Reed and Sydney Box were my early influences," Annakin disclosed. "Just as Walt Disney was always in a creating mode, so was Zanuck, and with a competitive wrinkle. When we would go out shooting in France during the filming of *The Longest Day*, Zanuck would challenge me to contests to see who could come up with the most creative ideas."

Location authenticity was sought as opposed to expense with original locations such as Omaha Beach, Utah Beach, Sword Beach and Ste. Mere Eglise being utilized. No expense was spared concerning casting either as a veritable "who's who" of international film greats donned uniforms. *The Longest Day,* an adaptation of the runaway bestseller by Cornelius Ryan, landed among the top grossers of 1962. The cast included Henry Fonda, John Wayne, Robert Mitchum, Rod Steiger, Richard Burton, Robert Ryan, Sean Connery, Curt Jurgens, John Gregson, Alexander Knox, Eddie Albert, Red Buttons and Peter Lawford, to name but a few. Zanuck tapped Annakin to film battle exteriors at a location 60 miles outside Paris as well as all of the studio shooting in Boulogne, France. "A great spirit of cooperation existed between us," Annakin said.

Annakin directed another World War II action epic, the 1965 release, *Battle of the Bulge.* It was originally produced in Cinerama with a running time of 164 minutes, just 15 minutes less than *The Longest Day.* The final version was cut 23 minutes. A battle spectacle highlighting one of the great conflicts of the war, the film delivers strongly in the area of action footage. "The battle footage is the best I've ever seen captured on film," an ecstatic Jack Warner cabled the movie's two line producers, Milton Sperling and Philip Yordan.

Annakin shot the war footage on location in Segovia, Spain, where he encountered a stern, seemingly unrelenting adversary, the weather. As he revealed, "It snowed in Segovia for six weeks. We had to patiently wait things out before we were able to accomplish what we had set out to do. The only other real obstacle we had was in locating a theme for the script. I had many story conferences with Phil Yordan, the brilliant screenwriter who won an Oscar for *Broken Lance.* We finally hit on our theme, which was anti-war. Robert Shaw delivered a powerful performance as Colonel Hessler, who maintained a robustly pro-war stance. The contrasting figure to Shaw was his adjutant, played by the fine German actor, Hans-Christian Blech. The actors got their exercise in the film as we had them all walking three miles daily."

Henry Fonda and Robert Ryan were repeaters from the glossy *The Longest Day* cast, while a young veteran of Annakin films, James MacArthur, also appeared. Among the other cast notables were Dana Andrews, Charles Bronson, Telly Savalas, George Montgomery and Pier Angeli.

Rank's Loss and Zanuck's Gain

Annakin and Zanuck became collaborative partners in what many critics regard as the finest effort of the veteran director's career in *Those Magnificent Men in Their Flying Machines*, but the winds of destiny needed to blow in the correct direction before they reunited and the successful 1965 release became a reality. The comedy-action epic became one of the top grossers of the year and netted Annakin an Academy Award nomination.

"J. Arthur Rank wanted to do the film but couldn't find the money," Annakin recalled. "At that point Darryl Zanuck stepped in. Darryl told me, 'This is your picture. You will be responsible for finding or building old airplanes which fly. Every detail of pre-production. I'll send you a sympathetic Line Producer.' He assigned Stan Margulies, who became my lifelong friend. This movie was my original idea and I co-scripted with Jack Davies, a great friend and veteran film writer with whom I had collaborated on eight other comedies."

The extra responsibility invested by Zanuck was a challenge to which Annakin responded. He secured Best Film honors from the New York Film Critics for 1965 while the script he co-authored with Jack Davies resulted in a Best Original Screenplay Oscar nomination. The movie won a British Academy Award for Best Costume Design in a Color Film.

Those Magnificent Men in Their Flying Machines plunged Annakin into two areas in which he was well versed and had accumulated much experience, adventure and comedy. The film, set in 1910, concerns a large air race between London and Paris being sponsored by a rich British newspaper publisher. With veteran Annakin compatriot James Robertson-Justice serving as narrator, it includes a star-studded international cast. Red Skelton and Terry-Thomas performed notable comic skits, while Robert Morley, James Fox, Sarah Miles, Sam Wanamaker, Stuart Whitman and Flora Robson also turned in solid efforts.

A quasi-sequel in which racecars were substituted for the flying machines of the earlier classic, *Those Daring Young Men in Their Jaunty Jalopies*, was released in 1969.

"I preferred the title *Monte Carlo or Bust* to the one that Robert Evans at

Paramount gave to the film," Annakin lamented. "Evans was seeking to find a commercial title that was close to *Those Magnificent Men in Their Flying Machines.*"

The comedy and competitive adventure elements were retained from the earlier blockbuster, the major exception being that this time cars rather than airplanes were featured. The action involves a 1,500 mile Monte Carlo auto rally in the early 1920s, in which Tony Curtis duels Terry-Thomas with the winner slated to gain outright the British auto factory they co-own after gambler Curtis won his share in a poker game. British comedy stars Dudley Moore and Peter Cook added appropriate laugh hysterics.

For Annakin, the thrill of directing films lies in the challenge presented. He observed, "When it comes to making films, we start out with nothing except a script, a cast and a camera, but one's personal experiences of real life and places are the things which will give the movie its individuality, and hopefully success, so long as one remembers it is the audience you have to excite, not just yourself."

Synopses of Major Films

The Maltese Falcon (1941) is generally regarded as the first noir film. Successful screenwriter John Huston convinced Warner Brothers studio head Jack Warner to allow him to make his directorial debut adapting to the screen for the third time the hard-hitting detective novel by San Francisco author Dashiell Hammett starring his legendary detective, Sam Spade. Huston believed that the earlier failures stemmed from the adaptations rather than the story itself. Humphrey Bogart surged to international stardom playing the honest, uncompromising Spade, who turns in the woman he loves, Mary Astor, to the police for killing his partner, Jerome Cowan, whom he disliked, believing nonetheless that the murder of one's partner involves a moral obligation. An offbeat criminal triumvirate of Sydney Greenstreet, Peter Lorre and Elisha Cook, Jr., clash repeatedly with Spade in their pursuit of the elusive Maltese Falcon, which Spade defines as "The stuff that dreams are made of."

Double Indemnity (1944) was director Billy Wilder's courageous tour de force presenting a raw, emboldened realism during an era when the forces of censorship embodied in the powerful Breen Office discouraged filmmakers from tackling life in the raw. With Raymond Chandler, the world's number one detective writer, Wilder adapted a trenchant script containing tough, acerbic dialogue from the best selling novel by James M. Cain. Barbara Stanwyck was at her most powerful playing the role of a predatory wife who will stop at nothing to get what she wants, including killing her husband. She enlists insurance salesman Fred MacMurray to assist her after he sells a life insurance policy with a double indemnity clause to her husband, Tom Powers. After the murder MacMurray is forced to sweat out the determined investigative efforts of the office's wily claims manager, played with resolute conviction by Edward G. Robinson.

Murder, My Sweet (1944) marked RKO's emergence into major noir ranks. Directed by Edward Dmytryk, the film marked former song and dance man Dick Powell's debut into the ranks of serious drama as he earned high praise in his role of wise cracking detective Philip Marlowe in scenarist John Paxton's adaptation of Raymond Chandler's novel *Farewell, My Lovely*. Chandler gave Powell glowing praise for capturing the essence of his famous detective Marlowe. Powell is dogged throughout the film by the shadowy, hulking presence of professional wrestler turned actor Mike Mazurki, who plays the crazed, homicidal Moose Malloy, who enlisted the detective to find his former girlfriend. Powell runs afoul of mobster Otto Kruger and resists the charms of bad girl Claire Trevor, preferring instead her stepdaughter, Anne Shirley, who was then married to the film's producer, Adrian Scott.

Crossfire (1947) was another brilliant RKO success directed by Edward Dmytryk with *Murder, My Sweet* collaborators John Paxton and Adrian Scott writing and producing. The film was adapted from the novel *The Brick Foxhole*, written by future directing giant Richard Brooks. The action takes place over one long evening in Washington, D.C., just after the end of World War II. Hate-filled anti–Semite Robert Ryan kills kindly Sam Levene in his apartment solely because he is Jewish. A former East St. Louis policeman and returning soldier, Ryan's hostility is evident to both investigating police officer Robert Young and Robert Mitchum, a sergeant in Ryan's unit. They realize he is the killer, despite Ryan's efforts to pin the murder on a vulnerable fellow soldier. In his efforts to avoid detection, Ryan then strangles fellow soldier Steve Brodie. Finally the wily Young lays a trap for the ruthless killer, creating a clever twist ending.

Out of the Past (1947) saw 22-year-old Washington, D.C., nightclub singer-model Jane Greer surge to stardom playing the role of the amoral, alluring *femme fatale* Kathie Moffett, who shifts her attentions strategically between mob boss Kirk Douglas and honest but mesmerized detective Robert Mitchum. Veteran screenwriter Daniel Mainwaring adapted his own novel, *Build My Gallows High*, using his sometime pen name of Geoffrey Homes, and receiving assistance from Frank Fenton. The dialogue crackles as the intricate plot evolves and Greer switches sides repeatedly, winning grudging admiration from Mitchum even as he recognizes the level of her treachery. Eventually the sultry brunette does in both Mitchum and Douglas after driving each man to the brink of lust-ridden futility. When her own end comes she faces it with the same sangfroid with which she has lived her life.

Laura (1944) was Twentieth Century–Fox's answer to Warner Brothers' *Casablanca*, an initially troubled B picture which overcame its difficulties, elevating itself to the ranks of a bona fide classic. When Twentieth boss Darryl F. Zanuck returned from the war he swore that Otto Preminger would never direct a film as long as he was head of the studio. This occurred after an angry clash which resulted in director Rouben Mamoulian's leaving the project. Zanuck expressed dissatisfaction with Dana Andrews as Detective Mark McPherson and initially spurned Preminger's recommendation that stage actor Clifton Webb be cast as smug New York society columnist-commentator Waldo Lydecker. Both choices proved superb and the intense psychological warfare between the determined detective and the Gotham socialite with the superiority complex emerges as a dramatic high point.

Gene Tierney is cast in her most memorable role as Laura Hunt, a Madison Avenue advertising executive who emerges as the intended victim of Webb. His clash with Andrews heightens when he realizes that the detective has fallen in love with the woman he considers to be his personal creation. A novel plot twist emerges as Andrews becomes infatuated at a time when Tierney is thought to have been murdered, prompting a bitter comment from Webb that he has fallen in love with a ghost. In reality, the victim, intended to be Laura Hunt, was instead a beautiful model. The film captures Manhattan society among Upper East Siders. Jay Dratler, Samuel Hoffenstein and Betty Reinhardt adapted Vera Caspary's novel. The haunting theme by David Raksin has become an enduring classic along with the film.

The Postman Always Rings Twice (1946) was another screen triumph adapted from a James M. Cain best-selling novel, along with other forties hits *Double Indemnity* and *Mildred Pierce*. Scenarists Harry Ruskin and Niven Busch retained the Depression flavor of Cain's work as John Garfield, filmdom's traditional rebel outcast and forerunner to James Dean, arrives penniless at the roadside restaurant-gas station run by Cecil Kellaway and his much younger wife, blonde bombshell Lana Turner. The first meeting between Garfield and Turner has been called one of the sexiest scenes in film history as he stares at her with open lust when she emerges in a scintillating white outfit. Turner is not a predatory opportunist in the manner of Barbara Stanwyck in *Double Indemnity* or Jane Greer in *Out of the Past*, but her trapped desperation prompts her to enlist Garfield's help in disposing of a man who has been like a father to him, prompting strong conscience pangs. The film's biting irony arises from Garfield and Turner's getting away with the murder of Kellaway, after which, with them now married and her pregnant, each vowing to go straight, she is killed in an automobile accident with Garfield driving. Garfield is then convicted of killing Turner. Tay Garnett directed with a steady hand and the cash registers rang cheerily as the film achieved quick blockbuster status with MGM contract player Turner soaring to new acclaim.

The Third Man (1949) was a co-production between Britain and America with colorful Hungarian émigré and London-based Alexander Korda joining forces with Hollywood partner David O. Selznick. Graham Greene, a master of the British thriller, crafted the screenplay with Carol Reed directing. The brilliant background zither music of Anton Karas provided the perfect backdrop for a post-war drama set in Vienna, in which the black market atmosphere results in nihilistic Orson Welles running a racket in which penicillin, valuable to preserve life, is stolen from hospitals, watered down, then sold illegally underground. Joseph Cotten, a pulp western fiction writer and old friend of Welles's, is invited to come to Vienna to assist him, with the trusting Cotten being told that he is involved in a medical charity enterprise. When a former colleague is killed and events are rigged to make it appear that Welles died after being hit by a car, Cotten becomes suspicious and begins his own investigation. Trevor Howard of the British military police realizes that Cotten is a babe in the woods flirting with death and seeks to save him.

Eventually he manages to enlist his help after it is learned that Welles is very much alive. The hauntingly beautiful Alida Valli, cast in the role of a Viennese stage actress, remains in love with Welles even after he has betrayed her, spurning the advances of Cotten, who is deeply enamored of her.

Across the Bridge (1957) was praised by reviewers upon its release as the greatest noir film to come out of England since *The Third Man* eight years earlier. Yorkshire's Ken Annakin, one of Walt Disney's leading directors and a protégé of Carol Reed, cast Rod Steiger in a sensitive role which mightily assisted him along the highway to international stardom. Steiger portrays an international business magnate based in London who learns when he is in New York on business that Scotland Yard has uncovered his fraudulent ways and he is slated for prosecution. He leaves New York immediately by train, hoping to reach Mexico to elude the grasp of authorities. On the train he drinks with another passenger, Bill Nagy, concocting an idea. Steiger steals Nagy's identity and knocks him out after he has consumed a large amount of whiskey, leaving the train in Texas near the Mexican border. On his departure he learns that he has inherited Nagy's dog, Dolores, which he is unable to shake. The script by Guy Elmes and Denny Freeman was adapted from a story by Graham Greene, who earlier penned *The Third Man*. The surprising plot twist emerges when Steiger learns that Nagy is wanted for killing the governor of a Mexican province, becoming a hero among the oppressed. While Steiger is pursued across the border in Texas by Scotland Yard police officer Bernard Lee, he becomes an object of hatred in the small Mexican town where he leads a bleak and isolated existence. Ultimately his only friend is the dog he once spurned, Dolores.

Bibliography

All-Movie Guide. Internet Film Site and Database, www.allmovie.com.

Behlmer, Rudy, editor. *Memo from Darryl F. Zanuck*. New York: Grove Press, 1993.

Brooks, Richard. *The Brick Foxhole*. Garden City, N.Y.: Sun Dial Press, 1946.

Brown, Peter Harry, and Pat H. Broeske, *Howard Hughes: The Untold Story*. New York: Dutton, 1996.

Cain, James M. *Cain X 3: The Postman Always Rings Twice, Mildred Pierce, Double Indemnity*. New York: Knopf, 1969.

Chandler, Raymond. *Four Complete Philip Marlowe Novels: The Big Sleep, Farewell, My Lovely, The High Window, The Lady in the Lake*. New York: Crown Publishers, 1986.

_____, *The Little Sister*. Boston: Houghton Mifflin, 1949.

Cotten, Joseph. *Vanity Will Get You Somewhere*. San Francisco: Mercury House, 1987.

DiOrio, Al. *Barbara Stanwyck: A Biography*. New York: Coward-McCann, 1983.

Dirks, Tim. *The Greatest Films*. Internet Film Site and Database, www.filmsite.org.

Drazin, Charles. *In Search of "The Third Man."* London: Methuen, 1999.

Hanna, Thomas. *The Thought and Art of Albert Camus*. Chicago: Regnery, 1958.

Hare, William. "Jane Greer: Out of the Past," *Films of the Golden Age*. Summer 2002.

_____,"The Ken Annakin Story," *Films of the Golden Age*. Fall 1998.

_____, "Rouben Mamoulian: Impeccable Style," *Films of the Golden Age*. Spring 1999.

_____, "Sir Carol Reed: The Man Behind 'The Third Man,'" *Films of the Golden Age*. Winter 2000–01.

Higham, Charles, and Joel Greenberg. *The Celluloid Muse: Hollywood Directors Speak*. Chicago: Henry Regnery, 1969.

Hiney, Tom. *Raymond Chandler: A Biography*. New York: Atlantic Monthly Press, 1997.

Hirschhorn, Clive. *The Warner Bros. Story*. New York: Crown, 1979.

Hoopes, Roy. *Cain: The Biography of James M. Cain*. New York: Holt, Rhinehart and Winston, 1982.

The Internet Movie Database. Internet Film Site and Database, www.imbd.com.

Larkin, Rochelle. *Hail Columbia*. New Rochelle, N.Y.: Arlington House, 1975.

LeRoy, Mervyn, as told to Dick Kleiner. *Mervyn LeRoy: Take One*. New York: Hawthorn Books, 1974.

MacFarlane, Brian. *An Autobiography of British Cinema*. London: Methuen, 1997.

MacShane, Frank. *The Life of Raymond Chandler*. New York: Dutton, 1976.

Maltin, Leonard, editor. *TV Movies and Video Guide*. New York: Signet, 1990.

Milne, Tom. *Mamoulian*. Bloomington: Indiana University Press, 1969.

Morella, Joe, and Edward Z. Epstein. *Lana: The Public and Private Lives of Miss Turner.* New York: Citadel Press, 1971.
_____, *Rita: The Life of Rita Hayworth.* New York: Delacorte Press, 1983.
Nolan, William F. *Hammett: A Life at the Edge.* New York: Congdon & Weed, 1983.
Perry, George. *The Great British Picture Show.* Boston: Little Brown, 1985.
Sennett, Ted. *Warner Brothers Presents: The Most Exciting Years—from "The Jazz Singer" to "White Heat."* New Rochelle, N.Y.: Castle Books, 1971.
Taylor, John Russell. (Introduction) *Masterworks of the British Cinema.* New York: Harper & Row, 1974.
Thomson, David. *A Biographical Dictionary of Film.* New York: Morrow, 1976.
_____, *Showman: The Life of David O. Selznick.* New York: Knopf, 1992.
Tierney, Gene, with Mickey Herskowitz. *Self-Portrait.* New York: Wyden, 1979.
TV Guide, Motion Picture Database. Internet Film Site and Database, www.tvguide.com.
Vaughn, Robert. *Only Victims.* New York: Limelight Editions, 1996.
Wakeman, John, editor. *World Film Directors: Volume One, 1890–1945.* New York: H.W. Wilson, 1987.
Wapshott, Nicholas. *The Man Between: A Biography of Carol Reed.* London: Chatto and Windus, 1990.
Yablonsky, Lewis. *George Raft.* New York: McGraw-Hill, 1974.

Personal Interviews

Ken Annakin
Guy Green
Jane Greer
Guy Hamilton
Mervyn LeRoy
Rouben Mamoulian
Mike Mazurki

Index

Adler, Luther 60
Aeschylus 144
Albert, Eddie 197
Ambler, Eric 150
Ames, Leon 136, 140
Anderson, Judith 121
Anderson, Maxwell 55
Andrews, Dana 4, 9, 90, 111, 113, 117–120, 127–129, 168, 195, 198, 202
Angeli, Pier 198
Annakin, Ken ix 4, 145, 151–152, 178–199, 204
Annakin, Pauline 196–197
Arden, Eve 134
Astaire, Fred 131
Astor, Mary 11, 18–21, 201

Ballard, Lucien 117
Barker, Lex 68
Bart, Lionel 178
Bartholomew, Freddie 107
Baxter, Anne 134, 183
Beauclerk, Charles 157, 159
Beery, Wallace 139
Bendix, William 102
Benedict, Richard 68
Bennett, Bruce 133
Bergman, Ingrid 90
Berkeley, Busby 52
Berle, Milton 108
Bickford, Charles 128
Blake, Robert 135
Blanke, Henry 17
Blech, Hans-Christian 198
Bleibtreu, Hedwig 162
Blondell, Joan 60
Blyth, Ann 132–133
Bogart, Humphrey 2, 10, 16–19, 21, 49, 119–120, 147, 201
Bond, Ward 20, 69
The Borgias 144, 161
Box, Betty 182
Box, Muriel 182
Box, Sydney 151, 182, 197
Brackett, Charles 25, 41
Brando, Marlon 4
Brazzi, Rosanno 185
Breen, Joseph (Breen Office) 24–25, 37, 44, 134, 138, 201
Breuer, Siegfried 169
Bridges, Jeff 103–104
Bridges, Mrs. Lloyd 104
Brodie, Steve 72, 78, 90, 95, 97, 100, 202
Bronson, Charles 198
Brooks, Richard 3, 65–67, 70, 202
Burnett, W.C. 15, 93
Burton, Richard 197
Busch, Niven 135, 203
Bushman, Francis X. 102
Buttons, Red 197

Cagney, James 47, 49, 103–104, 119
Cain, James M. 2–4, 22–30, 32–33, 35, 40–42, 44, 46, 68, 91–93, 132–137, 143, 201, 203
Calamai, Clara 134
Calleia, Joseph 11
Camus, Albert 1, 12–13, 29
Capone, Al 49
Capote, Truman 67
Capra, Frank 180
Carradine, John 93
Carroll, Madeleine 52
Caspary, Vera 106, 109–110, 114, 203
Chandler, Cissy 25
Chandler, Raymond 1–3, 7–8, 10, 13–15, 20–21, 25–28, 30–35, 37–42, 45–46, 52, 55–57, 59, 68, 91, 93, 144, 201–202
Chaney, Lon 103
Chiang Kai-shek, Madame 123
Christopher, Warren 69
Clifford, Dr. Hubert 162
Clutter Family 67
Cohn, Harry 130
Cole, Lester 75
Columbo, Russ 84
Como, Perry 84
Compton, Fay 149
Connery, Sean 197
Cook, Elisha, Jr. 11, 20–21, 47, 69, 79, 120, 201
Cook, Peter 199
Cooper, Gary 15
Cooper, George A. 68, 78
Corcoran, Kevin 196
Cotten, Joseph 4, 25, 157–158, 160–166, 168, 171, 176–177, 194, 203–204
Cowan, Jerome 19, 201
Coward, Noel 117, 149, 160
Crabtree, Arthur 183
Crawford, Joan 88, 129, 132–134, 183
Cregar, Laird 117
Crenna, Richard 37
Cronin, AJ. 149, 175
Cronyn, Hume 140
Crosby, Bing 45
Crowther, Bosley 164
Cruce, James 64
Curtis, Tony 195, 199
Curtiz, Michael 132–134

Danson, Ted 37

Dante 174
Darnell, Linda 127–128
Dassin, Jules 61
Davies, Jack 198
Davis, Bette 15, 103, 132–134, 183
Dean, Basil 148–149
Dean, James 136, 203
De Carlo, Yvonne 11
De Mille, Cecil B. 9, 64
De Sylva, Buddy 40
Deutsch, Ernst 167
Dickens, Charles 89, 151, 178
Dillinger, John 49, 77
Di Orio, Al 38–39
Disney, Roy 196
Disney, Walt 184, 195–197, 204
Dmytryk, Edward 3, 10, 14, 51–53, 60–61, 63–65, 67–68, 71–72, 74–77, 80, 103, 201–202
Douglas, Don 57
Douglas, Kirk 3, 47, 79–80, 82–83, 88–90, 93–94, 97–100, 104, 202
Dozier, William 25
Dratler, Jay 110, 203
Drayson, Gerald 102
Drazin, Charles 159, 172
Dreiser, Theodore 24
Dresdel, Sonia 155
Duff, Warren 88
Dunne, Irene 82
Duryea, Dan 11

Eastwood, Clint 103
Edwards, Blake 124, 177
Einstein, Albert 8
Elizabeth, Queen 6
Elmes, Guy 186, 204
Evans, Edith 181
Evans, Robert 198–199

Fairbanks, Douglas, Jr. 86
Faulkner, William 32
Faye, Alice 52, 128
Fenton, Frank 93, 202
Fernandel 13
Fields, Gracie 149
Finney, Jack 93
Fitzgerald, Barry 45
Fitzgerald, F. Scott 12, 32
Flynn, Errol 12, 51, 184
Fonda, Henry 129, 135, 195, 197–198
Forbes, Bryan 179
Ford, John 20, 55, 62, 100, 135
Forester, C.S. 26
Formby, George 149
Fox, James 198
Foy, Bryan 109, 112, 119, 122
Francis, Kay 139
Franz Josef 169
Freeman, Dennis 186, 204
Freeman, Mona 43
French, Harold 183
Freud, Sigmund 191
Friedrich, Otto 15, 75
Frings, Ketti 101
Fuller, Samuel 108

Gable, Clark 23, 139
Gardner, Ava 11–12, 77
Gardner, Erle Stanley 34
Garfield, John 4, 10, 17, 24, 29, 89, 93, 135–142, 203
Garland, Judy 11–12
Garner, James 30
Garnett, Tay 130–131, 135, 137–141, 203
Garson, Greer 139
George, Peter 93
Girotta, Massimo 134
Goetz, William 108–109
Goldwyn, Samuel 8, 100
Goodman, Benny 52
Goulding, Edmund 60–61
Goya y Lucientes, Francisco Jose 155
Grable, Betty 117, 128
Grahame, Gloria 69, 72, 74, 79
Granger, Farley 189, 192
Grant, Cary 77, 160
Gravet, Fernand 134
Gray, Coleen 60
Green, F.L. 154
Green, Guy 150–151, 179
Greene, Graham 4, 155–160, 164–165, 168–171, 176–177, 185–186, 191, 195, 203–204
Greenstreet, Sydney 11, 16, 19–21, 47, 69, 79, 201
Greer, Donn 104
Greer, Jane 3, 11, 19, 47, 76, 80–105, 125, 130, 133, 202
Greer, Robin 104
Gregson, John 197
Grey, Zane 171
Guinness, Alec 177, 182
Gwenn, Edmund 74

Hackford, Taylor 103–104
Hall, Jon 24
Halsey, William Frederick, Jr. 181
Hamilton, Guy 146–147, 152, 155–157, 160–163, 172, 175–177, 179
Hammett, Dashiell 1, 2, 13, 15, 17, 19–21, 24, 32–33, 41–42, 52, 68, 201
Harlow, Jean 128, 139
Harolde, Ralf 54, 57
Harrison, Joan 86–87
Harrison, Kathleen 182
Harrison, Rex 149
Hart, Moss 74, 120
Hartl, Carl 161
Haskell, Molly 116
Hawkins, Jack 155, 185
Hawks, Howard 15, 175
Hayward, Susan 76, 85, 87–88, 90, 103, 186
Hayworth, Rita 11, 25, 47, 124, 130
Head, Edith 40
Heather, Jean 43
Heatherton, Joey 103
Helmore, Tom 127
Hemingway, Ernest 12
Henrey, Bobby 155–156
Hepburn, Katharine 16
Hilton, James 65
Hiney, Tom 13
Hitchcock, Alfred 67, 97, 106, 127, 146–147, 149, 188
Hitler, Adolf 8, 11, 180
Hobson, Laura Z. 10
Hodiak, John 118
Hoerbiger, Paul 162, 166
Hoffenstein, Samuel 110, 115, 203
Holden, William 41
Holland, Marty 127
Holloway, Stanley 150
Holubar, Alan 139
Hoopes, Roy 23, 27, 45, 92
Hopper, Edward 1
Houseman, John 26, 34, 104
Howard, Esther 57
Howard, Leslie 183
Howard, Trevor 4,150, 158, 162–163, 166, 175–176, 194, 203
Hughes, Howard 65, 84, 86, 101–102
Humberstone, Bruce 117
Hurt, William 37, 47
Huston, John 1, 2, 15–21, 47, 52, 55, 79, 119–120, 149, 201
Huston, Virginia 93, 96, 98–99
Huston, Walter 2, 15–16, 20, 50, 183
Hyde, Wilfrid-Hyde 166

Indrisano, Johnny 58

Johns, Glynis 183, 185–186
Johnson, Nunnally 108
Johnson, Rita 87
Johnston, Eric 77
Johnston Office 134
Jolson, Al 50
Jones, Griffith 183
Jones, Jennifer 109–110
Jonson, Ben 4
Joyce, James 5, 97, 171
Jung, Carl 191
Jurgens, Curt, 197

Kael, Pauline 41, 57, 178
Karas, Anton 161–164, 203
Karloff, Boris 64
Kasdan, Lawrence 36–37
Katz, Ephraim 154–155
Kaufman, George S. 120
Kazan, Elia 74
Keeler, Ruby 52
Kellaway, Cecil 4,137, 140, 142, 203
Kelly, Paul 69–70, 72, 79
Kennedy, John F. 67
Kerima 175–176
Khrushchev, Nikita 8
Kinskey, Leonid 69
Kirk, Tommy 196
Kleiner, Harry 127
Knight, David 189, 192, 194
Knowles, Patric 102
Knox, Alexander 197
Koerner, Charles 46, 51–52
Korda, Alexander 152, 154–160, 175, 186, 203
Kramer, Stanley 77
Krasker, Robert 154–156, 163–164, 170, 174
Kruger, Otto 11, 53, 55, 61, 69, 79, 202
Kubrick, Stanley 21

Ladd, Alan 34, 38, 88
Lake, Veronica 34
Lamarr, Hedy 87, 109–110, 131
Lancaster, Burt 10, 67
Landi, Marla 190, 194
Landis, Carole 117
Lane, Lola 52
Lane, Rosemary 52
Lang, Fritz 20
Lang, Walter 112
Lange, Jessica 138
Langford, Frances 52
Lardner, Ring, Jr. 76
La Shelle, Joseph 117
Lasker, Edward 103
Lawford, Peter 197
Lawrence, Vincent 23, 143
Lean, David 145–146, 149–151, 181
Le Carre, John 163
Lee, Bernard 155, 162, 166, 191–194, 204
Lee, Gypsy Rose 93
Lee, Howard 110
Leonard, Sheldon 86
Leonardo de Vinci 144, 161
Le Roy, Mervyn ix, 130–131
Lester, Mark 178
Levene, Sam 67, 78, 202
Lewis, Ed "Strangler" 49
Lewis, Sinclair 67
Lewton, Val 89
Lippmann, Walter 22–23
Lockwood, Margaret 149
Lom, Herbert 61, 182
Lombard, Carole 38
Lorre, Peter 16, 18, 20–21, 47, 69, 79, 201
Loy, Myrna 64
Luce, Clare Booth 108
Luce, Henry 108
Luchaire, Cortinne 134
Lukas, Paul 90

MacArthur, James 195–196, 198
MacDonald, Jeanette 84
MacDonald, Kenneth 73
MacDougall, Ranald 134
MacLane, Barton 20–21
MacMurray, Fred 3, 10, 28, 33, 38–39, 42, 45, 47, 93, 133, 141, 201
MacShane, Frank 34
Madison, Guy 9, 64
Madriguera, Enrique 84
Mainwaring, Daniel (Geoffrey Homes) 80, 92, 96, 99, 101–103, 210
Malone, Dorothy 103
Maltin, Leonard 60, 103–104
Mamoulian (Newman), Azadia 112–113
Mamoulian, Rouben ix, 38, 107, 110, 112–117, 131, 155, 202
Mander, Miles 55
Mankiewicz, Joseph 175
Mannix, Eddie 75
March, Fredric 38, 64, 116
Marcuzzo, Elio 134
Margulies, Stan 198
Marlowe, Christopher 4, 144, 159
Marshall, Herbert 183
Mason, A.E.W. 26
Mason, James 154–155, 175, 182
Mature, Victor 50, 90
Maugham, Somerset 40, 60, 169, 183–185
Mayer, Louis B. 11, 130
Mazurki, Mike 3, 11, 48–53, 55, 58, 60–63, 79, 86, 124, 127, 202
McCarey, Leo 45
McGuire, Dorothy 196
McLaglen, Victor 62
Melville, Herman 32, 97
Mercer, Johnny 106
Michelangelo 144, 161
Miles, Sarah 198
Milestone, Lewis 112
Mills, John 65, 196
Milne, Tom 116
Mitchell, Cameron 139
Mitchum (Spence), Dorothy 91
Mitchum, Robert 3, 9, 10, 12, 14–15, 28, 39, 47, 64, 67–69, 71–72, 78–80, 82, 85, 88–92, 94–95, 97–105, 133, 160, 176, 197, 202
Molina, Julio 188
Montagu, Elizabeth 159
Montez, Maria 24
Montgomery, Bernard 181
Montgomery, George 198
Montgomery, Robert 10
Moody, Ron 178
Moore, Dickie 97–99
Moore, Dudley 199
Moore, Mary Tyler 104
Morgan, Michele 155
Morley, Robert 198
Muni, Paul 17
Munson, Ona 50
Musuraca, Nicholas 89, 91

Nagurski, Bronco 49
Nagy, Bill 189, 204
Neal, Tom 64
Neame, Ronald 150
Nelson, Baby Face 49
Nevins, Allan 22
Newton, Robert 154
Nicholson, Jack 138
Nimitz, Chester 181
Niven, David 150
Nolan, Lloyd 52
Nolan, William 19
Novarro, Roman 102
Novello, Ivor 149

Oberon, Merle 117, 152

O'Brien, Edmond 70
O'Donnell, Cathy 192
O'Hara, Maureen 86
O'Keefe, Dennis 104
Osborne, John 147
Ouspenskaya, Maria 50, 135

Parker, Cecil 184
Parsons, Louella 102
Patrick, Nigel 184
Paxton, John 57, 60, 65, 67, 70, 74–75, 77, 80, 201–202
Peck, Gregory 10, 77
Perinal, Georges 156
Phillips, Paul 57
Phipps, William 68, 73
Pichel, Irving 76, 87
Polansky, Abraham 135
Polony, Frank 114
Porter, Jean 61, 64
Powell, Dick 3, 10, 51–51–60, 64, 69, 77–79, 124, 201–202
Powell, Jane 99
Powell, Lawrence Clark 33
Powell, Michael 26, 175
Powell, William 139
Power, Tyrone 12, 60, 117, 183
Powers, Tom 33, 42, 201
Preminger, Otto 4, 107–120, 122–123, 126–129, 202
Preston, J.A. 37
Price, Vincent 115, 121
Proust, Marcel 26

Quinn, Anthony 86

Rafelson, Bob 138
Raft, George 16, 38, 49–50, 87
Raines, Ella 87
Raksin, David 106, 122, 203
Ralegh, Sir Walter 61
Rank, J. Arthur 187–188, 198
Rathvon, Peter 75
Ray, Nicholas 69, 192
Redford, Robert 135
Redgrave, Michael 149
Reed, Carol 4, 145–164, 170, 174–179, 181–182, 186–188, 194–195, 197, 203–204
Reed, Max 146
Reed, Oliver 178
Reinhardt, Betty 110, 203
Revere, Anne 134
Richardson, Ralph 155
Riesman, David 31
Righter, Carroll 91
Ritter, Thelma 134
Rivkin, Allen 17–18
Roach, Hal (studio) 139
Robertson-Justice, James 198
Robbins, Harold 103
Robinson, Dewey 57
Robinson, Edward G. 3, 17, 28, 39, 41, 47, 49, 201
Robson, Flora 198
Rogers, Peter 182
Romanoff, Mike 147
Rommel, Erwin 181
Rooney, Mickey 11–12
Roosevelt, Franklin D. 8, 134
Ruskin, Harry 135, 203
Russell, Harold 8–9
Russell, Rosalind 139
Rutherford, Margaret 151, 181
Ryan, Cornelius 197
Ryan, Kathleen 154–155, 175
Ryan, Robert 3, 66–68, 71–74, 76, 78, 197–198, 202

Sanders, George 52
Sartre, Jean Paul 12–13
Savalas, Telly 198
Schary, Dore 75–76
Schenck, Joseph 107–108
Schultz, Dutch 49
Scott, Adrian 54, 60, 65, 67, 74–77, 80, 202
Scott, Lizabeth 90, 101–102
Scott, Randolph 104
Scott, Zachary 133–134
Seaton, George 74
Sellers, Peter 123, 177–178
Selznick, David O. 89, 112, 119, 158–162, 164–165, 175–177, 203
Shakespeare, William 4, 12, 35, 61, 144, 159
Shaw, George Bernard 121, 144
Shaw, Robert 198
Sherriff, R.C. 154
Shirley, Anne 3, 54, 56, 202
Siegel, Don 85, 103
Simenon, George 13
Simon, Michael 134
Sinatra, Frank 84
Sistrom, Joseph 24–25, 27, 34
Skelton, Red 198
Slezak, Walter 86
Smart, Ralph 183
Smith, H. Allen 26
Smollet, Peter 159
Sophocles 144
Sperling, Milton 197
Stanwyck, Barbara 3, 19, 28, 33, 38–41, 45–46, 88, 93, 125, 132–134, 141, 201, 203
Steiger, Rod 4, 145, 187, 190–194, 197, 204
Steinbeck, John 135
Sternberg, Josef von 50–51
Stevenson, Adlai 67
Stewart, James 146, 160
Stone, Lewis 11
Stroheim, Erich von 64
Sturges, Preston 84
Swanson, Gloria 41
Swanson, H.N. 24–26
Swinburne, Nora 181, 184

Taylor, Laurette 108
Taylor, Robert 131
Temple, Shirley 8, 49
Terry, Ellen 146
Terry-Thomas 198
Thomson, David 133, 176
Tierney, Gene 4, 50, 61, 109–111, 114–118, 124, 129, 183, 203
Tobias, George 86
Todd, Ann 154, 182
Todd, Richard 184–185
Tolstoy, Leo 5, 97
Tone, Franchot 87
Totter, Audrey 142
Tourneur, Jacques 3, 14, 80, 83, 89–92
Tourneur (Thomas), Maurice 89
Tree, Sir Herbert Beerbohm 146–148
Trevor, Claire 3, 11, 19, 54–56, 77–78, 125, 202
Truman, Harry 10, 66
Trumbo, Dalton 75
Turner, Kathleen 37
Turner, Lana 4, 11, 24, 47, 88, 130, 134–142, 203
Twain, Mark 32

Ustinov, Peter 147–148, 150

Valentine, Paul 97–98
Vallee, Rudy 84, 87, 104
Valli, Alida 4, 157–158, 160, 162, 164, 166–168, 171, 176, 204
Van Upp, Virginia 86
Vane, Sutton 108
Velazquez, Diego Rodriguez de Silva y 155
Velez, Lupe 50
Visconti, Luchino 134

Wald, Jerry 132
Walker, Robert 189
Wallace, Edgar 148, 152
Wallace, Henry 10

Wallace, Richard 86
Wallis, Hal 17, 102
Walsh, Raoul 2, 15, 64
Walton, Douglas 55
Wannamaker, Sam 198
Wapshott, Nicholas 149, 157, 159, 176
Ward, Penelope Dudley 148–149
Ward, Rachel 103–104
Warner, Jack 182
Warner, Jack L. 2, 17–18, 132, 197, 201
Waxman, Harry 195
Wayne, John 55, 62, 139, 197
Webb, Clifton 4, 110–111, 115, 117–120, 122, 126–127, 203
Webb, Richard 99
Welles, Orson 4, 144, 158–162, 168, 171–173, 176–177, 194, 203–204
Wellman, William 64
Werker, Alfred 107
West, Mae 50
West, Nathaniel 29
Whistler, James McNeill 172–173
White, Jacqueline 70, 72
Whitman, Stuart 198
Widmark, Richard 61–62, 108, 127
Wild, Jack 178
Wilde, Oscar 144
Wilder, Billy 2–3, 17, 23–25, 27–28, 34–35, 37–46, 52, 56, 93, 188, 201
Williams, Bill 9
Willman, Noel 190–192
Wilson, Carey 131–138
Winchell, Walter 118–119
Windsor, Marie 21
Wise, Robert 74
Withers, Googie 61, 183
Wodehouse, P.G. 26
Wolfe, Thomas 32
Wood, Sam 75
Woolcott, Alexander 110
Woolley, Monty 120
Wormser, Richard 103
Wyler, Robert 149
Wyler, William 9, 15, 64, 100, 139, 183
Wynyard, Diana 148, 151, 154, 181

Yordan, Philip 197–198
Young, Robert 3, 68, 71–72, 76, 78, 85, 87–88, 202

Zanuck, Darryl F. 3–4, 10, 60, 65, 74, 76, 107–114, 116–120, 122, 127–128, 197–198, 202
Zbysko, Stanislaus 61
Zolotow, Maurice 23